Basic BASIC

An Introduction to Computer Programming in BASIC Language

Hayden Computer Programming Series

BASICS OF DIGITAL COMPUTER PROGRAMMING (Second Ed.)
John S. Murphy

BASIC BASIC: An Introduction to Computer Programming in BASIC Language (Second Ed.)
James S. Coan

ADVANCED BASIC: Applications and Problems
James S. Coan

DISCOVERING BASIC: A Problem Solving Approach
Robert E. Smith

PROGRAMMING PROVERBS
Henry F. Ledgard

PROGRAMMING PROVERBS FOR FORTRAN PROGRAMMERS
Henry F. Ledgard

FORTRAN WITH STYLE: Programming Proverbs
Henry F. Ledgard and Louis J. Chmura

COBOL WITH STYLE: Programming Proverbs
Louis J. Chmura and Henry F. Ledgard

BASIC WITH STYLE: Programming Proverbs
Paul Nagin and Henry F. Ledgard

FORTRAN FUNDAMENTALS: A Short Course
Jack Steingraber

THE BASIC WORKBOOK: Creative Techniques for Beginning Programmers
Kenneth E. Schoman, Jr.

BASIC FROM THE GROUND UP
David E. Simon

APL: AN INTRODUCTION
Howard A. Peelle

Basic BASIC
SECOND EDITION

An Introduction to Computer Programming in BASIC Language

JAMES S. COAN

Community Computer Corporation
Germantown Friends School

HAYDEN BOOK COMPANY, INC.
Rochelle Park, New Jersey

Library of Congress Cataloging in Publication Data

Coan, James S
   Basic BASIC: an introduction to computer
programming in BASIC language.

   (Hayden computer programming series)
   Includes indexes.
   1.   Basic (Computer program language).
2.   Electronic digital computers—Programming.
I.   Title.
QA76.73.B3C62   1978   001.6'424   77-14640
ISBN   0-8104-5107-7
ISBN   0-8104-5106-9   pbk.

5	6	7	8	9	PRINTING

79	80	81	82	83	84	85	YEAR

Preface

With the increasing availability of computer access through remote terminals and time sharing, more and more schools and colleges are able to introduce programming to substantial numbers of students.

This book is an attempt to incorporate computer programming, using BASIC language, and the teaching of mathematics. I believe the two activities support each other.

Flowcharts are used throughout the text. The general approach is to begin with short complete programs and then simply and methodically build them into larger programs. Each new capability or new organization of capabilities is presented to create a desired effect in a program. Details are introduced only as they become necessary or useful for the writing of a program, rather than as sets of facts to be memorized in case a particular situation should ever arise. Over 125 programs are used to achieve this.

All of the elementary BASIC language capabilities are presented in the first five chapters and Chap. 7. Chapter 6 and Chaps. 8–13 emphasize applications. The first seven chapters may be studied in conjunction with, or at any time following, a first-year algebra course. Chapters 8–13 are applications oriented, covering many of the popular topics of precalculus mathematics, with all of the required algorithms developed in the text. Thus, this text is suitable for use either as a supplementary text to be incorporated into existing mathematics courses, or as the text for a course or unit to cover programming alone.

Appendices A and B, respectively, present information for the operation of programs on paper tape and a few comments on error diagnosis. Appendix C introduces two formatting capabilities that are available on some time-sharing systems. Flowchart shapes are summarized in Appendix D. A summary of BASIC statement types is provided in Appendix E and an index of all the programs in Chaps. 2–13 is provided in Appendix F.

Many of the problems in the book are intended to enable the student to develop interesting mathematical concepts upon seeing the printed results of program RUNS. Possible solution programs are given in Appendix G for the even-numbered problems to give the student an indication of the correctness of his program without being required to run every program. However, particularly at the beginning, students derive greater benefit from seeing programs run (or not run) than from any other programming activity.

I wish to thank Germantown Friends School for its support in the preparation of this text. Thanks are due Mrs. Geoffrey Wilson for test teaching and numerous students for test learning portions of the manuscript.

JAMES S. COAN

Philadelphia

Preface to the Second Edition

The First Edition of this book has been significantly enhanced by presenting character string handling and the use of data files. Since strings and files involve language differences which depend on the computer, two versions are presented. Demonstration programs are presented in Chap. 7 for both General Electric Information Services BASIC and Hewlett-Packard BASIC.

The little used statement RESTORE is no longer discussed, and the INPUT statement is now presented in Chap. 1.

Thanks are due to the Community Computer Corporation for assistance in the preparation of material for this Second Edition.

JAMES S. COAN

Philadelphia

Contents

Basic BASIC

An Introduction to Computer Programming in BASIC Language

CHAPTER 1

Introduction to BASIC

In working with a computer, you, the programmer, must communicate with the computer. In order to do that you will have to use a language that the computer will understand. There are many languages written for this purpose. The language of this text is called BASIC. The actual physical communication is rather complicated and we will ignore most of the mechanics except for the apparatus at our end of things. The device we will be using is called a *remote terminal*. It will have a specific name depending on the manufacturer. The remote terminal has a keyboard, which is the part we are most concerned about.

1-1 PRINT

No matter how complicated a particular set of instructions is, you will have to tell the computer to put the results into some form discernible to yourself. Therefore, let us begin with a discussion of the PRINT statement. If you want the computer to write the following statement "THIS IS A SHORT PROGRAM," you will type on the keyboard of the terminal as follows:

```
10   PRINT "THIS IS A SHORT PROGRAM."
20   END
```

The computer, on proper instruction, will do exactly what you have set out to do.

The two lines 10 and 20 constitute a complete program. Several comments are in order here.

1) Note that every line in a program must begin with a positive integer.
2) The statement that we want to write out is in quotes; this may be used to good advantage, for example, for headings and labels.
3) In many time-share systems, every program must have as its highest numbered line the END statement. In some systems, the END statement is optional.

4) Note that all the letters are capitals. The terminal you may use or may not be restricted in this way. Note also that the letter "O" has a slash mark to distinguish it from the digit "0." On some terminals the reverse is true, the digit "0" has a slash and the letter "O" does not. On some printers one is more nearly a circle than the other or one is nearly diamond shaped. You can easily determine the method used by your equipment by examining some sample output on your screen or "hard copy."

5) It is conventional although not required to use intervals of 10 for the numbers of adjacent lines in a program. This is because any modification in the program must also have line numbers. So you can use the in-between numbers for that purpose. It should be comforting to know at this point that the line numbers do not have to be typed in order. No matter what order they are typed in, the computer will follow numerical order in executing the program.

6) Each line of a program is called a *program statement*.

You probably think of the computer as something that more commonly produces numerical results and you are partly correct. Suppose you wish to multiply 23.4 by 91. One way of doing this on the computer would be to write a program like this:

```
10   PRINT 23.4*91
20   END
```

Then on proper instruction the computer will type out the following and stop.

```
2129.4
DØNE
```

Computers vary as to the message that gets printed here. Notice the absence of quotes. In this case you have instructed the computer to perform an operation. Had you in fact wanted 23.4 * 91 typed out, then you would change the program. You might write the following:

```
10   PRINT "23.4*91=",23.4*91
20   END
```

This time the result will be as follows:

```
23.4*91=        2129.4
DØNE
```

You have succeeded in instructing the computer not only to perform an operation, but to print out the result in easily understandable form, which is desirable throughout mathematics. Notice the use of the comma here. The comma may be used to separate the different parts of a PRINT statement. Used in this way, a comma is called a *delimiter*. Notice too, that there are eight spaces between the equals sign and the number. A way to eliminate all but one of them will be explained later. There are many fine points that we will discuss as we progress, but for now we will take it in small quantities.

If we were limited to the PRINT and the END instructions, we would quickly return to using pencil and paper or an ordinary desk calculator. Without some additional capability, the computer would soon disappear. This brings us to the READ and DATA statements.

PRINT
Characters in quotes will be printed exactly as typed. Computed results will be typed as decimal numbers or as integers.

1-2 READ–DATA

The READ statement says to look for DATA as in the following:

```
10    DATA 23.4, 91, 83, 19, 87, 94, 76, 5.98, 876, 918
20    READ A, B
30    PRINT A*B
35    GØTØ 20
40    END
```

The computer ignores the DATA statement until it finds a READ, then it takes the first number in the first DATA statement and assigns that value to the first variable in the READ statement. Then, if there is a comma and another variable in READ as in our example, the computer assigns the second number in the DATA line to it; were there a third variable, the computer would continue until it ran out of variables. In our program, the first time through, A = 23.4 and B = 91. The next line says PRINT the product. Having printed the product the computer looks for the next instruction, which is GØTØ 20. This is a new one that means exactly what it says. So the computer will GØTØ line 20 and execute that instruction again. At this point the computer "knows" that it has already read and used the first two numbers in the DATA line. So it goes to the third and fourth numbers and assigns them to A and B in order and proceeds to print the product of 83 and 19, then goes back and assigns the fifth and sixth numbers to A and B, and so on until it runs out of numbers in the DATA line. There may be any number of DATA lines in a given program; all you need to realize for the time being is that a comma must be used to separate each discrete item of data and a comma should not be placed after the last item in a particular DATA line. Also, be careful not to use commas to designate thousands, millions, etc. *Warning:* You may not put variables or operation symbols in a DATA line. Only numbers in decimal form are allowed so far. Here is the computer's response to the above program:

```
2129.4
1577
8178
454.48
804168.
```

ØUT ØF DATA IN LINE 20

Note the explicit message at the completion of the print-out. This will vary from computer to computer.

In our examples so far, we have used only multiplication (°). The other arithmetic operations that you may use are addition (+), subtraction (−), division (/), and exponentiation (raising to a power). There are two symbols in common use for exponentiation: one is an upwards arrow (↑), and the other is a double asterisk (°°). Symbols used to instruct the computer to perform some operation are called *operators*. The symbols listed here are specifically designated as the arithmetic operators. The numbers on which the operation is to be performed are called *operands*. Contrary to convention in algebra, the multiplication symbol must be present. AB in algebra must be written A ° B for the computer. The computer assigns the same priorities to arithmetic operations as are assigned in algebra. If there are several operations of the same priority to be performed on the same line, the computer does them from left to right. Several sample programs will be given soon.

READ

The READ statement looks for numbers in a DATA statement. READ X, Y, Z looks for numbers in groups of three.

DATA

The DATA statement supplies values for the variables designated in the corresponding READ statement. Items of data must be separated by a comma. Numbers only are allowed.

1-3 SYSTEM COMMANDS

There are two kinds of instructions of which you should be aware. We have already discussed an instruction given by a program that you have written. We have not yet mentioned an equally important kind of instruction, the *system command*. We must realize that the computer does nothing by itself. Therefore, there must be what is called an *executive program* which will respond to your wishes. You need not worry about the executive program; it is taken care of by the people who maintain the computer.

The first system command required is referred to as the *sign-on* or *log-on*. The exact form of this varies from computer to computer. So we really cannot be specific here. It simply notifies the computer that you would like to use it.

Once you are signed on, the next most important command is RUN. After you have typed out your program, the computer must have a way of knowing that you want it to execute the program. So you must type RUN and then touch the return key on the keyboard. Only then will it respond to the programmed instructions.

Possibly next in importance is the command SCR (SCRub or SCRatch) or

CLE (CLEar) followed by depressing the return key. (Which you use will depend on the computer you are connected with.) Suppose you have run a program and someone else would like to run his. The old program may be erased by using the SCR command. So whenever you begin a new program it might be wise to simply type SCR and touch the return key. The system command must *not* be preceded by a number. There are several other commands that we will take up as they seem appropriate.

RUN
    Notifies the computer to execute the program instructions. Must not have a number in front of it.

SCR or CLE
    Notifies the computer that you are not going to use the current program. The current program is erased from the working area of the computer. Must not have a number in front of it.

1-4 LET

At this point you do have enough information to write quite a few programs. However, another statement type that may be used to make life easier is the LET statement. The LET statement may be used to assign any number or any algebraic expression to any variable. Using a LET statement, the last program would look like this:

```
10   DATA 23.4,91,83,19,87,94,76,5.98,876,918
20   READ A,B
30   LET C=A*B
40   PRINT C
50   GOTO 20
60   END
RUN

 2129.4
 1577
 8173
 454.48
 804168.

OUT OF DATA  IN LINE 20
```

We obtain the same results as before. In this particular program, we really did not save anything. However, in any situation where we need to write the value of A ° B several times or the expression is more involved, we will see that a saving may result. There are many things that you could not do without a LET capability.

LET
May be used to assign explicit values to a variable as LET X = 4.56, or may be used to assign algebraic expressions to a variable as LET V = X * F + Y * G. *Note:* All variables on the right-hand side must have been previously evaluated. On some computers LET is optional. Such systems permit Z = 4.56, for example.

1-5   INPUT

The INPUT statement serves much the same purpose as the READ statement in that it permits us to provide numbers for the computer to work with. For example, 100 INPUT A will cause the computer to print a question mark and stop at line 100. The question mark is a signal to whoever is operating the terminal that he or she is to type the desired value for A on the keyboard and press the carriage return key to resume the run of the program. Likewise, 100 INPUT A, B, C will call for three numbers separated by commas to be typed at the keyboard. It is advisable to have the computer print a label so that the operator can determine the nature of the numbers required. In the following program, note that the semicolon at the end of line 100 enables us to type the values for A and B on the same line as the printed label. The input numbers 15, 17 following the question mark were typed at the keyboard by the program operator.

```
100   PRINT "INPUT TWØ NUMBERS:";
110   INPUT A,B
120   PRINT " THE NUMBERS ARE:";A;B
130   PRINT "     THEIR SUM IS:";A+B
140   PRINT "THEIR PRØDUCT IS:";A*B
150   END
RUN

INPUT TWØ NUMBERS:?15,17
  THE NUMBERS ARE: 15      17
     THEIR SUM IS: 32
THEIR PRØDUCT IS: 255

DØNE
```

INPUT
Causes the computer to request data from the keyboard.

1-6   SAMPLE PROGRAMS

If we want the computer to obtain a decimal value for a compound fraction, there may be several programs that will do the job. Here we will have to use our knowledge of the order of operations as determined in algebra.

Three programs follow that find a decimal value for

$$\frac{2/5 + 3/7}{3/4 - 1/3}$$

```
10   LET N=2/5+3/7
20   LET D=3/4-1/3
30   PRINT N/D
40   END
RUN

 1.98857

DØNE
```

```
10   LET F=(2/5+3/7)/(3/4-1/3)
20   PRINT F
30   END
RUN

 1.98857

DØNE
```

```
10   PRINT (2/5+3/7)/(3/4-1/3)
20   END
RUN

  1.98857

DØNE
```

Parentheses serve as a powerful tool in grouping terms properly for the desired results. Keep in mind that priorities are exactly as they are in algebra and that if several operations of the same priority appear in the same line, they are executed from left to right.

Carefully study the programs which follow to see how the placement of the parentheses affects the results.

```
10   PRINT "3/5/3/5=";3/5/3/5
20   PRINT "3/(5/3/5)=";3/(5/3/5)
30   PRINT "3/5/(3/5)=";3/5/(3/5)
40   PRINT "(3/5)/(3/5)=";(3/5)/(3/5)
50   PRINT "(3/5/3)/5=";(3/5/3)/5
60   PRINT "(3/5)/3/5=";(3/5)/3/5
70   END
RUN

3/5/3/5= .04
3/(5/3/5)= 9.
3/5/(3/5)= 1
(3/5)/(3/5)= 1
(3/5/3)/5= .04
(3/5)/3/5= .04

DØNE
```

```
10   PRINT "A=";2↑3+1+3↑2+1
20   PRINT "B=";2↑(3+1)+3↑2+1
30   PRINT "C=";2↑3+(1+3)↑2+1
40   PRINT "D=";2↑3+1+3↑(2+1)
50   PRINT "E=";2↑(3+1+3)↑2+1
60   END
RUN
```

```
A=  19
B=  26
C=  25
D=  36
E=  16385

DØNÈ
```

It is important to know the capacity of the computer you are working with. Notice that according to the computer, $(2/5 + 3/7)/(3/4 - 1/3) = 1.98857$. If we work that out longhand, the result would be 1.98857142. BASIC provides from 6 to 15 digits, if they are needed, depending on the computer, with the last digit rounded off in decimal numbers, if it is the capacity digit.

If the results require more than the digit capacity of the computer, the computer prints in scientific notation as follows:

```
10   LET  A=98781.
20   LET  A1=8976
30   LET  P=A*A1
40   PRINT A,"*",A1,"=",P
50   END
RUN
```

```
98781.          *          8976          =          8.86658E+08

    DØNE
```

The E + 08 means "times ten to the eighth power" and the decimal number is rounded off to the sixth digit. When the computer uses this notation, it is called *E-format*. Again we get large spaces using the comma to delimit the printed results. We will discuss this before we wind up chapter one.

A new item A1 appears in the above program in line 20. There you will find the statement LET A1 = 8976. The computer treats this as a new variable. In BASIC you may use any letter of the alphabet and any letter of the alphabet followed by a single digit as a variable. Some computers have additional simple variables. Thus a large number of variables are available.

Probably the best way to learn how the computer handles scientific notation is by experience. So, let us run a sample program to see what happens.

```
5    PRINT "X","Y","Q","P","S"
10   DATA 1.31E+10,2.13E+11,1.16132E-05,2.83E+06
20   READ X,Y
26   LET Q=X/Y
40   LET P=X*Y
50   LET S=X+Y
60   PRINT X,Y,Q,P,S
65   GØTØ 20
70   END
RUN
```

X	Y	Q	P	S
1.31000E+10	2.13000E+11	6.15023E-02	2.79030E+21	2.26100E+11
1.16132E-05	2.83000E+06	4.10360E-12	32.8654	2.83000E+06

ØUT ØF DATA IN LINE 20

Notice the use of Q for quotient, P for product, etc. This is a technique that is useful not only on the computer, but throughout mathematics.

Suppose you wish to write a program to find the total cost of a purchase in which there are different numbers of items at various prices, say 2 @ $.35, 3 @ $2.65, 11 @ $.25, 1 @ $9.49, and 35 @ $1.59. We could have many more, but for a sample this should suffice. This program could of course be written in several ways, but here is one possibility:

```
10    PRINT "ITEMS","UNIT PRICE","CØST","SUBTØTAL"
20    DATA 2,.35,3,2.65,11,.25,1,9.49,35,1.59
25    LET T=0
30    READ N,P
40    LET T=T+N*P
45    PRINT N,P,N*P,T
50    GØTØ 30
70    END
RUN
```

ITEMS	UNIT PRICE	CØST	SUBTØTAL
2	.35	.7	.7
3	2.65	7.95	8.65
11	.25	2.75	11.4
1	9.49	9.49	20.89
35	1.59	55.65	76.54

ØUT ØF DATA IN LINE 30

The single figure we set out to obtain is in the lower right-hand corner. The result is $76.54; however, the other information is bound to be useful in at least some situations. Besides, even if we only print the right-hand column, we do not yet know how to dispose of the first four figures in that column. If you only want to print the right-hand column, then lines 10 and 45 may be altered thus:

```
10    PRINT "SUBTØTAL"
45    PRINT T
```

and only that column will be printed. Notice that line 10 is executed only once and line 45 is executed five times. The GØTØ statement in line 50 only returns the computer back to line 30. So the computer only prints the headings once and only lets T = 0 once.

Still, in the last program, the combination of lines 25 and 40 may seem strange, but it will not as soon as you gain a little more insight into how the computer works. Line 25 is said to initialize the value of T at 0, i.e., give it an initial value of 0. When the computer executes the initializing statement, line

25 LET T = 0, it "says" that there is a location in the computer storage area which this program will call T and that this program also requires that the number zero be stored in that location for now. If we then say 26 LET T = 5, then the computer will put the number 5 in that location designated as T and zero will no longer be there. If we write a program that says 25 LET T = 0 followed by 26 LET T = T + 1, then the computer goes to the location where it is storing the value for T, "sees" 0, adds 1 to it, and returns the result to the location from which it just got 0, thereby replacing 0 (the old value) with 1 (the new value). So we see that in BASIC (as in other computer languages) = does not mean "two names for the same thing." It means, instead, that the number on the right is to be placed in a location whose name is specified on the left. Thus we see that the equals sign as used here really specifies an operation for the computer to perform. So the equals sign is called an *assignment operator* or a replacement operator, and the LET statement is called the *assignment statement* or replacement statement.

Let us go through the program line by line. The lowest numbered line is a PRINT statement. So, right off, the computer prints the headings. Then it recognizes that the next statement is a DATA statement and ignores it. Line 25 assigns the value 0 to T. Then in line 30 the computer reads the first two numbers in the DATA line. Line 40 says that the previous value of T is to be taken out of storage and added to N times P. So, the first time through line 40, the value of T on the left will be 0 (from storage) plus the cost of two items at $.35, or .70, and the computer returns the value .70 to the location in storage called T. Line 50 sends the computer back to read the next two numbers in the DATA line and to add their product (7.95) to .70 to get 8.65. It should be clear that we are printing the values of N, P, N times P, and T each time we read two new numbers. This process continues until the computer finds no more data. This causes the computer to terminate the RUN.

1-7 COMMA AND SEMICOLON IN PRINT STATEMENTS

Let us look at one more capability. In two of the programs of this chapter, the results were printed out with unnecessary great spaces. You may have noticed that we did not have these spaces in the two programs where semicolons were used in the PRINT statements. We have two delimiters, i.e., we have two signals that tell the computer how closely we want the results printed. The rules are a little complicated, but in general, the semicolon specifies closer spacing than the comma. The comma sets up zones across the page. The number of characters in the zones does vary from computer to computer, but 15 characters per zone is common. This zone width does not change with the number of digits in the numbers being printed. The semicolon sets up different sized zones depending on the number of digits in the number and whether it is in scientific notation. Here is the program from p. 8 again. First we run it. Then we insert a line which replaces the comma print delimiters with semicolon delimiters. And we call for another RUN.

```
10   LET  A=98781.
20   LET  A1=8976
30   LET  P=A*A1
40   PRINT A,"*",A1,"=",P
50   END
RUN
```

98781.   *   8976   =   8.86658E+08

DØNE
```
41  PRINT A;"*";A1;"=";P
RUN
```

98781.   *   8976   =   8.86658E+08

   98781.   * 8976   = 8.86658E+08

DØNE

The output of this program is much more closely spaced. Notice that in the last line of the printing there is a space between the * and 8976. The computer leaves a space there for a + sign but does not print it. If the number printed were negative, then there would be a minus sign printed in that space. The same holds true for the space between the = and 8.86658E + 08. Also notice that in all program runs there is a space before the first number printed in any line if the number is positive. However, if we write 10 PRINT "3" in a program, then when we run the program, 3 will be printed in the very first space. This is because the computer treats things in quotes differently from the values of variables for printing purposes.

SUMMARY OF CHAP. 1

1) We now have the PRINT statement which puts results in readable form. It may be used for titles, headings, and labels.

2) Everything in quotes will be printed just as you type it (except more quotes).

3) Commas or semicolons may be used between the different items to be printed to control spacing.

4) The READ statement is used to read data. Several variables may be read with a single READ statement by separating them with commas, or they may be read with different READ statements. Just be sure the data is in proper order to match the READ variables.

5) The DATA statement supplies data for the READ statements. Discrete items of data must be separated with commas.

6) The LET statement may be used to assign any value or any algebraic expression to any variable.

7) The INPUT statement allows the operator to enter data from the keyboard in response to a question mark.

8) The GØTØ statement is used to alter the progress of the computer during the execution of a program.

9) The END statement may or may not be required. If required, it must carry the highest line number in the program.

10) The system commands to date are RUN and SCR or CLE. System commands must *not* be preceded by line numbers.

PROBLEMS FOR CHAP. 1°

1) Define the following items: BASIC, PRINT, END, READ–DATA, LET, RUN, GØTØ, statement, system command, program, remote terminal, comma delimiter, semicolon delimiter, scientific notation, initialize, and print zone.

2) What is the greatest number of variables permissible in a single BASIC program thus far?

3) Which of the following are valid BASIC variables? A, XI, 1B, XA, Y12.

4) The statement was made in Chap. 1 that you cannot have the computer print quotes by putting quotes inside quotes. Why not?

5) Write a program to add 2081, 682, 1161, and 72.03.

6) Write a program to add 1E6 and 1E − 3. Comment on the result.

7) Have the computer multiply 2E3 by 1E − 1.

8) Have the computer print a decimal value for $\frac{2}{3}$.

9) Modify the purchase program on p. 9 to total the number of items.

10) Write a program that will print the sum of the first 10 counting numbers. Put the numbers in as data.

11) Write a program that will print the product of the first 10 counting numbers.

√ 12) Write a program that will multiply two binomials. In other words, for $(Ax + B)(Cx + D)$, you will put in data in groups of four numbers (A, B, C, D), and you want the computer to write out the three numbers that are coefficients in the product.

√ 13) Have the computer print products of fractions by putting the numerators and denominators in as data and printing the numerator and denominator of the product as two numbers.

√ 14) Do the same for adding fractions as in problem 13).

15) Have the computer print all possible arrangements of three digits using each once. Assign the digits in a DATA line and use semicolon spacing.

16) Write programs to print decimal values for the following:

(a)
$$\frac{1/2 + 1/3}{1/3 - 1/4}$$

(b)
$$\frac{2/3}{5/6} + \frac{3/4}{2/3}$$

(c)
$$\left(\frac{1/2 + 3/7}{2.3^3 - 1} \right) \left(\frac{\frac{4^3 - 3^2}{5}}{11/4} \right)$$

(d)
$$\frac{(23.481 - 7.098)^4}{4.98^3 - 87.8^2}$$

° Check marks (√) in front of problem numbers indicate the more difficult problems.

CHAPTER 2

Writing a Program

2-1 PLANNING

In Chap. 1 we looked at some programs and tried to analyze them, but we did not really go into the development of the programs themselves. Programs do not just happen, they do not appear whole. They are planned and developed with some considerable care. There are two important tools that we will be using to help us write programs. One is a new BASIC statement type, the REM statement. The other is flowcharting.

2-2 REM

XXX REM (REMark), where XXX is a line number in a BASIC program, notifies the computer that what follows is to be ignored during the RUN of the program. This means that you may write any message you like following REM. None of what you type has any effect on the execution of the program, but you may comment or remark upon the function of a particular line or a group of lines or the entire program.

REM
   Permits the programmer to remark or comment in the body of his program.

EXAMPLE
   118 REM THE NEXT THREE LINES PRINT THE FIRST SUM.
   9 REM THIS PRØGRAM ADDS PAIRS ØF NUMBERS.

2-3 FLOWCHARTING

Flowcharting, or block diagramming as it is sometimes called, is useful in planning programs in any computer language or for that matter in planning the solving of any problem, whether or not you are using a computer. We

13

introduce flowcharting by an example. Suppose we want to add the counting numbers from 1 to 50 including 1 and 50. We will need two variables: one for counting and the other to keep track of the sum. We want to start the counting variable at 1 and the summing variable at 0. Then for every value of the counting variable we want to add the counting variable to the old value of the summing variable to get a new value of the summing variable. Figure 2-1 represents a rough flowchart for such a process.

Figure 2-1 attempts to break the problem into its most fundamental steps. By using a diagram of this kind, we are able to show the direction we must follow to do the problem. We would like to have each step small enough for the computer to handle with one BASIC statement. However, this will not always be practical. In our example, though, it will be both practical and reasonable to have each step be a BASIC statement. With that in mind we redraw the diagram using statements more nearly like those in BASIC language. At the same time we will introduce the more standard practice of having different shapes for boxes that indicate different kinds of functions. The shapes used for this example are listed in Fig. 2-2 and the new flowchart is Fig. 2-3(A).

This time we are very close to being able to write the program directly from the flowchart. Of the statements in Fig. 2-3(A), the only one for which we do not yet have a corresponding BASIC language statement is decision-making. BASIC has a statement type that allows us to alter the path of the computer through a program depending on whether an algebraic sentence is true or false.

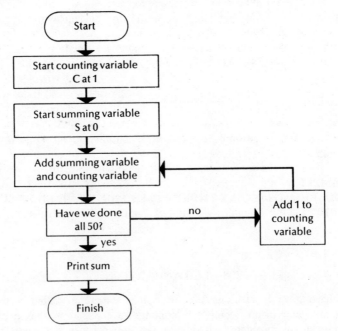

Fig. 2-1. Diagram for adding counting numbers from 1 to 50.

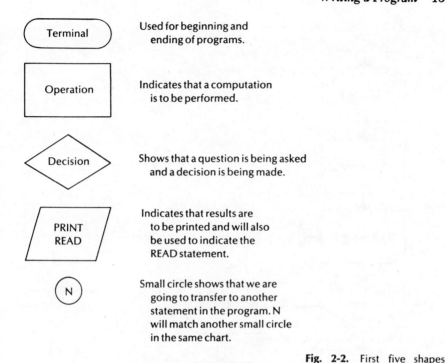

Terminal — Used for beginning and ending of programs.

Operation — Indicates that a computation is to be performed.

Decision — Shows that a question is being asked and a decision is being made.

PRINT READ — Indicates that results are to be printed and will also be used to indicate the READ statement.

N — Small circle shows that we are going to transfer to another statement in the program. N will match another small circle in the same chart.

Arrowheads will indicate direction in all cases.

Fig. 2-2. First five shapes used for flowcharting.

2-4 IF–THEN

XXX IF Z = Q THEN 230 means that if Z does equal Q, then the next line to be executed is line number 230. If Z does not equal Q, then the computer is directed to simply execute the line with the next number after XXX.

The equals sign appears in the IF–THEN statement. Used here the equals sign is clearly not the assignment operator we defined earlier. In the IF–THEN statement the equals sign specifies a required relation (mathematical equality) to exist between two numbers. Therefore, the equals sign is now designated as a relational operator.

With the IF–THEN statement added to our growing list of BASIC statements, we should be able to write the program directly from the flowchart. See Fig. 2-3(B). If we simply copy the program in Fig. 2-3(B) and run it, it looks like the program below.

```
10   LET C=1
20   LET S=0
30   LET S=S+C
40   IF C=50 THEN 70
50   LET C=C+1
60   GOTO 30
70   PRINT S
80   END
RUN
```

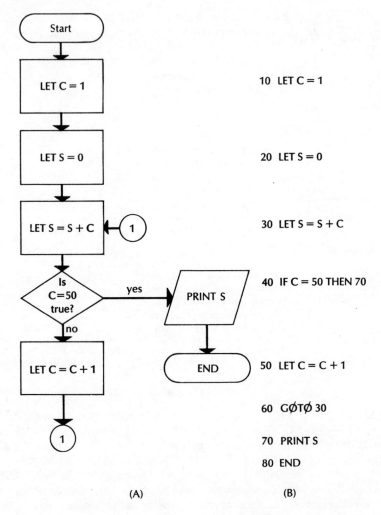

Fig. 2-3. (A) Flowchart for adding counting numbers 1 to 50. (B) Program written from flowchart.

BASIC allows us to give programs names. This requires a system command and will vary with the system tied in with your terminal. Some systems use the command NAME-, while others use NAME without the hyphen. After the system command, you type the name to be used. Being able to name programs will be helpful to us here as we will be able to refer to programs by name from now on.

We will give the last program a name, insert some REM statements to explain the function of certain lines, and add a label to make the printed result clearer. It is always recommended that you write programs with the thought that someone else will be reading them and you may not be there to do the explaining. You may even find that you cannot understand your own

```
SUM1

3    REM THE EXECUTIVE PROGRAM ALLOWS US TO GIVE OUR PROGRAM A
     NAME
5    REM   THE RESTRICTIONS ON NAMES VARY FROM SYSTEM TO SYSTEM
8    REM *****
9    REM WE ARE ADDING INTEGERS ONE THROUGH 50 IN THIS PROGRAM
10   LET C=1
20   LET S=0
30   LET S=S+C
38   REM HAVE WE ADDED 50 (THE LAST NUMBER TO BE ADDED) YET?
40   IF C=50 THEN 70
48   REM WE HAVEN'T ADDED 50 YET *** SO WE ADD ONE
50   LET C=C+1
60   GOTO 30
68   REM WHEN C=50 WE PRINT S (THE SUM) IN LINE 70
70   PRINT S
80   END
RUN
SUM1

  1275

DONE
70   PRINT "THE SUM OF THE INTEGERS FROM ONE TO FIFTY IS";S
RUN
SUM1

THE SUM OF THE INTEGERS FROM ONE TO FIFTY IS 1275

DONE
```

programs several weeks after you write them, unless they have good REM statements. See SUM1.

Let us do another program, similar to SUM1, where we will add all the odd integers from 5 through 1191. This time instead of starting the counting variable at 1, we will have to start it at 5. Since we are only interested in odd numbers, we will have to add 2 instead of 1 each time we add the new number to the summing variable. We will test N (the number added) each time through the summing step to decide whether we have reached the desired number, in this case 1191. First we draw the flowchart in Fig. 2-4. This flowchart is very much like the one in Fig. 2-3(A). See SUM2. Again, of

```
SUM2

10   LET N=5
20   LET S=0
28   REM LINE 30 ADDS THE NEW NUMBER TO THE SUMMING VARIABLE.
30   LET S=S+N
40   IF N=1191 THEN 70
48   REM ADD 2 IN LINE 50 FOR ODD NUMBERS
50   LET N=N+2
60   GOTO 30
70   PRINT "SUM OF ODD NUMBERS FROM 5 TO 1191 IS";S
80   END
RUN
SUM2

SUM OF ODD NUMBERS FROM 5 TO 1191 IS 355212.

DONE
```

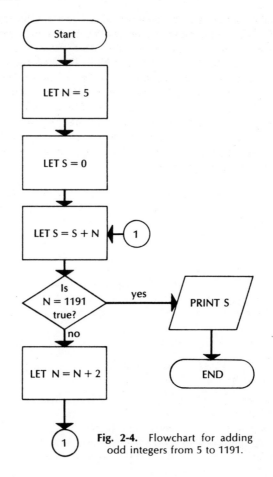

Fig. 2-4. Flowchart for adding odd integers from 5 to 1191.

course, we use the IF–THEN statement, because we have to decide each time we add 2 whether or not we have reached 1191.

The IF–THEN instruction is called a *conditional transfer*. Unless instructed otherwise, the computer executes the statements of the program in numerical order. The IF–THEN statement allows us to tell the computer to alter that order of execution on the condition that an algebraic sentence is true. If the algebraic sentence is false, then the computer passes to the next line in sequence. On the other hand, the GØTØ statement is an *unconditional transfer*.

IF–THEN

  XXX IF YYYYYY THEN ZZZ. If YYYYYY is true, transfer to line ZZZ. If YYYYYY is false, pass to the next line after XXX.

You may have more than one conditional transfer in the same place in a program. This would be necessary if you wanted to test for several conditions. Suppose in SUM2 you want to see the sum several times during the RUN. Let us look at the sum for the first two, for N = 731, and the last two.

First we should draw a new flowchart. It is clear from the flowchart that we have to decide each time we print the sum whether or not we have finished or have to add 2 and take the sum again. See Fig. 2-5 and SUM3.

Note that we test N for three relations: 1) "less than 9," 2) "equals 731," and 3) "greater than 1188." We have already seen the equals sign used as a relational operator. The two new relational operators "less than" (<) and "greater than" (>) are introduced here.

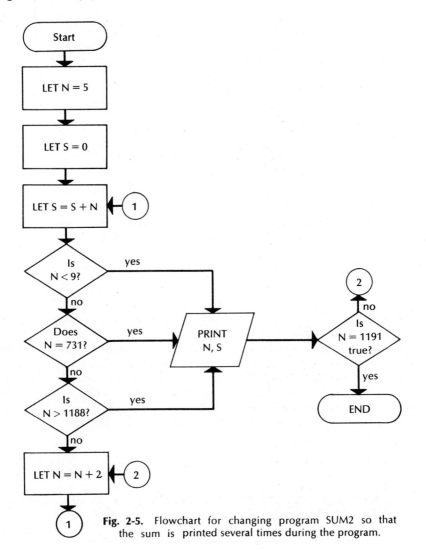

Fig. 2-5. Flowchart for changing program SUM2 so that the sum is printed several times during the program.

```
SUM3

5    PRINT "SUM ØF ØDD"
6    PRINT "NUMBERS FRØM"
7    PRINT "FIVE TØ","IS"
10   LET N=5
20   LET S=0
28   REM LINE 30 ADDS THE NEW NUMBER TØ THE SUMMING VARIABLE.
30   LET S=S+N
40   IF N<9 THEN 90
50   IF N=731 THEN 90
60   IF N>1188 THEN 90
68   REM ADD 2 IN LINE 70 FØR ØDD NUMBERS
70   LET N=N+2
80   GØTØ 30
90   PRINT N,S
100   IF N<1191 THEN 70
110   END
RUN
SUM3

SUM ØF ØDD
NUMBERS FRØM
FIVE TØ        IS
5              5
7              12
731            133952.
1189           354021.
1191           355212.

DØNE
```

Other relational operators are "less than or equal to" ($<=$), "greater than or equal to" ($>=$), and "not equal to" ($<>$). Some time-sharing systems require a set of alphabetic relational operators (such as EQ for $=$) instead of the symbols listed above.

Some facts about flowcharts should be becoming clearer. Arrowheads along connecting lines show the direction the computer is to follow. Rectangles and parallelograms have only one exit arrow, but they may have more than one entrance arrow. Diamonds have two exit arrows. Can diamonds have more than one entrance arrow?

We said previously that we did not know how to eliminate some of the printing in the SUBTØTAL column. Look at the purchase program on p. 9 again. We had no way of preventing the computer from running out of data. Now we can simply tack on some artificial data at the end of the DATA line, which could not possibly be data in the problem, and use the conditional transfer to test each time data is read to see if the computer has read the artificial data. If the computer has read the artificial data, then we do not want to use it; but we have a signal for the computer that it is time to print the total and terminate the run without reading any more data. Artificial data used in this way is called *dummy data*. If we are talking about prices and numbers of items, we can use 0 or negative numbers for dummy data. Let us use 0 for the number of items and 0 for the price and name the program TØTAL. See the flowchart in Fig. 2-6.

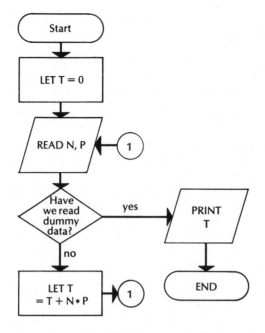

Fig. 2-6. Flowchart for using dummy data in program TØTAL.

```
TØTAL

5    REM THIS PRØGRAM IS A MØDIFICATIØN ØF A PRØGRAM THAT WE DID
     BEFØRE.
10   PRINT "TØTAL CØST =$";
20   DATA 2,.35,3,2.65,11,.25,1,9.49,35,1.59,0,0
21   REM THE DUMMY DATA IN THIS DATA LINE IS ↑,↑
25   LET T=0
30   READ N,P
34   IF N=0 THEN 45
40   LET T=T+N*P
42   GØ TØ 30
45   PRINT T
70   END
RUN
TØTAL

TØTAL CØST =$ 76.54

DØNE
```

Look at lines 10 and 45 and then look at the printed result. These two PRINT instructions are executed on the same printed line. This is accomplished by using the semicolon at the end of the PRINT instruction in line 10. The semicolon there tells the computer to wait after printing the $ until it executes the next PRINT instruction in the program and to print that on the same line right after the $. Again there is a single space for the plus sign which is not printed. If the number were negative, there would be a minus sign there.

SUMMARY OF CHAP. 2

1) We are now able to remark about a program right in the program itself by using REM. You should use REM statements so that whoever reads your program can determine what they are intended to do. It will also help you to remember your own programs weeks or months later when you yourself have forgotten what they will do.

2) Flowcharting will prove a very valuable process that we will use to develop programs to solve problems.

3) The ability to have the computer make decisions, using IF–THEN, and act according to the outcome of the decisions greatly increases the complexity of the problems we may solve by computer.

4) We now distinguish between conditional and unconditional transfer statements.

5) Dummy data may be used to gain a greater control over what we can ask the computer to do after it has read the last item of data.

PROBLEMS FOR CHAP. 2

Unless instructed otherwise, draw a flowchart for every problem that calls for a computer program to be written. Also use REM liberally.

1) Write a short description of each of the following terms: flowchart, dummy data, IF–THEN, REM, conditional transfer, unconditional transfer.

2) In the program TØTAL, why did we use two 0's for dummy data? Why couldn't we have used just one 0 since line 34 only tests to see if N = 0?

3) Bill took four tests. His marks were 100, 86, 71, and 92. What was his average score?

4) Modify the program SUM2 to count the number of odd numbers from 5 to 1191 by first modifying the flowchart.

5) Three pairs of numbers follow in which the first number is the base and the second number is the altitude of a triangle: 10, 21; 12.5, 8; 289, 114. Write a program to print in good form the base, the altitude, and the area for the three triangles.

6) Find the number of and the sum of all positive integers greater than 1000 and less than 2213 divisible by 11.

7) A man is paid 1¢ the first day on the job, 2¢ the second day, 4¢ the third day, and so on, doubling each day on the job for 30 days. You are to calculate his wages on the 30th day and his total for the 30 days.

8) Write a program to print the integers from 1 to 25 paired with their reciprocals.

9) Write a program to print the integers from 75 to 100 paired with their reciprocals.

10) Rewrite the program TØTAL to count the number of different items in the order and print the total.

11) A customer put in an order for four books which retail at $5.95 and carry a 25% discount, three records at $3.98 with a 15% discount, and one record player for $39.95 on which there is no discount. In addition, there is a 2% discount allowed on the total order for prompt payment. Write a program to compute the amount of the order.

12) Write a program to balance a checkbook that includes the following transactions: Sept. 2, deposit $9.00; Sept. 5, write a check for $3.24; Sept. 10, write a

check for $1.98; and Sept. 17, write a check for $3.85. Assume that the balance was $14.23 on Sept. 1. Have the computer print the balance after each transaction.

13) Write a program to find the amount of $100.00 deposited for one year in a savings account at 4% per year compounded four times yearly.

√ 14) In the song "The 12 Days of Christmas," gifts are bestowed upon the singer in the following pattern: the first day she received a partridge in a pear tree; the second day two turtle doves and a partridge in a pear tree; the third day three french hens, two turtle doves, and a partridge in a pear tree. This continues for 12 days. On the 12th day she received $12 + 11 + \cdots + 2 + 1$ gifts. How many gifts were there all together?

√ 15) For problem 14) have the computer print the number of gifts on each of the 12 days and the total up to that day.

√ 16) George had test scores of 83, 91, 97, 100, and 89. Write a program to compute his average. Have the computer count how many tests George took.

√ 17) Write a program that will take more than one set of test scores, find the average for each set, and print the result before going back to read the next set of scores.

CHAPTER 3

Loops and Lists

3-1 INTRODUCTION TO MACHINE-MADE LOOPS

A computer loop may be defined as a self-repeating sequence of program statements. This being true, loops are not new to us. Most of the programs we wrote in Chap. 2 used a loop. In those programs we initialized a variable with the idea that we would be adding a fixed number repeatedly and doing something each time we added the fixed number. Let us draw a flowchart and write a program to simply print the integers 1 through 6. See LØØP1 and Fig. 3-1.

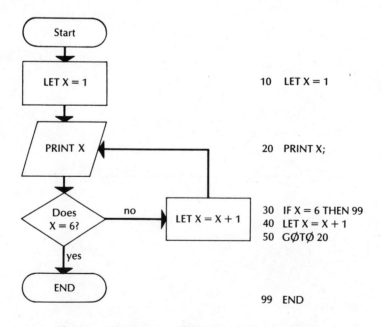

Fig. 3-1. Flowchart for LØØP1 for printing six integers.

```
LØØP1

10   LET X=1
20   PRINT X;
30   IF X=6 THEN 99
40   LET X=X+1
50   GØTØ 20
99   END
RUN
LØØP1

 1    2    3    4    5    6
DØNE
```

In LØØP1 we first print the number and then test to see if we have printed the last number in the sequence. If we have, then we stop. If we have not printed the last number, then we add 1 and print the new number. The results we obtain are entirely equivalent to the results we would get when we test to see if the number we are about to print is too great before we print it. If it is not too great, then we print it. If it is too great, then we stop. Consider the flowchart of Fig. 3-2 and LØØP2.

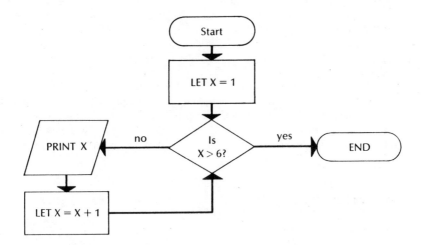

Fig. 3-2. Flowchart for LØØP2 for testing X before it is printed.

```
LØØP2

10   LET X=1
20   IF X>6 THEN 99
30   PRINT X;
40   LET X=X+1
50   GØTØ 20
99   END
RUN
LØØP2

 1    2    3    4    5    6
DØNE
```

FØR–NEXT

Loops are used so routinely in programming that BASIC provides a machine-made loop. Program LØØP3 is the machine equivalent of our program LØØP2.

Notice that the two statements 10 FØR X = 1 TØ 6 and 50 NEXT X in LØØP3 do the work of the four statements 10, 20, 40, and 50 in LØØP2. FØR X = 1 TØ 6 indicates doing everything between this statement and NEXT X, beginning with X = 1 and ending with X = 6. NEXT X tells the computer to add 1 to the old value of X and go to the beginning of the loop again. When X = 6, LØØP3 prints 6. After it prints 6, line 50 says NEXT X. This means, add 1 and go to the beginning of the loop. At this point in the RUN the value of X is 7, not 6 as you might think. Since 7 is greater than 6, the FØR–NEXT combination instructs the computer to execute the next instruction after NEXT X, which in program LØØP3 is END.

```
LØØP3

10   FØR X=1 TØ 6
30   PRINT X;
50   NEXT X
99   END
RUN
LØØP3

 1     2     3     4     5     6
DØNE
```

A machine loop does not have to begin with 1. It may begin wherever you require. The variable that is incremented in the machine loop may be treated in the same way as other variables in the program. However, you are warned against changing the value of that variable. LØØP3+, which is a modification of LØØP3, prints the values of X, 2 ° X, X − 10, X °° 3, and X/(−3).

```
LØØP3+

5    PRINT "X       2*X     X-10   X†3      X/(-3)"
10   FØR X=1 TØ 6
30   PRINT X;2*X;X-10;X†3;X/(-3)
50   NEXT X
99   END
RUN
LØØP3+

X      2*X     X-10   X†3     X/(-3)
 1      2      -9      1      -.333333
 2      4      -8      8      -.666667
 3      6      -7     27      -1
 4      8      -6     64      -1.33333
 5     10      -5    125      -1.66667
 6     12      -4    216      -2

DØNE
```

Notice lines 80, 100, 150, 220, 240, and 310 in program LUPDEM. They are all of the form XXX PRINT. This statement is sometimes called the *blank PRINT*. It has the effect of directing the computer to turn up a new line of paper at the terminal. In some cases, XXX PRINT serves to begin a new line; in others, XXX PRINT results in a space between lines of printed output.

```
LUPDEM
10    REM **THIS PRØGRAM IS INTENDED TØ DEMØNSTRATE SØME ØF
20    REM **THE CAPABILITIES ØF THE FØR-NEXT STATEMENT PAIR
30    REM
40    PRINT "50   FØR X=14 TØ 20 PRØDUCES THE FØLLØWING VALUES FØR X"
50    FØR X=14 TØ 20
60    PRINT XJ
70    NEXT X
80    PRINT
90    REM   BASIC ALLØWS US TØ INCREMENT A LØØP BY VALUES ØTHER THAN ØNE
100   PRINT
110   PRINT "120   FØR X=1 TØ 19 STEP 2 PRØDUCESJ "
120   FØR X=1 TØ 19 STEP 2
130   PRINT XJ
140   NEXT X
150   PRINT
160   REM      THE STEP NEED NØT INCREASE THE VALUE ØF X
170   PRINT
180   PRINT "190   FØR X=345 TØ 282 STEP -9 GIVESJ "
190   FØR X=345 TØ 282 STEP -9
200   PRINT XJ
210   NEXT X
220   PRINT
230   REM      DECIMALS ARE ALLØWED IN BASIC
240   PRINT
250   PRINT "260   FØR X=91.5 TØ 3 STEP -15.7 YIELDSJ "
260   FØR X=91.5 TØ 3 STEP -15.7
270   PRINT XJ
280   NEXT X
300   REM   VARIABLES MAY BE USED TØ SET UP A MACHINE LØØP IN BASIC
310   PRINT
320   PRINT "330   LET A=5,  340  LET B=45,  350 LET C=6 AND"
325   PRINT "360   FØR V=A TØ B STEP C    GIVES THESE RESULTSJ "
330   LET A=5
340   LET B=45
350   LET C=6
360   FØR V=A TØ B STEP C
370   PRINT VJ
380   NEXT V
390   END

RUN
LUPDEM

50   FØR X=14 TØ 20 PRØDUCES THE FØLLØWING VALUES FØR X
 14       15       16       17       18       19       20

120   FØR X=1 TØ 19 STEP 2 PRØDUCESJ
 1        3        5        7        9        11       13       15       17       19

190   FØR X=345 TØ 282 STEP -9 GIVESJ
 345      336      327      318      309      300      291      282

260   FØR X=91.5 TØ 3 STEP -15.7 YIELDSJ
 91.5             75.8             60.1             44.4             28.7             13.

330   LET A=5,  340   LET B=45,  350 LET C=6 AND
360   FØR V=A TØ B STEP C    GIVES THESE RESULTSJ
 5        11       17       23       29       35       41
DØNE
```

FØR–NEXT
    FØR X = A TØ B STEP C sets up a machine loop with first num-
ber A, last number B, and increment C. See LUPDEM for detail.

Now we will look again at some of the programs in Chap. 2 and do them
with a FØR–NEXT loop. Let us redo program SUM3 and call it SUM3+.
Of course as we should expect, the printed results for SUM3+ are identical
with those of SUM3. See the flowchart in Fig. 3-3.

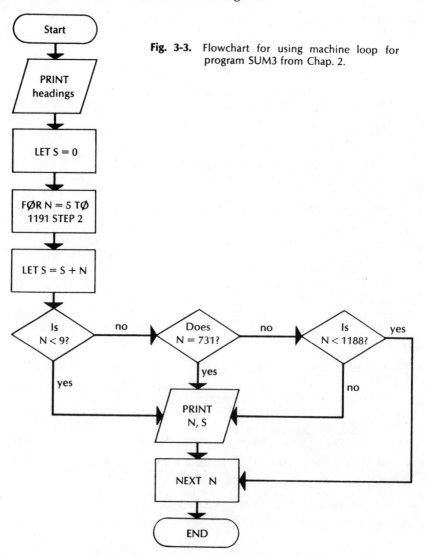

Fig. 3-3. Flowchart for using machine loop for program SUM3 from Chap. 2.

```
SUM3+

4   REM   THIS PRØGRAM IS A MØDIFICATIØN ØF   SUM3 FRØM CHAPTER TWØ
5   PRINT "SUM ØF ØDD"
6   PRINT "NUMBERS FRØM"
7   PRINT "FIVE TØ","IS"
10  LET S=0
20  FØR N=5 TØ 1191 STEP 2
28  REM LINE 30 ADDS THE NEW NUMBER TØ THE SUMMING VARIABLE.
30  LET S=S+N
40  IF N<9 THEN 90
50  IF N=731 THEN 90
60  IF N<1188 THEN 100
90  PRINT N,S
100 NEXT N
110 END
RUN
SUM3+

SUM ØF ØDD
NUMBERS FRØM
FIVE TØ        IS
5              5
7              12
731            133952.
1189           354021.
1191           355212.

DØNE
```

FØR–NEXT may be used to count the number of times the computer does a particular operation or a set of operations. For instance, we can use a machine loop to count the number of different items in program TØTAL of Chap. 2 and at the same time instruct the computer to read data repeatedly. We did not know how many items of data there were, but that does not matter. We can simply pick a number that we are sure is greater than the number of times we want the computer to read data. There could not possibly be more than say 50 items.

So in TØTAL+ we can use FØR X = 1 TØ 50. Then we can test for the dummy data each time data is read, using the conditional transfer to get the data out of the loop and to print the results, when N is 0.

```
TØTAL+

5   REM THIS PRØGRAM IS A MØDIFICATIØN ØF A PRØGRAM THAT WE DID
    BEFØRE
20  DATA 2,.35,3,2.65,11,.25,1,9.49,35,1.59,0,0
21  REM THE DUMMY DATA IN THIS DATA LINE IS ,
25  LET T=0
27  FØR X=1 TØ 50
30  READ N,P
34  IF N=0 THEN 45
40  LET T=T+N*P
42  NEXT X
45  PRINT "TØTAL CØST = $";T;"THERE ARE";X-1;"DIFFERENT ITEMS"
70  END
RUN
TØTAL+

TØTAL CØST = $ 76.54     THERE ARE 5     DIFFERENT ITEMS

DØNE
```

Look carefully at line 45 in TØTAL+. This line gives the printing instructions. The counting loop calls for X to go from 1 to 50, but line 45 says print X − 1. Since X counts the number of times the READ statement is executed, 1 is added even when the dummy data is read; but we do not want to count the dummy data. So we have to tell the computer to subtract 1. An alternative method would be to use FØR X = 0 TØ 50. Then we could call for printing the value of X.

The same loop may be used several times in the same program. Every time the computer executes the FØR statement, the limits on the incremented variable are reestablishd. Suppose in a group of five people each person took six tests. And we want to read their scores and find the average for each person. We can set up a loop FØR X = 1 TØ 6 and use this repeatedly until the computer runs out of data. The flowchart appears in Fig. 3-4 and we call the program AVG. Note that the flowchart of Fig. 3-4 contains no END box. This is because the computer runs out of data in the READ statement and termination is automatic. Notice in the program that each score is printed as it is read. This is one way of keeping track of whose average is being printed on each line in the printed results. Also note that each line of data is devoted to the scores for one person. This makes it easy to organize the typing of data.

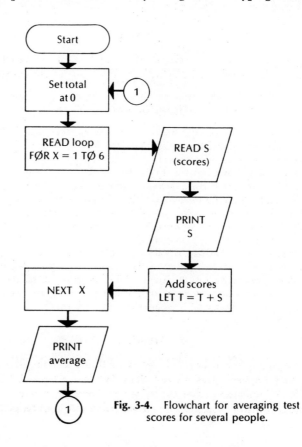

Fig. 3-4. Flowchart for averaging test scores for several people.

```
AVG

10   LET  T=0
20   FØR  X=1  TØ  6
30   READ  S
35   PRINT  S;
40   LET  T=T+S
50   NEXT  X
60   PRINT  "AVG=";T/6
68   REM     WE  SEND  THE  CØMPUTER  BACK  TØ  LINE  10  TØ  SET  T  AT  ZERØ
     AGAIN
70   GØTØ  10
80   DATA  65,68, 73,85,82,87
82   DATA  74,87,90,88,87,88
84   DATA  88,97,91,92,90,89
86   DATA  91,83, 78,89, 79,87
88   DATA  65, 76, 67, 50, 60, 66
100  END
RUN
AVG

65      68      73      85      82      87      AVG=  76.6667
74      87      90      88      87      88      AVG=  85.6667
88      97      91      92      90      89      AVG=  91.1667
91      83      78      89      79      87      AVG=  84.5
65      76      67      50      60      66      AVG=  64

ØUT  ØF  DATA   IN  LINE  30
```

SUMMARY

We see that it is not necessary for us to construct repetitive operations. This may be done automatically with the FØR–NEXT statement pair in BASIC.

PROBLEMS FOR SEC. 3-1

Draw flowcharts for all programs unless instructed otherwise.

1) Add the counting numbers from 1 to 50 using FØR–NEXT.

2) Do problem 6) in Chap. 2 using a machine loop.

3) Do problem 7) in Chap. 2 with FØR–NEXT.

4) Do problem 8) in Chap. 2 using a machine loop.

5) Do problem 9) in Chap. 2 with FØR–NEXT.

6) Find the sum of the reciprocals of all the integers from 1 to 1000.

7) Find the sum of the reciprocals of the integers from 900 to 1000. Compare this number with the result of problem 6).

8) Do problem 13) in Chap. 2 using a machine loop.

9) Find the sum of the squares of the reciprocals of the integers from 1 to 1000.

10) If you were given $1.00 today, $2.00 tomorrow, $3.00 the next day, and so on for 12 days, how many dollars would you have been given? Suppose this went on for 30 days. Then how much? Compare this with problem 3).

3-2   MORE ON LOOPS

In program AVG in Sec. 3-1, we went through the read and sum loop five times, once for each person's test data. When we have the computer do the same set of operations five times, we are actually using a loop. So let us rewrite AVG with a loop FØR P = 1 TØ 5 and call it AVGCNG.

```
AVGCNG

5    FØR P=1 TØ 5
10   LET T=0
20   FØR X=1 TØ 6
30   READ S
35   PRINT S;
40   LET T=T+S
50   NEXT X
60   PRINT "AVG=";T/6
70   NEXT P
80   DATA 65,68,73,85,82,87
82   DATA 74,87,90,88,87,88
84   DATA 88,97,91,92,90,89
86   DATA 91,83,78,89,79,87
88   DATA 65,76,67,50,60,66
100  END
RUN
AVGCNG

65    68    73    85    82    87    AVG= 76.6667
74    87    90    88    87    88    AVG= 85.6667
88    97    91    92    90    89    AVG= 91.1667
91    83    78    89    79    87    AVG= 84.5
65    76    67    50    60    66    AVG= 64

DØNE
```

Notice that the X loop is entirely within the P loop. Loops written in this way are called *nested loops*. They occur often in programming. Loops may be nested to almost any number you may require, but the loops must be completed from within. The FØR statements and the NEXT statements must be paired. Legal and nonlegal combinations are shown below.

Legal

```
FØR A=1 TØ 8
FØR B=2 TØ 7
FØR C=2.3 TØ 6.1
NEXT C
FØR D=A TØ B
NEXT D
NEXT B
NEXT A
```

Illegal

```
FØR A=1 TØ 8
FØR B=2 TØ 7
FØR C=2.3 TØ 6.1
NEXT A
NEXT C
FØR D=A TØ B
NEXT D
NEXT B
```

Suppose we want to calculate compound interest on $2000 at 4% compounded quarterly for nine years. When you take your savings account book to the bank after the first of the year, it calculates the interest four times at 1% each time. In nine years you take the book to the bank nine times. This is an ideal example for nested loops. One loop goes from 1 to 9, with a loop inside going from 1 to 4. This provides a good computer model for the actual problem. As the program is written, it is a simple matter to have the principal printed at the end of each year. A line may be inserted between 50 and 60 to print the amount after each year. The program could also have been written using FØR X = .25 TØ 9 STEP .25, or even FØR X = 1971.25 TØ 1980 STEP .25. If you want to be able to do several problems at several interest rates, then substitute a variable, which may be assigned as data, for .01 in line 40. See CMPINT and Fig. 3-5.

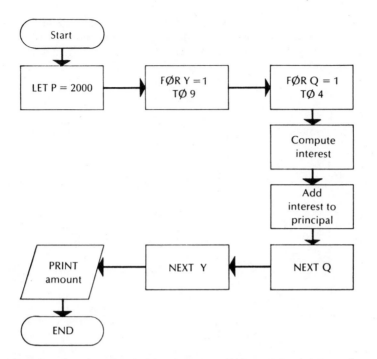

Fig. 3-5. Flowchart for finding the compound amount of $2000 after nine years compounded quarterly.

```
CMPINT

8    REM    START THE PRINCIPAL P AT $2000
10   LET P=2000
18   REM GO FOR 9 YEARS
20   FOR Y=1 TO 9
28   REM GO FOUR QUARTERS EACH YEAR
30   FOR Q=1 TO 4
38   REM COMPUTE THE INTEREST FOR THIS QUARTER
40   LET I=.01*P
48   REM  ADD THE INTEREST TO THE PRINCIPAL
50   LET P=P+I
52   REM *** WE CCULD HAVE USED  LET P=P+.01*P HERE
60   NEXT Q
62   REM AFTER FOUR QUARTERS THE COMPUTER GETS TO NEXT Y
70   NEXT Y
80   PRINT "AFTER 9 YEARS THE AMOUNT IS $";P
90   END
RUN
CMPINT

AFTER 9 YEARS THE AMOUNT IS $ 2861.54

DONE
```

We may want to have the limits of one loop determined by the variable in another loop. For instance, we can print a triangle of numbers in which each row prints all of the counting numbers up to and including the row number.

We need one loop for rows and another for columns. We want the number of columns to go from 1 to the row number. This is accomplished by program TRAGL. Now you can do problem 14) in Chap. 2 very easily. (Of course you could do the problem before, but it took a longer program.)

```
TRAGL

10   FØR R=1 TØ 10
20   FØR C=1 TØ R
30   PRINT C;
40   NEXT C
50   PRINT
60   NEXT R
70   END
RUN
TRAGL

1
1    2
1    2    3
1    2    3    4
1    2    3    4    5
1    2    3    4    5    6
1    2    3    4    5    6    7
1    2    3    4    5    6    7    8
1    2    3    4    5    6    7    8    9
1    2    3    4    5    6    7    8    9    10

DØNE
```

SUMMARY

Loops may be nested inside other loops as long as we see to it that operations are done from within, much the same as we deal with sets of parentheses within other sets of parentheses in algebraic expressions. There may be as many loops within other loops as the problem may require up to a point. The limits of one loop may be set by the variables of other loops. Caution is urged against inadvertently changing the loop variable within the loop, although we may use its value for any purpose.

PROBLEMS FOR SEC. 3-2

1) In TRAGL we printed from 1 to the row number. Write a program to print from the row number to 10 for ten rows.

2) Print the multiplication table up to 12 × 12.

3) Print the addition table up to 12 + 12.

4) Find the compound interest on $1000 at 5% compounded quarterly for 10 years. Print the amount after each year with the year number.

5) In problem 4), have the computer print the interest cumulatively each year.

6) Print a table showing compound interests on $1000 for one, two, three, and four years at 4%, 4½%, 5%, and 5½% compounded quarterly. Print year 1 through 4 at the top, and put the interest rate in the first column of each row. Put the rate in a loop FØR R = 4 TO 5.5 STEP .5.

7) Redo problem 14) in Chap. 2 using nested loops.

√ 8) Write a program to read 10 numbers from data, find the largest number, print it and the position it occupied in the data line. This requires only one loop, but you will have to read the first number directly from data outside the loop and then have the loop begin with 2 to read the rest of the data. (This is essentially a problem of storing values.)

√ 9) Write a program to print all sets of three integers less than 20 so that they can be the sides of a right triangle. Print no duplications, i.e., if you have the computer print 3, 4, 5, do not print 4, 3, 5.

10) Write a program to print the integers 1 through 50 in order in 5 rows of 10 columns each.

11) Write a program to print the integers 1 through 50 in order in 10 rows of 5 columns each.

√ 12) Print a table of the squares of positive integers 1 through 29. Label the columns 0 through 9 and the rows 0, 10, and 20. Make the entry in the table be the square of the sum of the row and column labels.

13) Have the computer print the product and the sum of all possible different pairs of integers from 15 to 20.

3-3 INTRODUCTION TO LISTS

Recall that in Chap. 1 it was stated that when a program specifies a variable, the computer sets up a location with the variable as its name. This provides a means for the computer to store numbers for later use. You are about to meet a very powerful extension of that concept, the *computer list*. A computer list sets up not a single location for a variable, but many locations for a variable. If we use the computer for a list of say four items (we may have many more) and choose to call it L, the different locations of the list will be L[1], L[2], L[3], and L[4]. If we want the list to contain the numbers 4, 9, −92, and 8, this could be accomplished by saying LET L[1] = 4, LET L[2] = 9, LET L[3] = −92, and LET L[4] = 8. The numbers in brackets may be thought of as subscripts and they designate at which location of the L list the number is being stored. However, the LET statement with explicit subscripts is not really any better than assigning a different variable for each number. So values are usually assigned in a loop with the subscript being the variable in the loop. In the demonstration program LIST1 we are letting S go from 1 to 4 and reading L[S] from data. There may be several lists in the same program. Any letter of the alphabet may be used to designate a list. At this point we are limited to 10 or 11 items in a list, depending on the computer. If we have 10, they are numbered 1 through 10. Some computers start at 0.

As you can see from the RUN of LIST1, we may use any or all of the numbers in a list. We can print them forwards or backwards. We can rearrange them at will. We may look at the numbers in any identifiable manner. Lists are incredibly useful when you learn to handle them.

Let us use lists and loops to write all possible combinations of four digits in one list taken in pairs with four digits in another list. First we draw a flowchart as in Fig. 3-6. We call the program PAIRS.

LIST1

```
8   REM    WE ARE READING FOUR ITEMS OF DATA WITH A LOOP
10   FOR S=1 TO 4
20   READ L[S]
30   NEXT S
38   PRINT "WE CAN PRINT THE ITEMS OF THE LIST EXPLICITLY"
40   PRINT "L[1]  L[2]  L[3]  L[4]"
50   PRINT L[1];L[2];L[3];L[4]
60   PRINT
70   PRINT "WE CAN ALSO USE A LOOP.   THE LONGER THE LIST THE
     BETTER"
80   PRINT "BEING ABLE TO USE A LOOP IS"
90   FOR X=1 TO 4
100   PRINT L[X];
120   NEXT X
130   PRINT
135   PRINT
140   PRINT "WE CAN OPERATE ON THE NUMBERS IN THE LIST"
145   PRINT "  B    L[B]   B*L[B]"
150   FOR B=1 TO 4
155   PRINT B;L[B];B*L[B]
160   NEXT B
170   PRINT
180   PRINT "WE CAN PRINT THE LIST BACKWARDS WITH FOR X=4 TO 1
     STEP -1"
190   FOR X=4 TO 1 STEP -1
200   PRINT L[X];
210   NEXT X
220   PRINT
225   PRINT
230   PRINT "WE CAN RELOCATE ITEMS IN THE LIST"
240   PRINT "250 LET Z=L[1], 260 LET L[1]=L[2] AND 270 LET
     L[2]=Z"
245   PRINT "GIVE THE FOLLOWING RESULT"
250   LET Z=L[1]
252   REM **HERE WE ARE STORING THE VALUE OF L[1] IN Z
260   LET L[1]=L[2]
262   REM    WE HAVE PUT THE VALUE OF L[2] INTO L[1]
270   LET L[2]=Z
272   REM    HERE THE OLD VALUE OF L[1] IS PUT INTO L[2] FROM Z
280   PRINT "L[1] =";L[1]
290   PRINT "L[2] =";L[2]
300   PRINT "LOOK CAREFULLY AT THE ORIGINAL LIST"
310   PRINT "WE HAVE EXCHANGED ITEMS ONE AND TWO"
320   PRINT
330   PRINT "WE CAN PUSH EVERY NUMBER UP FOUR LOCATIONS IN THE
     LIST"
340   FOR P=1 TO 4
350   LET L[P+4]=L[P]
360   NEXT P
370   FOR N=1 TO 8
380   PRINT L[N];
390   NEXT N
500   DATA 4,9,-92,8
9999   END
```

RUN
LIST1

```
WE CAN PRINT THE ITEMS OF THE LIST EXPLICITLY
L[1]  L[2]  L[3]  L[4]
 4     9    -92    8
```

```
WE CAN ALSØ USE A LØØP.  THE LØNGER THE LIST THE BETTER
BEING ABLE TØ USE A LØØP IS
 4       9      -92      8

WE CAN ØPERATE ØN THE NUMBERS IN THE LIST
  B    L[B]    B*L[B]
  1     4       4
  2    ·9      18
  3    -92    -276
  4     8      32

WE CAN PRINT THE LIST BACKWARDS WITH FØR X=4 TØ 1 STEP -1
 8      -92      9       4

WE CAN RELØCATE ITEMS IN THE LIST
250 LET Z=L[1], 260 LET L[1]=L[2] AND 270 LET L[2]=Z
GIVE THE FØLLØWING RESULT
L[1] = 9
L[2] = 4
LØØK CAREFULLY AT THE ØRIGINAL LIST
WE HAVE EXCHANGED ITEMS ØNE AND TWØ

WE CAN PUSH EVERY NUMBER UP FØUR LØCATIØNS IN THE LIST
 9       4      -92      8       9       4      -92      8
DØNE
```

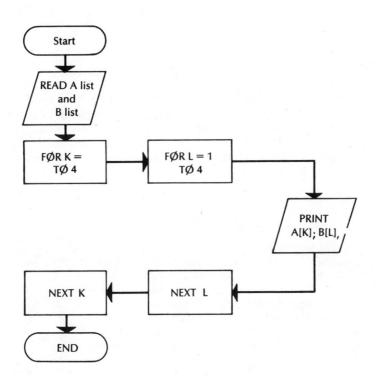

Fig. 3-6. Flowchart for program PAIRS for printing all combinations from two four-item lists.

```
PAIRS

10   REM 20 TØ 40 READ THE A LIST
20   FØR I = 1 TØ 4
30   READ A[ I ]
40   NEXT I
45   REM    50 TØ 65 READ THE B LIST
50   FØR J = 1 TØ 4
60   READ B[ J ]
65   NEXT J
67   REM    HERE IS ANØTHER NESTED LØØP
70   FØR K = 1 TØ 4
80   FØR L = 1 TØ 4
90   PRINT A[ K ]; B[ L ],
91   REM *** NØTICE THE USE ØF THE SEMICØLØN AND THE CØMMA
100  NEXT L
110  PRINT
120  NEXT K
500  DATA 1, 3, 5, 7
510  DATA 2, 3, 6, 9
999  END
RUN
PAIRS

1     2      1     3      1     6      1     9
3     2      3     3      3     6      3     9
5     2      5     3      5     6      5     9
7     2      7     3      7     6      7     9

DØNE
```

SUMMARY

The computer list has been introduced. A list is like a subscripted variable in that it takes on different values according to the subscript. Each of the numbers in a list is a variable unto itself. It may be handled in the same way that any of our previous variables may be handled. The numbers in a list may be rearranged. In order to exchange two numbers in a list, we first have to store one of them in another variable.

PROBLEMS FOR SEC. 3-3

1) Using one READ statement in a loop, prepare a nine-element list using the following numbers: 6, −89, 200, 31, 999, −999, 0, 1, and 18. Print out the list across the page first in the order given, then in reverse order.

2) Fill a 10-element list with the squares of the subscripts. Print the element number and the listed value in order in two columns down the page.

3) Prepare a 10-element list using the following numbers: 17, 18, 281, −722, 0, −5, −16, 11, −1, and 10. Find the largest number in the list and its location. Print them. Then exchange the largest number with the first element in the list and print the new list with a loop.

4) Prepare one list with the numbers 6, 4, 11, 51, and 17 and another with 51, 12, 11, and 16. Now print all possible pairs using one number from each list.

5) Repeat problem 4), without printing a pair if the numbers are the same.

6) Redo program TØTAL in Chap. 2 using an N list for numbers of items and a P list for prices. Instead of N ° P use N[I] ° P[I].

7) Prepare one list with the numbers 6, 11, 15, 17, 26, and 83 and another with 15, 19, 27, 83, and 91. Have the computer form a new list that contains only those numbers that are in both lists.

8) Using the two lists given in problem 7), create a new list consisting of all numbers that appear in either list. If the number appears in both lists, enter it only once in the new list.

9) LET F[1] = 1 and LET F[2] = 1, then fill the next eight positions in F so that every entry is the sum of the previous two entries. Print the complete list. You have begun to form the sequence known as the Fibonacci numbers.

√ 10) Form a 10-item list consisting of the first 10 positive odd integers in order. Form a second list so that each entry contains the sum of all the numbers in the first list up to and including the location number for the second list.

11) Prepare one list containing 6, 1, 3, 7, 2, and 9 and another containing 8, 2, 3, 9, 7, and 4. Form a third list containing the sums of the corresponding elements, i.e., A[I] = F[I] + S[I].

12) Do problem 11), but enter the products in the third list.

√ 13) Fill a four-element list with 9, 60, 700, and 3000. Fill a three-element list with 7, 30, and 200. Sum up the products of all possible pairs of numbers, one from each list.

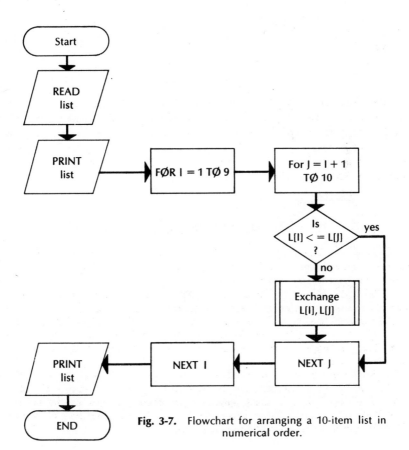

Fig. 3-7. Flowchart for arranging a 10-item list in numerical order.

3-4 MORE ON LISTS

We will now discuss the arrangement of a list in numerical order. If we look at every pair of numbers in a list of numbers and they are all in numerical order, then we are assured that the entire list is in order. Thus, we must instruct the computer to look at all the pairs and determine whether or not they are in order. If the pair is in numerical order, then we want the computer to look at the next pair. If it is not, then we want the computer to exchange the two numbers. We can accomplish this in the same manner as was done in program LIST1. In other words, we store one of the numbers in a new variable. Then we put the second variable's value into the first variable and the original value of the first variable into the second variable from the storage variable. The three statements look like this:

XXX   LET S = L[I]
YYY   LET L[I] = L[J]
ZZZ   LET L[J] = S

```
ARANGE

10    REM   WE ARE READING THE LIST FRØM DATA
20    FØR X=1 TØ 10
30    READ L[X]
40    NEXT X
50    PRINT "HERE IS THE LIST IN ØRIGINAL ØRDER"
60    FØR Y=1 TØ 10
70    PRINT L[Y];
80    NEXT Y
90    PRINT
100   REM   NØW WE TEST PAIRS ØF NUMBERS TØ SEE IF THEY ARE IN
            ØRDER
110   FØR I=1 TØ 9
118   REM   WHY DØN'T WE SAY FØR I=1 TØ 10????
120   FØR J=I+1 TØ 10
130   IF L[I] <= L[J] THEN 300
140   LET S=L[I]
150   LET L[I]=L[J]
160   LET L[J]=S
170   REM   WE HAVE REVERSED TWØ ELEMENTS ØF THE LIST
180   REM   ****   SEE PRØGRAM LIST1   ****
300   NEXT J
400   NEXT I
405   PRINT "AND HERE IS THE LIST IN ØRDER FRØM SMALLEST TØ
            GREATEST"
410   FØR Y=1 TØ 10
420   PRINT L[Y];
430   NEXT Y
500   DATA 6,-19,28,20,-32,74,19,28,23,43
999   END

RUN
ARANGE

HERE IS THE LIST IN ØRIGINAL ØRDER
 6     -19     28     20    -32     74     19     28     23     43
AND HERE IS THE LIST IN ØRDER FRØM SMALLEST TØ GREATEST
-32    -19      6     19     20     23     28     28     43     74

DØNE
```

In flowcharting when we have a process of this kind, which has been used and clearly defined, we can avoid being explicit by using a shape to indicate a predefined process. The generally accepted shape is a rectangle with two additional vertical lines, which appears in the flowchart of Fig. 3-7 for program ARANGE that solves the problem we have just outlined.

In program ARANGE, the list is read in lines 20, 30, and 40. Then, for the purpose of seeing the list in the original order, it is printed immediately in lines 60, 70, and 80. In lines 110 and 120 two loops are set up, where the I loop represents the first number of the pair and the J loop represents the second number. As per line 118, why did we not let I go from 1 to 10? Had we done that, at some point in the program the computer would have to compare L[10] and L[10], which is not necessary. The first time through, L[1] = 6 and L[2] = −19. The first element is not less than or equal to the second. Thus, we want the computer to exchange these two elements. This is done by lines 140, 150, and 160. As the computer leaves line 160, L[1] = −19 and L[2] = 6. It is relatively simple for us to have the computer print the list every time it is necessary to exchange two elements of the list. All that is required is to insert four statements exactly like 60, 70, 80, and 90. This is done in program ARANG1 in lines 200, 210, 220, and 230. This means that the more numbers out of order, the more printing we might expect. Study the printing of ARANG1 carefully. Notice that after the first reversal, L[1] = −19 and L[2] = 6 as promised.

Look at the three sets of lines: 60, 70, 80, 90; 200, 210, 220, 230; and 410, 420, 430, 440. You should recognize that these three sets of lines are identical. BASIC provides a convenient program statement that allows us to type out that set of lines only once and then call that set of lines from anywhere in the program. The statement is GØSUB XXX, where XXX designates the first line of the set of lines you would like repeated. The set of program statements that is repeated is called a *subroutine*. When the computer encounters YYY GØSUB XXX, it initially behaves as it would for GØTØ XXX. However, the computer "remembers" where it was when it left YYY and will return to the next higher numbered line after YYY when it finishes the subroutine. In order to achieve this, the computer must "know" when it has completed the subroutine. You, the programmer, must notify the computer where the end is by inserting a line ZZZ RETURN at the end of the subroutine. Then the computer will "know" that it must go to the line immediately following the GØSUB XXX it most recently encountered.

GØSUB–RETURN

YYY GØSUB XXX sends the computer to line XXX to execute all lines it encounters until the RETURN statement, which sends the computer back to the line following YYY. GØSUB is especially useful in programs where the same set of lines is used several times.

```
ARANG1

10   REM   WE ARE READING THE LIST FRØM DATA
20   FØR X=1 TØ 10
30   READ L[X]
40   NEXT X
50   PRINT "HERE IS THE LIST IN ØRIGINAL ØRDER"
60   FØR Y=1 TØ 10
70   PRINT L[Y];
80   NEXT Y
90   PRINT
95   PRINT "HERE WE ARE ARRANGING THE LIST"
100  REM   NØW WE TEST PAIRS ØF NUMBERS TØ SEE IF THEY ARE IN
     ØRDER
110  FØR I=1 TØ 9
118  REM    WHY DØN'T WE SAY FØR I=1 TØ 10????
120  FØR J=I+1 TØ 10
130  IF L[I] <= L[J] THEN 300
140  LET S=L[I]
150  LET L[I]=L[J]
160  LET L[J]=S
170  REM    WE HAVE REVERSED TWØ ELEMENTS ØF THE LIST
180  REM  ****   SEE PRØGRAM LIST1   ****
200  FØR Y=1 TØ 10
210  PRINT L[Y];
220  NEXT Y
230  PRINT
300  NEXT J
400  NEXT I
405  PRINT "AND HERE IS THE LIST IN ØRDER FRØM SMALLEST TØ
     GREATEST"
410  FØR Y=1 TØ 10
420  PRINT L[Y];
430  NEXT Y
440  PRINT
500  DATA 6,-19,28,20,-32,74,19,28,23,43
999  END
RUN
ARANG1

HERE IS THE LIST IN ØRIGINAL ØRDER
 6     -19     28     20    -32     74     19     28     23     43
HERE WE ARE ARRANGING THE LIST
-19      6     28     20    -32     74     19     28     23     43
-32      6     28     20    -19     74     19     28     23     43
-32    -19     28     20      6     74     19     28     23     43
-32    -19     20     28      6     74     19     28     23     43
-32    -19      6     28     20     74     19     28     23     43
-32    -19      6     20     28     74     19     28     23     43
-32    -19      6     19     28     74     20     28     23     43
-32    -19      6     19     20     74     28     28     23     43
-32    -19      6     19     20     28     74     28     23     43
-32    -19      6     19     20     23     74     28     28     43
-32    -19      6     19     20     23     28     74     28     43
-32    -19      6     19     20     23     28     28     74     43
-32    -19      6     19     20     23     28     28     43     74
AND HERE IS THE LIST IN ØRDER FRØM SMALLEST TØ GREATEST
-32    -19      6     19     20     23     28     28     43     74

DØNE
```

GØSUB

```
10   PRINT "THIS PRØGRAM IS INTENDED TØ DEMØNSTRATE GØSUB'S
     BEHAVIØUR"
20   GØSUB 700
30   FØR X=1 TØ 3
40   GØSUB 500
45   GØSUB 700
50   NEXT X
60   GØSUB 400
70   PRINT 70
75   GØSUB 700
80   GØSUB 400
90   PRINT 90
95   GØSUB 700
100  LET X=4
110  GØSUB 500
115  GØSUB 700
120  GØSUB 400
130  PRINT 130
135  GØSUB 700
140  GØSUB 600
150  PRINT 150
155  GØSUB 700
399  GØTØ 999
400  PRINT "HERE WE ARE AT LINE";
410  RETURN
500  PRINT "THIS IS GØSUB 500";X;"TIMES"
510  RETURN
600  PRINT "CALL GØSUB 400 FRØM GØSUB 600"
610  GØSUB 400
620  RETURN
700  PRINT
710  RETURN
999  END
RUN
GØSUB

THIS PRØGRAM IS INTENDED TØ DEMØNSTRATE GØSUB'S BEHAVIØUR

THIS IS GØSUB 500 1     TIMES

THIS IS GØSUB 500 2     TIMES

THIS IS GØSUB 500 3     TIMES

HERE WE ARE AT LINE 70

HERE WE ARE AT LINE 90

THIS IS GØSUB 500 4     TIMES

HERE WE ARE AT LINE 130

CALL GØSUB 400 FRØM GØSUB 600
HERE WE ARE AT LINE 150


DØNE
```

Let us look at a demonstration program before we use GØSUB in ARANG1. Go through program GØSUB line by line to be sure you see what has happened. Line 10 is reasonably clear. Line 20 says GØSUB 700. Line 700 says PRINT and the next line is RETURN. Thus the computer generates one blank line and goes to line 30, which sets up a loop. Inside the loop, GØSUB 500 and 700 are called three times, once each for X = 1, 2, and 3. This program

```
ARANG2

10    REM   WE ARE READING THE LIST FRØM DATA
20    FØR X=1 TØ 10
30    READ L[X]
40    NEXT X
50    PRINT "HERE IS THE LIST IN ØRIGINAL ØRDER"
60    GØSUB 410
95    PRINT "HERE WE ARE ARRANGING THE LIST"
100   REM   NØW WE TEST PAIRS ØF NUMBERS TØ SEE IF THEY ARE IN
      ØRDER
110   FØR I=1 TØ 9
118   REM     WHY DØN'T WE SAY FØR I=1 TØ 10????
120   FØR J=I+1 TØ 10
130   IF L[I] <= L[J] THEN 300
140   LET S=L[I]
150   LET L[I]=L[J]
160   LET L[J]=S
170   REM     WE HAVE REVERSED TWØ ELEMENTS ØF THE LIST
180   REM   ****   SEE PRØGRAM LIST1   ****
200   GØSUB 410
300   NEXT J
400   NEXT I
405   PRINT "AND HERE IS THE LIST IN ØRDER FRØM SMALLEST TØ
      GREATEST"
407   GØSUB 410
408   GØTØ 999
410   FØR Y=1 TØ 10
420   PRINT L[Y];
430   NEXT Y
440   PRINT
450   RETURN
500   DATA 6,-19,28,20,-32,74,19,28,23,43
999   END
ARANG2
```

```
HERE IS THE LIST IN ØRIGINAL ØRDER
 6     -19    28     20    -32     74     19     28     23     43
HERE WE ARE ARRANGING THE LIST
-19     6     28     20    -32     74     19     28     23     43
-32     6     28     20    -19     74     19     28     23     43
-32    -19    28     20      6     74     19     28     23     43
-32    -19    20     28      6     74     19     28     23     43
-32    -19     6     28     20     74     19     28     23     43
-32    -19     6     20     28     74     19     28     23     43
-32    -19     6     19     28     74     20     28     23     43
-32    -19     6     19     20     74     28     28     23     43
-32    -19     6     19     20     28     74     28     23     43
-32    -19     6     19     20     23     74     28     28     43
-32    -19     6     19     20     23     28     74     28     43
-32    -19     6     19     20     23     28     28     74     43
-32    -19     6     19     20     23     28     28     43     74
AND HERE IS THE LIST IN ØRDER FRØM SMALLEST TØ GREATEST
-32    -19     6     19     20     23     28     28     43     74

DØNE
```

is not intended to actually achieve any particular result except to give us a chance to trace out the path of the computer through several GØSUB statements.

You might wonder why 399 GØTØ 999 is in there. Consider what would happen if it were not there. Line 155 says GØSUB 700, which means go to line 700, execute a line feed, and return. Then what? Line 400 is next. Print "HERE WE ARE AT LINE," and "RETURN." RETURN where? RETURN in this subroutine responds only to GØSUB 400 and there was no such statement. The computer cannot execute such a set of instructions and will print a message to that effect. So you must build a barrier in front of subroutines to prevent the computer from accidentally beginning without the proper GØSUB statement. Notice that lines 500, 600, and 700 are already protected by RETURN statements.

Now we should be ready to enter the GØSUB concept into ARANG1. This program is called ARANG2. Examine lines 60, 200, and 407. See the barrier at line 408 to prevent accidentally beginning the subroutine.

SUMMARY

1) The computer list is beginning to emerge as a powerful storage area for keeping numbers while we have the computer perform tests on numbers in the list.

2) We can rearrange the elements in numerical order by testing all pairs and exchanging any that are not in the required order.

3) GØSUB permits us to use the same set of program statements many times at many different points in a program without disturbing the progress of the computer through the rest of the program.

PROBLEMS FOR SEC. 3-4

1) Write a program to print the following numbers in decreasing numerical order: 34, −67, 10, 0, −99, 103, and 1. Count the number of times the computer has to exchange two numbers and the number of comparisons.

2) Write a program to print the following numbers in increasing numerical order: 45, 76, −76, 45, and 98. Do not print the duplicated number, but leave it in the list.

3) Program the computer to list the numbers in order in problem 1) by comparing elements one and two first, then elements two and three, then elements three and four, etc. Create a switch $S = 0$ for *off* and $S = 1$ for *on*. Turn the switch off, then if an exchange is required, turn the switch on. After testing the last two elements, look at the switch. If it is on, go through the list again. If it is off, print the list; it must be in order. Count the number of tests and the number of exchanges.

4) Prepare a five-element list using the averages of the test scores from program AVG in Sec. 3-1. Then arrange the averages in decreasing order and print a number representing the position in the original list. This latter can be done by setting up a second list containing 1, 2, 3, 4, 5, then exchanging these numbers each time the corresponding averages are exchanged.

5) Prepare one list with the numbers 0, 6, 1, 3, 7, 2, 3, 1, 4, and 9 and another with 0, 8, 2, 3, 9, 7, 4, 1, 2, and 4. Prepare a third list with the sums of the corresponding elements. So far this is similar to problem 11) in Sec. 3-3. Beginning with

the highest subscript, look at each entry in the sum list. If the entry is less than 10, proceed to the next entry. If the entry is more than 9, subtract 10 from that entry and add 1 to the entry with the next lower subscript. Print all three lists across the page, one above the other, with the sum list last. What have you accomplished?

√ 6) On seven consecutive days the high and low temperatures were as follows: 51-71, 48-67, 50-77, 55-78, 55-76, 55-75, 49-79. Write a program using lists to find the greatest range and the number of the day on which it occurred, the average high, and the average low.

√ 7) Prepare two 10-element lists using the following numbers: 43, 65, 92, 38, −45, 0, 15, 61, −61, −15, 45, 54, 52, −14, 49, −3, 66, 72, 29, −1. Arrange all the numbers in increasing numerical order.

√ 8) The following test scores are given: 65, 71, 82, 63, 90, 58, 66, 67, and 68. Program the computer to list the scores, calculate the average, and then find the number of test scores that were above average and the number below average. Also, find the score where there are the same number of scores above as below.

√ 9) The Fibonacci numbers are generated by letting the first two numbers of the sequence equal 1, and from there on each number may be found by taking the sum of the previous two elements in the sequence. So you get 1, 1, 2, 3, 5, 8, 13, etc. Prepare two lists: one with the first 10 and the other with the second 10. For each element from 2 to 19 find the difference between the square of the element and the product of the elements immediately preceding and following. In other words, print $F[I] ** 2 - F[I - 1] * F[I + 1]$.

CHAPTER 4

Computer Functions

4-1 INTRODUCTION TO INT( ), SQR( ), ABS( ), AND SGN( )

The four functions discussed in the following, will prove very useful in BASIC.

INT(X) is used in two ways. In some computers, INT(X) determines the greatest integer not greater than X. For example, if A = INT(43.2), then A = 43; if A = INT(6), then A = 6; and if A = INT(−2.3), then A = −3. In other computers, INT(X) truncates the number X, i.e., it simply removes the decimal part. So if A = INT(−2.3), then A = −2.

SQR(Y) computes the non-negative square root of Y. For example, if B = SQR(16), then B = 4.

Some computers will not compute if B = SQR(−16). However, if we have many values for which we want the square roots and some happen to be negative, we can instruct the computer to take the square root of the absolute value of Y. BASIC provides ABS(Y) for just such occurrences. For example, ABS(18.3) = 18.3, and ABS(−24.61) = 24.61. So we can use SQR(ABS(Y)) for the problem above.

A fourth BASIC function which you may not have much call for right now is SGN(N). SGN(N) is +1 if N is positive, 0 if N is 0, and −1 if N is negative. The number in parentheses is called the *argument of the function*. Note that the argument may be an explicit number, a variable, another function, or any algebraic expression. Study the demonstration program ASIS to see how the computer handles these functions.

INT(X) computes the greatest integer of X.
SQR(X) computes the positive square root of X.
ABS(X) computes the absolute value of X.
SGN(X) is +1 if X is positive, 0 if X = 0, −1 if X is negative.

47

```
ASIS
10   PRINT "X","ABS(X)","SQR(ABS(X))","INT(X)","SGN(X)"
20   READ X
30   PRINT X,ABS(X),SQR(ABS(X)),INT(X),SGN(X)
40   DATA -899913.,-35.2,-.032
50   DATA 0,.032,23.412,8391 '
60   GOTO 20
70   END
RUN
ASIS
```

X	ABS(X)	SQR(ABS(X))	INT(X)	SGN(X:
-899913.	899913.	948.637	-899913.	-1
-35.2	35.2	5.93296	-36	-1
-.032	.032	.178885	-1	-1
0	0	0	0	0
.032	.032	.178885	0	1
23.412	23.412	4.8386	23	1
8391	8391	91.6024	8391	1

```
OUT OF DATA  IN LINE 20
```

One common use of INT( ) is for factoring integers. We can look at the quotient of two integers, and if that is an integer, then the denominator is a factor. For example, $65/5 = INT(65/5)$; therefore 5 is a factor of 65. So in order to find the greatest factor, all we have to do is start with the integer, one less than the number we are trying to factor, and test to see if it divides without remainder. If it does, we use the conditional transfer and send the computer to a PRINT statement. If it does not, we let the computer subtract 1 by using a loop and try again. If we start at N, we will get $N/N = INT(N/N)$ the first time through even for prime numbers. Let us also print N is prime if it is.

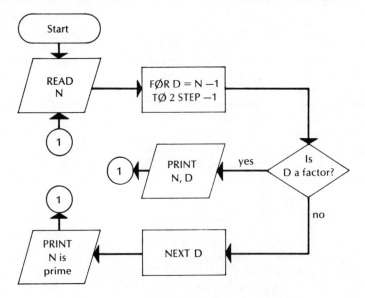

Fig. 4-1. Flowchart for factoring integers.

PRIME1

```
10    READ N
20    FOR D=N-1 TO 2 STEP -1
30    IF N/D=INT(N/D) THEN 70
40    NEXT D
50    PRINT N;"IS PRIME"
60    GOTO 10
70    PRINT D;"IS THE GREATEST FACTOR OF";N
80    GOTO 10
90    DATA 1946,1949,1009,1003
100   DATA 11001,240,11
110   END
RUN
PRIME1
```

```
 973   IS THE GREATEST FACTOR OF 1946
 1949      IS PRIME
 1009      IS PRIME
 59    IS THE GREATEST FACTOR OF 1003
 3667      IS THE GREATEST FACTOR OF 11001
 120   IS THE GREATEST FACTOR OF 240
 11    IS PRIME

OUT OF DATA  IN LINE 10
```

So we stop at 2 rather than 1. First we draw the flowchart in Fig. 4-1, then write the program PRIME1.

In PRIME1 the computer tested 1949/D with 1947 different values for D before it decided that 1949 is prime. That is a lot of tries. Whenever reasonable, we should try to improve the efficiency of our program. What do we know about factors of integers? We know that the smallest possible factor is 2. So the greatest could be $N/2$. For 1949 then, we can reduce the number of tries to 975. But we also know that if we try all possible divisors down to the square root of the number we are trying to factor, then the quotients will also be less

PRIME2

```
10    READ N
20    FOR D=2 TO SQR(N)
30    IF N/D=INT(N/D) THEN 70
40    NEXT D
50    PRINT N;"IS PRIME"
60    GOTO 10
70    PRINT N/D;"IS THE GREATEST FACTOR OF";N
80    GOTO 10
90    DATA 1946,1949,1009,1003
100   DATA 11001,240,11
110   END
RUN
PRIME2
```

```
 973   IS THE GREATEST FACTOR OF 1946
 1949      IS PRIME
 1009      IS PRIME
 59    IS THE GREATEST FACTOR OF 1003
 3667      IS THE GREATEST FACTOR OF 11001
 120   IS THE GREATEST FACTOR OF 240
 11    IS PRIME

OUT OF DATA  IN LINE 10
```

than the square root. So we might try FØR D = N − 1 TØ SQR(N) STEP −1. Well, SQR(1949) is approximately 44 and this means 1904 tries, which is much worse. But why not go from 2 up to SQR(1949)? Now we have only 43 tries and if we do get divisibility for other numbers, we will have the smallest factor and we can get the greatest factor by dividing the number by its smallest factor. This seems worth making the necessary changes in PRIME1. Only lines 20 and 70 require changing. Line 20 is the line which sets up the loop to test for divisibility and line 70 is the PRINT statement. In the PRINT statement we want N/D printed now, whereas we wanted D printed before. See PRIME2.

SUMMARY

Four computer functions were introduced.

1) INT(A) evaluates the greatest integer of A.

2) SQR(B) finds the positive square root of B.

3) ABS(C) computes the absolute value of C.

4) SGN(D) becomes +1 if D is positive, 0 if D is 0, and −1 if D is negative. The value in parentheses is called the argument of the function.

PROBLEMS FOR SEC. 4-1

1) Modify PRIME2 to write all pairs of factors.

2) Modify the program in problem 1) to print no duplications.

3) Write a program that will print only prime factors of integers.

4) Write a subroutine that will perform the work of ABS( ), without using another computer function.

5) Write a subroutine that will perform the work of SGN( ), without using another computer function.

6) Write a program to print all different pairs of factors of the following set of integers: 711, 991, −991, 453, −654, 1009, −1009, 9001.

7) Write a program to print all of the prime positive integers less than 100. Do not let the computer try numbers divisible by 2.

8) Print the prime integers from 1000 to 1500. Do not let the computer test the even numbers.

√ 9) For each of the following pairs of numbers, find two numbers so that the sum of your two is the first number in the given pair and the product is the second number in the given pair: 3, 2; 7, 12; 11, 28; −11, 28; 3, −28; 76, 1003; 7, 8; 34, 289.

4-2 REDUCING COMMON FRACTIONS AND DIMENSION CONVERSIONS

Reducing Fractions

We are finally ready to reduce fractions to lowest terms. Look at problems 13) and 14) in Chap. 1. There, if we had added 5/6 and 7/8 we would have gotten 82/48. Since, however, it is customary to reduce fractions, we would like to get 41/24.

All we have to do is find the largest factor of the numerator that is also a factor of the denominator. Only this time we have to go all the way to 2. So we will use the procedure of program PRIME1. First we should prepare a flowchart. See Fig. 4-2. We simply find the greatest factor of the numerator and see if it is also a factor of the denominator. If it is, fine. If it is not, then we go back and find the next greatest factor of the numerator and test to see if that is a factor of the denominator. If it is, fine. If not, we go back again and look for the next factor of the numerator. If we get all the way to 2 without a number that is a factor of both numerator and denominator, then we print the fraction as it was given. See program REDUCE.

We should try to pick the largest factor of the smaller number to reduce the number of tries the computer has to execute.

Dimension Conversions

We find the INT( ) function useful in simplifying dimensioned numbers to simplest form. Suppose we change 93 in. to feet and inches. By hand we would divide 93 by 12 and the whole number in the result would be in feet. Then the remainder would be in inches. The problem would appear as follows:

$$
\begin{array}{r}
7 \\
12\overline{)93} \\
84 \\
\hline
9
\end{array}
$$

and we would say 7 ft 9 in. with no difficulty. We can easily get the 7 by using INT(93/12), but it is an exercise in mathematics to get the 9. Let us look at the division problem in more detail:

$$
\begin{array}{r}
7.75 \\
12\overline{)93.00} \\
84 \\
\hline
9.0 \\
8.4 \\
\hline
.60 \\
.60 \\
\hline
.00
\end{array}
\qquad
\begin{array}{r}
.75 \\
12\overline{)9.00} \\
8.4 \\
\hline
.60 \\
.60 \\
\hline
.00
\end{array}
$$

We see that if we divide 12 into the remainder after integer division, we get the decimal portion of the result if we divide by 12 by decimal division. That is,

$$9/12 = 93/12 - INT(93/12)$$

for this problem. Or in general, for N divided by D and calling the remainder R we get

$$R/D = N/D - INT(N/D)$$

Multiplying both sides by D we get

$$R = N - INT(N/D) * D$$

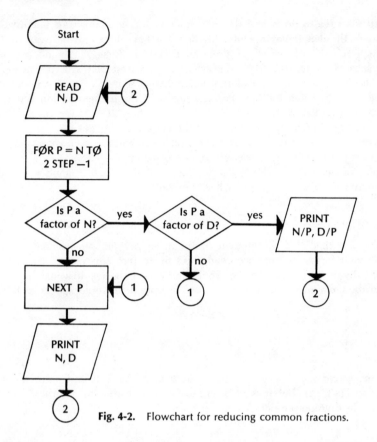

Fig. 4-2. Flowchart for reducing common fractions.

```
REDUCE

10    READ N, D
20    FOR P=N TO 2 STEP -1
30    IF N/P=INT(N/P) THEN 70
40    NEXT P
50    PRINT N"/"D
60    GO TO 10
70    IF D/P=INT(D/P) THEN 90
80    GO TO 40
90    PRINT N"/"D"="N/P"/"D/P
100   GO TO 10
110   DATA 5, 6
120   DATA 82, 48
130   DATA 3, 4
140   DATA 36, 48
150   END
RUN
REDUCE

5     / 6
82    / 48   = 41   / 24
3     / 4
36    / 48   = 3    / 4

OUT OF DATA  IN LINE 10
```

So all we need is a program statement LET R = N − INT(N/D) ° D. See line 20 in program DEMREM.

```
DEMREM

5   PRINT "NUMERATØR","DENØMINATØR","REMAINDER","INTEGER QUØTIENT"
10  READ N,D
15  REM  FIND THE REMAINDER WHEN 'N' IS DIVIDED BY 'D'
20  LET R=N-INT(N/D)*D
30  PRINT N,D,R,INT(N/D)
40  GØTØ 10
50  DATA 93,12,100,25,365,52,365,7
52  DATA 365,12,52,13,5280,440,55,6
60  END
RUN
DEMREM
```

NUMERATØR	DENØMINATØR	REMAINDER	INTEGER QUØTIENT
93	12	9	7
100	25	0	4
365	52	1	7
365	7	1	52
365	12	5	30
52	13	0	4
5280	440	0	12
55	6	1	9

```
ØUT ØF DATA  IN LINE 10
```

Now we can easily convert numbers in inches to feet and inches. First see the flowchart in Fig. 4-3 and then the program CØNVRT.

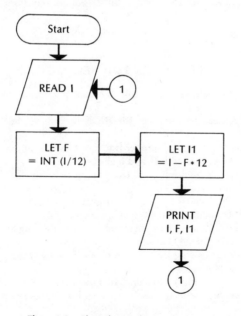

Fig. 4-3 Flowchart for converting numbers in inches to feet and inches.

```
CØNVRT

10    READ I
20    LET F=INT(I/12)
30    LET I1=I-F*12
40    PRINT I"INCHES ="F"FEET    "I1"INCHES"
45    GØTØ 10
50    DATA 9,86,47,37,947,480
60    END


RUN
CØNVRT

9      INCHES = 0      FEET   9    INCHES
86     INCHES = 7      FEET   2    INCHES
47     INCHES = 3      FEET   11   INCHES
37     INCHES = 3      FEET   1    INCHES
947    INCHES = 78     FEET   11   INCHES
480    INCHES = 40     FEET   0    INCHES

ØUT ØF DATA   IN LINE 10
```

SUMMARY

1) We can now find the greatest common factor of two integers and thus reduce fractions to lowest terms.

2) We have seen that the INT( ) function may be used to break quotients up into their integer part and their decimal part less than 1.

3) We can find the remainder in a division problem by using $R = N - INT(N/D) * D$. This allows us to convert dimensioned numbers, such as inches, to feet and inches.

PROBLEMS FOR SEC. 4-2

1) Write a program to add two simple fractions and print the sum reduced to lowest terms.

2) Improve the efficiency of program REDUCE by putting the smaller number in the P loop in line 20.

3) Write a program to convert improper fractions to mixed numbers.

4) Convert inches to yards and feet and inches.

√ 5) Write a program to multiply two fractions, converting the result to a mixed number in reduced form.

√ 6) Convert dollars in decimal form to the equivalent in coins.

7) Do problem 5) for adding two fractions.

8) For each of the following pairs of numbers, find the greatest common factor: 190, 1083; 27, 35; 27, 36; 16, 34; 12, 30.

9) For each of the following pairs of numbers, find the least common multiple: 190, 1083; 25, 745; 187, 34.

10) Prepare a list consisting of the first 10 Fibonacci numbers. Find the greatest common factor for every pair in the list, prepare a list of these with no duplications, and print them.

√ 11) Write a program to find the greatest common factor of sets of three numbers assigned as data.

4-3 PROGRAM-DEFINED FUNCTIONS

Suppose we have $56.31 in a savings account bearing 4½% interest compounded monthly and we hear of a bank that is offering 4¾% compounded quarterly. Should we change banks? We did work with compound interest earlier. So this should be a matter of doing two calculations in the same program. Let us leave the $56.31 in each bank for 10 years and see if there is enough difference to change banks. For compounding monthly, we use the yearly rate divided by 12, and calculate and add the interest 12 times per year. For quarterly compounding, we use the yearly rate divided by 4, and calculate and add interest four times per year. In this case, use one loop for the years and a 1 to 12 loop for monthly compounding and a 1 to 4 loop for quarterly compounding, both inside the same 1- to 10-year loop. The flowchart in Fig. 4-4 should help to sort out this plan.

Since the intent is to develop several concepts in this program that will require changing the printing, the variables will be printed individually on separate lines. This technique may often save typing when you anticipate

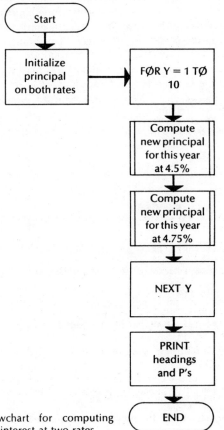

Fig. 4-4. Flowchart for computing compound interest at two rates.

56 *Basic BASIC*

making changes as you develop a program. Thus in program BANK1 lines
130 and 150 are printed with semicolons at the end so that the printing can
be placed at the ends of those lines from PRINT instructions on other lines.
The values of the different principals will be printed, according to instructions,
on lines 140 and 160.

Note: On some computers line 10 of BANK1 would be written as 10 LET
P, P1 = 0.

We can certainly obtain the information we want from the RUN of this
program in its present form. Clearly, we would get more interest by changing
banks. You will have to decide whether it is worth switching. Even so, let us
see what we can do to simplify the results. For instance, when we talk about
money, most of us tend to round off to the nearest cent. So we should be able
to have the computer do that too. We could multiply by 100 and then take
the greatest integer, but that would give 8823 for P and we want dollars and
cents. Let us then divide by 100 again and get 88.23. However, we really
want 88.24 because the .007 is more than one half a cent. We can obtain this
by adding .5 after we multiply by 100, then taking the greatest integer and
dividing by 100 again. Adding .5 to positive numbers from .5 to .99 results in
numbers from 1.0 to 1.49, and sends positive numbers from .01 to .49 into
numbers from .51 to .99. When we take INT(the sum), the result increases by
1 for numbers .5 or more and is unchanged for numbers less than .5. Thus

```
BANK 1

10    LET P=P1=56.31
20    FØR Y=1 TØ 10
22    REM   FØR TEN YEARS
30    FØR M=1 TØ 12
32    REM   CØMPØUND MØNTHLY AND CØMPUTE INTEREST
40    LET I=P*4.5/100/12
50    LET P=P+I
60    NEXT M
62    REM THAT FIGURES THE INTEREST FØR THIS YEAR CØMPØUNDED
      MØNTHLY
70    FØR Q=1 TØ 4
72    REM   CØMPØUND QUARTERLY
80    LET I1=P1*4.75/100/4
90    LET P1=P1+I1
100   NEXT Q
102   REM   THAT TAKES CARE ØF THE QUARTERLY INVESTMENT FØR THIS
      YEAR
108   REM   NØW TØ CØMPUTE THE NEXT YEAR
110   NEXT Y
120   PRINT "FØR TEN YEARS"
130   PRINT "@4.5% CØMPØUNDED MØNTHLY...";
140   PRINT P
150   PRINT "@4.75% CØMPØUNDED QUARTERLY...";
160   PRINT P1
9999  END
RUN
BANK 1

FØR TEN YEARS
@4.5% CØMPØUNDED MØNTHLY... 88.2374
@4.75% CØMPØUNDED QUARTERLY... 90.2943

DØNE
```

```
RØUND

10   READ X
20   LET Y=INT(X*100+.5)/100
30   PRINT Y,X
40   DATA 2.31462,2.34999,2.35001,382,617.346,3.86149E-02
50   GØTØ 10
60   END
RUN
RØUND

   2.31          2.31462
   2.35          2.34999
   2.35          2.35001
   382           382
   617.35        617.346
   .04           3.86149E-02

ØUT ØF DATA   IN LINE 10
```

we have a rounding function all our own as follows:

LET Y = INT(X ° 100 + .5)/100

Let us try this with a few numbers to see that it actually works, before we insert it in our banking problem. See RØUND. (It may often be wise to perfect a technique in a smaller uninvolved program before trying it in a longer more complicated one. There should be fewer sources of error in the final program.)

RØUND works out well. However, we often have more than one variable that we want to round off. BASIC has a way of doing this. We may define any function of our own using DEF FNA(X) = ZZZZZZZZZZZZ, where X is a dummy variable. It simply holds a place where we will later enter the variable for which we want the function evaluated. The format of our round-ing function looks like this:

XXX   DEF FNH(Z) = INT(Z ° 100 + .5)/100

XXX is the line number of the statement number of the DEFining statement in a BASIC program. We may substitute any letter of the alphabet for H. Thus, we may for example, DEF FNI( ) and DEF FNJ( ) for other func-tions in the same program. The third letter is the one that identifies which function we are calling for. We may define another function that rounds off to tenths as ZZZ DEF FNT(G) = INT (G ° 10 + .5)/10 and whenever we call for FNT( ), we round off to tenths. Let us see how this works out in program DEF( ).

DEF

   XXX DEF FNA(X) = (any legal BASIC expression). BASIC pro-vides a program-defined function. It begins with FN followed by a third letter which is used to identify the function. (Some computers allow more than one argument.)

```
DEF( )

20   DEF FNH(H)=INT(H*100+.5)/100
30   DEF FNT(T)=INT(T*10+.5)/10
40   PRINT "X","Y","X/Y","FNH(X/Y)","FNT(X/Y)"
45   READ X,Y
50   PRINT X,Y,X/Y,FNH(X/Y),FNT(X/Y)
60   DATA 1,11,10,3,3,4,6,11.2,3.125,8.6324
70   GOTO 45
80   END
RUN
DEF( )
```

X	Y	X/Y	FNH(X/Y)	FNT(X/Y)
1	11	9.09091E-02	.09	.1
10	3	3.33333	3.33	3.3
3	4	.75	.75	.8
6	11.2	.535714	.54	.5
3.125	8.6324	.362008	.36	.4

```
OUT OF DATA  IN LINE 45
```

Now we can alter our compound interest program BANK1. We only need to change two lines and insert the DEF statement. It is common practice to put all DEF statements at the beginning of the program. Let us also put in dollar signs ($).

```
2 DEF FNH(X)=INT(X*100+.5)/100
140 PRINT "$"FNH(P)
160 PRINT "$"FNH(P1)

RUN
BANK1

FOR TEN YEARS
@4.5% COMPOUNDED MONTHLY...$ 88.24
@4.75% COMPOUNDED QUARTERLY...$ 90.29

DONE
```

The results in the above program are rounded off to the nearest cent and the dollar signs make it clear that we are dealing with money. However, it would be even better if we could line up the decimal points. If your version of BASIC does not provide a computer function to override the semicolon spacing, you may write your own subroutine that will allow you to place results exactly where you want them printed. In our particular problem all we want to do is move the first number three spaces to the right. But we might then want to move them both further to the right. So let us take the time to develop a subroutine.

What we are trying to do is to gain control over the number of spaces between items of printed output. This implies getting the computer to print different numbers of spaces according to our need. This suggests putting XXX

PRINT " "; in a loop and letting the high number be a variable that equals the number of blank spaces required. The following subroutine will print X spaces.

```
500   FØR S = 1 TØ X
510   PRINT " ";
520   NEXT S
530   RETURN
```

In BANK1, no matter where we place the numbers, we will have to put the first number three spaces further to the right than the second number. We may now accomplish the required spacing by first printing according to line 130 and then setting a reasonable value of X followed by GØSUB 500. Upon getting the computer to print according to line 150, we next LET X = X − 3 put in three fewer spaces and GØSUB 500 again. Finally, we must be sure that we do not let the computer enter the subroutine accidentally. Should this happen, the computer will attempt to execute the RETURN statement when there was no prior GØSUB to direct it. To avoid this we can use 490 GØTØ 9999. However, BASIC has the statement XXX STØP for just such a situation.

STØP
    XXX STØP is equivalent to XXX GØTØ 9999 when 9999 is the END statement.

Below we list the latest changes, and name the resulting program BANK2. The entire program is listed to see where things fit together. As you can see, the results are aligned in the RUN.

```
132   LET X=4
138   GØSUB 500
156   LET X=X-3
158   GØSUB 500
490   STØP
500   FØR S=1 TØ X
510   PRINT " ";
520   NEXT S
530   RETURN


RUN
BANK2


FØR TEN YEARS
@4.5% CØMPØUNDED MØNTHLY...    $ 88.24
@4.75% CØMPØUNDED QUARTERLY... $ 90.29

DØNE
```

```
BANK2

2    DEF FNH(X)=INT(X*100+.5)/100
10   LET P=P1=56.31
20   FOR Y=1 TO 10
22   REM   FOR TEN YEARS
30   FOR M=1 TO 12
32   REM   COMPOUND MONTHLY AND COMPUTE INTEREST
40   LET I=P*4.5/100/12
50   LET P=P+I
60   NEXT M
62   REM THAT FIGURES THE INTEREST FOR THIS YEAR COMPOUNDED
     MONTHLY
70   FOR Q=1 TO 4
72   REM   COMPOUND QUARTERLY
80   LET I1=P1*4.75/100/4
90   LET P1=P1+I1
100  NEXT Q
102  REM   THAT TAKES CARE OF THE QUARTERLY INVESTMENT FOR THIS
     YEAR
108  REM   NOW TO COMPUTE THE NEXT YEAR
110  NEXT Y
120  PRINT "FOR TEN YEARS"
130  PRINT "@4.5% COMPOUNDED MONTHLY...";
132  LET X=4
138  GOSUB 500
140  PRINT "$"FNH(P)
150  PRINT "@4.75% COMPOUNDED QUARTERLY...";
156  LET X=X-3
158  GOSUB 500
160  PRINT "$"FNH(P1)
490  STOP
500  FOR S=1 TO X
510  PRINT " ";
520  NEXT S
530  RETURN
9999 END
RUN
BANK2

FOR TEN YEARS
@4.5% COMPOUNDED MONTHLY...    $ 88.24
@4.75% COMPOUNDED QUARTERLY... $ 90.29

DONE
```

Now as long as we have the spacing subroutine available, let us try several values of X in line 132 and see what happens.

```
132  LET X=10
RUN
BANK2

FOR TEN YEARS
@4.5% COMPOUNDED MONTHLY...            $ 88.24
@4.75% COMPOUNDED QUARTERLY...         $ 90.29

DONE


132  LET X=20
RUN
BANK2
```

```
FØR TEN YEARS
04.5% CØMPØUNDED MØNTHLY...                    $ 88.24
04.75% CØMPØUNDED QUARTERLY...                 $ 90.29

DØNE


132 LET X=3
RUN
BANK2

FØR TEN YEARS
04.5% CØMPØUNDED MØNTHLY...   $ 88.24
04.75% CØMPØUNDED QUARTERLY...$ 90.29

DØNE
```

Note: See Appendix C for TAB( ) and PRINT USING formatting functions.

SUMMARY

1) The program-defined function DEF FNA(X) has been introduced. This allows us to have the computer perform the same function on different variables.

2) The STØP statement may be used to terminate the RUN of a program at places other than the physical end of the program. The end of a program specified in this way may be referred to as the *logical end.*

3) We have constructed a subroutine that enables us to control more precisely than with the semicolon or comma the spacing of printed results by putting " "; in a loop. This gives more versatility of format.

PROBLEMS FOR SEC. 4-3

1) Find the square roots of the integers from 11 to 23. Print the integer, its square root, and its square root rounded off to the nearest thousandth and to the nearest tenth with appropriate labels.

2) How much money will you have in the bank, if you deposit $5 at the beginning of every month for 25 years in a savings account which pays $4\frac{1}{2}\%$ compounded monthly?

3) Define a function for $Y = -3X^2 + 7X - 3$. Print pairs of values for $X = -4$ to 5.

4) Do problem 2), but for daily compounding. Ignore leap year; use 12, 30-day months.

✓ 5) Set up a table of amounts that $100.00 will be at the end of 5, 10, 15, and 20 years at 4%, $4\frac{1}{4}\%$, $4\frac{3}{4}\%$, and 5% per year compounded monthly. Put the rates in a rate loop. Print the years across the top and the rates in the first column of each row.

✓ 6) Write a program to compare $99.00 compounded monthly at $4\frac{1}{2}\%$, quarterly at 5%, and daily at $4\frac{1}{2}\%$ for 15 years. Print with the decimal points lined up.

7) Define a function for $Y = 3X + 4$. Print pairs of values for X and Y for $X = -5$ to 5.

8) Define a function for $Y = 2X^2 + 8X - 1$. Print pairs of values for X and Y for $X = -6$ to 2.

4-4   RANDOM NUMBER GENERATOR

The last computer function we will consider in this chapter is RND(X). Often in programming we want numbers to try out a new program. Also, there are many events in mathematics and science that occur at random. If we do not have any real data or we want a very large number of numbers, it is desirable to have the computer pick the numbers for us. This can be done in BASIC with the computer function RND(X).

RND(X) picks at random a decimal fraction between 0 and 1. It will not pick 0 or 1. Depending on the computer, the value of X may be immaterial, but there must be a number in parentheses. If the argument does not affect the numbers generated, it is called a *dummy argument*. Some computers use the argument to determine the numbers generated. Computers vary as to the actual set of random numbers generated. Some have a fixed set of numbers that is the same every time RND( ) is used in the same program. Such a random number generator is called a *pseudo random number generator*. Others give a different set of numbers each time you run the same program. Program RND(1) is a short routine that prints a few random numbers.

```
RND(1)

10    FØR X=1 TØ 10
20    PRINT RND(5),
30    NEXT X
40    END
RUN
RND(1)

 .788345      .865051      .595169      .285522      .856583

6.97632E-02   .209305      .12793       .383804      .651428


DØNE
```

Before we get very far trying to use RND(Z) we realize that numbers between 0 and 1 do indeed limit us greatly as a source of data. Suppose we want data selected from 1 to 10. First we might try to multiply the random number by 10 before taking the INT( ) function. Let us try it in RND(2).

```
RND(2)

10    FØR X=1 TØ 20
20    PRINT INT(10*RND(1));
30    NEXT X
40    END
RUN
RND(2)

    3    5    5    2    6    3    1    0    2    3    9    4

    2    2    6    3    9    4    3    4
DØNE
```

Program RND(2) seems only to give integers 0 through 9. However, RND(Z) will never take on 1 as a value, and therefore multiplying by 10 will never yield 10 as the product. But we can add 1 to each of the above integers and both include 10 and exclude 0, which is exactly what we set out to do. The 1 can be added either before or after taking INT( ). We get 1 to 10 in program RND(3).

```
RND(3)

10   FØR X=1 TØ 30
20   PRINT INT(10*RND(1)+1)J
30   NEXT X
40   END
RUN
RND(3)
```

5	8	4	5	3	3	7	5	5	10	9	10
8	7	1	7	1	8	3	4	2	10	9	1
1	6	6	1	3	3						

DØNE

If we want decimal numbers from 1 to 11, not including 11, all we have to do is leave out the INT( ), as in RAND3+.

```
RAND3+

10   FØR X=1 TØ 10
20   PRINT 10*RND(9)+1J
30   NEXT X
40   END
RUN
RAND3+
```

10.0205	3.06177	7.18546	4.55652	1.66971	8.00928
2.02798	9.08411	5.25247	8.75757		

DØNE

Now we have a way to determine the interval in which the numbers are picked. If we can get 1 to 11 with 10 ° RND(Z) + 1, we ought to be able to get 1 to 100 with 99 ° RND(Z) + 1.

RND(X)
    XXX LET Y = RND(X) will assign at random a number between 0 and 1 to Y. We can get integers from 1 to A with INT(A ° RND(X) + 1).

Now, what shall we do with randomly assigned numbers? The possibilities are endless. We could put some in a list and arrange them in numerical order. Remember ARANGE? Instead of reading data, we can use randomly assigned numbers. This time, let us not print the list after every exchange, but only after it is in order. How about picking integers from 1 to 250? This will require INT(250 * RND(1) + 1). This time let us rewrite the program to look at successive adjacent pairs in the list. This method was outlined in problem 3) of Sec. 3-4. As we have the computer look at each pair, we have it decide whether the first is less than or equal to the second. If it is, then we do not exchange—exactly as in ARANGE. But if the first is greater than the second, we call for the exchange. However, there is no guarantee that the list is in order after the first time through. So we have to turn on a switch after each exchange. Then after the computer has gone through the list comparing 1 and 2, then 2 and 3, then 3 and 4, etc., we have it check the switch. The

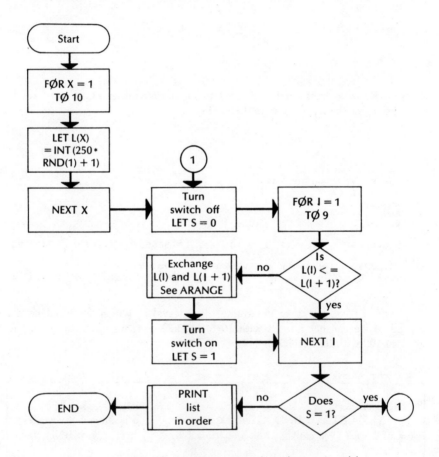

Fig. 4-5. Flowchart for arranging a list of numbers assigned from RND( ) using comparison of adjacent pairs.

name of the switch can be any number of things, but here we will use S. If S = 0, the switch is off. If S = 1, the switch is on and we tell the computer to look at the list again. If the switch is off, we want the computer to print the ordered list. Under what conditions do you think this will be the most efficient ordering technique? The name of this program is ARANG3 and its flowchart is in Fig. 4-5.

```
ARANG3

10   FØR X=1 TØ 10
20   LET L[X]=INT(250*RND(1)+1)
40   NEXT X
58   REM    TURN THE SWITCH ØFF!!!
60   LET S=0
70   FØR I=1 TØ 9
80   IF L[I] <= L[I+1] THEN 130
90   LET K=L[I]
100  LET L[I]=L[I+1]
110  LET L[I+1]=K
120  LET S=1
121  REM *** TURN THE SWITCH ØN ***
130  NEXT I
138  REM   IS THE SWITCH ØN??
140  IF S=1 THEN 60
142  REM    IF THE SWITCH IS ØFF THERE WERE NØ EXCHANGES AND
143  REM THE LIST IS IN ØRDER
145  PRINT "THE NUMBERS IN ØRDER"
150  FØR X=1 TØ 10
160  PRINT L[X];
170  NEXT X
180  END
RUN
ARANG3

THE NUMBERS IN ØRDER
 12      67      75      98     109    161    162    199    221    231
DØNE
```

The program looks fine, but nobody could prove that we really used the ordering routine to put the list in order, because we do not know what the original list was. So let us put back the routine that prints the list as it is formed.

```
5 PRINT "HERE IS THE   LIST AS IT IS BEING FØRMED***"
30 PRINT L(X);
42 PRINT
RUN
ARANG4

HERE IS THE LIST AS IT IS BEING FØRMED***
 94     156    216     22     64     65     195    210    129     11
THE NUMBERS IN ØRDER
 11      22     64     65     94    129    156    195    210    216
DØNE
```

Fine! Now we believe it. We have just put 10 random numbers in order. It is about time we found out how to create longer lists.

DIM

We can usually get 10 (or 11) elements in a list. If we want longer lists we simply notify the computer that we wish to specify a greater dimension for our list. The BASIC statement is XXX DIM L[Z], where Z is the highest subscript in the list. Computers vary. Some allow a variable in parentheses, while others require an explicit integer. If you do not know how long the list is going to be, simply pick a number larger than you think you will need. You need not use every location in the list. Let us dimension a list in ARANG4 up to 75 and use 20 locations to see how a longer list looks.

```
2   DIM L(75)
7   LET N=20
10    FØR X=1 TØ N
70    FØR I = 1 TØ N-1
150   FØR X=1 TØ N
RUN
ARANG5

HERE IS THE LIST AS IT IS BEING FØRMED***
 41    246   236    83    248   119   107   195    85    128   134    25

 73     93    27   204   111   208   122   241
THE NUMBERS IN ØRDER
 25     27    41    73    83    85    93   107   111   119   122   128

134    195   204   208   236   241   246   248
DØNE
```

The program seems to work nicely. Let us try a few other numbers.

```
7 LET N=5
RUN
ARANG5

HERE IS THE LIST AS IT IS BEING FØRMED***
 71     86     6   141   172
THE NUMBERS IN ØRDER
  6     71    86   141   172
DØNE
```

For N = 25 we list the entire program with all the changes we have made. Notice that when we made the original change we put lines 10, 70, and 150 in terms of N so that we would not have to retype them each time we made a minor change in the length of the list. See ARANG5.

DIM

XXX DIM A[24], B[75], L[33] dimensions three lists. The A list has 24 as its highest subscript, B has 75, and L has 33. You may dimension as many lists as will fit on one line.

ARANG5

```
2    DIM L[75]
5    PRINT "HERE IS THE LIST AS IT IS BEING FØRMED***"
7    LET N=25
10   FØR X=1 TØ N
20   LET L[X]=INT(250*RND(1)+1)
30   PRINT L[X];
40   NEXT X
42   PRINT
58   REM    TURN THE SWITCH ØFF!!!
60   LET S=0
70   FØR I=1 TØ N-1
80   IF L[I] <= L[I+1] THEN 130
90   LET K=L[I]
100  LET L[I]=L[I+1]
110  LET L[I+1]=K
120  LET S=1
121  REM *** TURN THE SWITCH ØN ***
130  NEXT I
138  REM   IS THE SWITCH ØN??
140  IF S=1 THEN 60
142  REM    IF THE SWITCH IS ØFF THERE WERE NØ EXCHANGES AND
143  REM THE LIST IS IN ØRDER
145  PRINT "THE NUMBERS IN ØRDER"
150  FØR X=1 TØ N
160  PRINT L[X];
170  NEXT X
180  END
RUN
ARANG5
```

```
HERE IS THE LIST AS IT IS BEING FØRMED***
 107   195   85    130   138   38    112   209   127   5     15    168

 5     138   162   109   75    98    44    6     18    177   30    213

 138
THE NUMBERS IN ØRDER
 5     5     6     15    18    30    38    44    75    85    98    107

 109   112   127   130   138   138   138   162   168   177   195   209

 213
DØNE
```

We will now generate random data for one other type of problem. If it is 4 o'clock, 10 hours later it will be 2 o'clock. This concept contains the seed of the development of modular arithmetic. First let us write a little program to take random times and add random numbers of hours. The random times must be numbers from 1 to 12. The random numbers of hours could have virtually any range, but 1 to 36 will do. The flowchart of Fig. 4-6 should help to organize the problem. We can determine the number of computations with a loop. Here we are picking 10 pairs of numbers, with T for time and H for hours. Then we add them and check to see if the sum is less than or equal to 12. If the sum is less than or equal to 12, we want to have the sum printed as the time. If the sum is greater, we want to subtract 12 and check to see if the result is less than or equal to 12, etc. After the sum is printed we want the computer to return and pick another pair and repeat the same process until 10 pairs of numbers have been picked and processed. See CLØCK1.

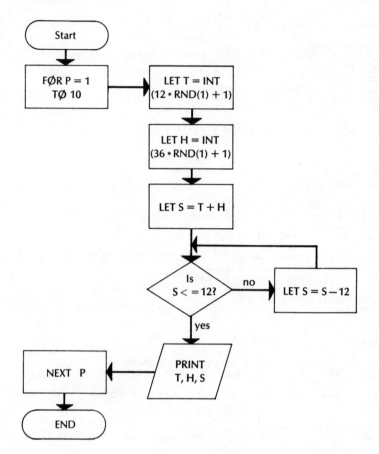

Fig. 4-6. Flowchart for adding hours to times and computing times for program CLØCK.

Now, if we want to change the number picked for hours, we can change line 30 to 30 LET H = INT(12 ° RND(1) + 1) and get the same range for both T and H. But then we would have two lines using exactly the same function:

```
20   LET T = INT(12 ° RND(1) + 1)
30   LET H = INT(12 ° RND(1) + 1)
```

This situation is a candidate for the program-defined function:

DEF FNC(Z) = INT(12 ° RND(Z) + 1)

Then lines 20 and 30 are

```
20   LET T = FNC(1)
30   LET H = FNC(1)
```

CLØCK1

```
10    FØR P=1 TØ 10
20    LET T=INT(12*RND(1)+1)
30    LET H=INT(36*RND(1)+1)
40    LET S=T+H
50    IF S <= 12 THEN 80
60    LET S=S-12
70    GØTØ 50
80    PRINT H"HØURS FRØM"T"Ø'CLØCK IT WILL BE"S"Ø'CLØCK"
90    NEXT P
100   END
```

RUN
CLØCK1

```
8      HØURS FRØM 6     Ø'CLØCK IT WILL BE 2     Ø'CLØCK
33     HØURS FRØM 9     Ø'CLØCK IT WILL BE 6     Ø'CLØCK
27     HØURS FRØM 5     Ø'CLØCK IT WILL BE 8     Ø'CLØCK
33     HØURS FRØM 5     Ø'CLØCK IT WILL BE 2     Ø'CLØCK
31     HØURS FRØM 9     Ø'CLØCK IT WILL BE 4     Ø'CLØCK
32     HØURS FRØM 12    Ø'CLØCK IT WILL BE 8     Ø'CLØCK
2      HØURS FRØM 9     Ø'CLØCK IT WILL BE 11    Ø'CLØCK
28     HØURS FRØM 4     Ø'CLØCK IT WILL BE 8     Ø'CLØCK
8      HØURS FRØM 10    Ø'CLØCK IT WILL BE 6     Ø'CLØCK
4      HØURS FRØM 11    Ø'CLØCK IT WILL BE 3     Ø'CLØCK
```

DØNE

In CLØCK2 we change lines 20 and 30 and insert line 5 to define FNC( ) and list the program in full.

CLØCK2

```
5     DEF FNC(Z)=INT(12*RND(Z)+1)
10    FØR P=1 TØ 10
20    LET T=FNC(1)
30    LET H=FNC(1)
40    LET S=T+H
50    IF S <= 12 THEN 80
60    LET S=S-12
70    GØTØ 50
80    PRINT H"HØURS FRØM"T"Ø'CLØCK IT WILL BE"S"Ø'CLØCK"
90    NEXT P
100   END
```

RUN
CLØCK2

```
6      HØURS FRØM 6     Ø'CLØCK IT WILL BE 12    Ø'CLØCK
7      HØURS FRØM 8     Ø'CLØCK IT WILL BE 3     Ø'CLØCK
7      HØURS FRØM 12    Ø'CLØCK IT WILL BE 7     Ø'CLØCK
8      HØURS FRØM 3     Ø'CLØCK IT WILL BE 11    Ø'CLØCK
5      HØURS FRØM 7     Ø'CLØCK IT WILL BE 12    Ø'CLØCK
4      HØURS FRØM 4     Ø'CLØCK IT WILL BE 8     Ø'CLØCK
7      HØURS FRØM 5     Ø'CLØCK IT WILL BE 12    Ø'CLØCK
4      HØURS FRØM 11    Ø'CLØCK IT WILL BE 3     Ø'CLØCK
11     HØURS FRØM 3     Ø'CLØCK IT WILL BE 2     Ø'CLØCK
10     HØURS FRØM 12    Ø'CLØCK IT WILL BE 10    Ø'CLØCK
```

DØNE

Modular Arithmetic

From the clock program we can easily develop the concept of modular addition. The biggest difference between modular addition and the last program is that for modulo 12 addition mathematicians define the set of integers as {0, 1, 2, 3, 4, 5, 6, 7, 8, 9, 10, 11}, dropping 12 and appending 0. Now we may not allow sums of 12 as before. So we will have to change line 50 to test for less than or equal to 11 not 12. But we must not change line 60 which subtracts 12. Why? Since we defined a function in CLØCK2, we need change only line 5 to generate integers from 0 to 11. As we wrote CLØCK1, we would have had to change two lines. Of course, we will have to change the printing and name the new program MØD12.

```
MØD12

 5   DEF FNC(Z)=INT(12*RND(Z))
10   FØR P=1 TØ 10
20   LET T=FNC(1)
30   LET H=FNC(1)
40   LET S=T+H
50   IF S <= 11 THEN 80
60   LET S=S-12
70   GØTØ 50
80   PRINT H"+"T"="S"MØD 12"
90   NEXT P
100  END
RUN
MØD12

 7   +  6   =  1     MØD 12
 8   +  5   =  1     MØD 12
 2   +  9   =  11    MØD 12
 8   +  6   =  2     MØD 12
10   +  8   =  6     MØD 12
 1   +  1   =  2     MØD 12
 1   +  3   =  4     MØD 12
 7   +  11  =  6     MØD 12
10   +  9   =  7     MØD 12
 1   +  7   =  8     MØD 12

DØNE
```

```
MAMD12

 5    DEF FNC(Z)=INT(12*RND(Z))
10    FØR P=1 TO 5
20    LET A=FNC(1)
30    LET B=FNC(1)
40    LET S=A+B
50    PRINT A"+"B"=    ";
60    GØSUB 500
70    LET S=A*B
80    PRINT A"*"B"=    ";
85    GØSUB 500
87    PRINT
90    NEXT P
490   STOP
500   IF S <= 11 THEN 530
510   LET S=S-12
520   GOTO 500
530   PRINT S"MØD 12    ";
540   RETURN
9999  END
```

```
RUN
MAMD12

10   +  4   =  2    MØD 12      10   *  4   =  4     MØD 12
 1   +  2   =  3    MØD 12       1   *  2   =  2     MØD 12
 6   +  1   =  7    MØD 12       6   *  1   =  6     MØD 12
 3   +  10  =  1    MØD 12       3   *  10  =  6     MØD 12
 1   +  10  =  11   MØD 12       1   *  10  =  10    MØD 12

DØNE
```

Where there is addition, multiplication is bound to follow. Suppose we multiply 5 by 7. We are accustomed to getting 35. But for MØD12 we only allow 0 through 11, so we subtract 12 and get 23, which is still too large. Subtract 12 again to get 11. Thus we are going to use the subtraction routine in the multiplication part of MØD12 also. This is a GØSUB situation. In the flowchart of Fig. 4-7, the GØSUB predefined process is the subroutine of lines 50, 60, and 70 in MØD12. Of course, there are more changes in printing. We call the program MAMD12 (Multiply and Add MoD 12).

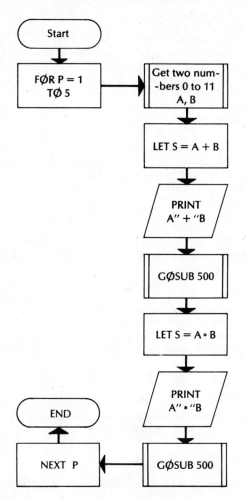

Fig. 4-7. Flowchart for adding and multiplying mod 12 for program MAMD12.

SUMMARY

Two major expansions in our programming capability have occurred in this section. We are now able to generate random numbers in any range we like. They can be limited to integers or they can be decimal numbers. And lists may now be dimensioned to the length that we require. We have also used the GØSUB statement to good advantage in a modular arithmetic program.

PROBLEMS FOR SEC. 4-4

1) Print a list of 30 randomly assigned numbers from 2.00 to 20.00 with tenths and hundredths permitted but no digits to the right.

2) Print a list of 25 integers from −200 to 200 assigned by a random number function in increasing order.

3) Print the list in problem 2) to guarantee that there are no duplications. In other words, if you generate a number that has already been used, generate another.

4) Prepare a list of the first 18 Fibonacci numbers. For all nonequal pairs find the greatest common factor. Enter the greatest common factors in a list with no duplications and print the result.

5) Prepare a list of the first 20 Fibonacci numbers. For $1 = 2$ to 19 print F[I] ** 2 − F[I − 1] * F[I + 1].

6) Use three lists to add two 20-digit numbers. Use one list for each number and enter the digits one by one as elements in the list. Use the third list as the sum list. Be sure to carry if the sum of the two corresponding digits is 10 or more.

7) Do problem 6) using two lists instead of three.

√ 8) Use three lists to multiply two 10-digit numbers digit by digit. (Could this be done with two lists?)

9) Modify program MAMD12 to find the remainder after dividing the value of S by 12 to replace the subroutine that uses successive subtraction.

10) Write a program to do arithmetic mod 5 and mod 6, five problems each. Put 5 and 6 in a data line and write one random function so that it generates 0 to 4 for mod 5 and 0 to 5 for mod 6.

11) Have the computer print the addition table and the multiplication table for mod 6.

12) Have the computer do subtraction mod 7.

13) Write a program in which the mod and the number of problems are selected at random, and the problems are generated with random data.

14) Have the computer generate pairs of integers and find the greatest common factor.

15) Have the computer generate sets of three integers and find the greatest common factor.

16) Generate pairs of integers and find the least common multiple.

17) Generate sets of four integers and treat them as coefficients of two binomials and find the three coefficients of the product; i.e., generate A, B, C, and D in $(AX + B)(CX + D)$ and find E, F, and G in EX ** 2 + FX + G. Print all five numbers in two groups, one group for A, B, C, and D and another for E, F, and G.

√ 18) Form two 20-element lists with integers in the same range. Form two other lists. One list is to contain all numbers that appear in both lists, i.e., the intersection of the two lists. The other list is to contain a number if it is in either of the original two lists, but only entering it once if it is in both lists. In other words, find the union.

19) Fill a 25-element list with the first 25 positive odd integers. Fill a second 25-element list with the sum of all the entries of the first list up to and including the subscript number of the second list.

20) Modify CLØCK1 to handle times in hours and minutes.

CHAPTER 5

Elementary Data Processing

5-1 INTRODUCTION TO DATA PROCESSING

One of the very common uses of computers is for data processing. There is no clear cut definition for data processing that distinguishes it from other kinds of computer activity. In a sense, all computer work is data processing. However, data processing often implies that the computer is being used to sort, collate, tabulate, and/or otherwise process data. Such activities as processing questionnaires fall in this category.

Tabulating One Item

Let us ask some families how many television sets they have in their homes. The answers will be numbers, one number per family. We can set up a list so that the first element counts the number of families with one set and the Nth element counts the number of families with N sets. Before we begin counting, there will be zero families having each number of sets. So we will have to initialize each element of the list at 0. Then when the number for a family is read, we will add 1 to the element in the list corresponding to that number of television sets. If the first family has one set, then we have the computer look at T[1]. T[1] = 0 to start, and adding 1 makes T[1] = 1. The next time a family has one set we have the computer add 1 to T[1], and then T[1] will equal 2. The process is repeated until all data is read. We will have to use dummy data, since we want to print the results only after we have tabulated all data. We can draw a simple flowchart. See Fig. 5-1.

Of course we could allow for a larger number of sets by simply using a longer list. We could have provided for zero sets by letting T[1] tabulate 0, T[2] tabulate 1, T[3] tabulate 2, etc. Then line 60 in program TV'S would read

$$60 \quad \text{LET } T[N + 1] = T[N + 1] + 1$$

because, when N is 0, you want T[1] and when N is 1, you want T[2], etc. Or we could use 0 subscripts if they are available.

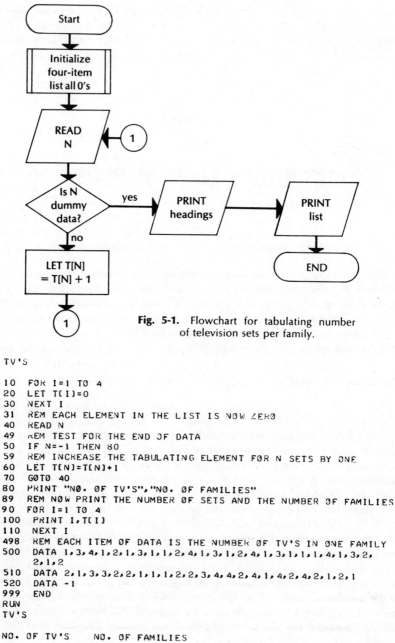

Fig. 5-1. Flowchart for tabulating number of television sets per family.

```
TV'S

10    FOR I=1 TO 4
20    LET T[I]=0
30    NEXT I
31    REM EACH ELEMENT IN THE LIST IS NOW ZERO
40    READ N
49    REM TEST FOR THE END OF DATA
50    IF N=-1 THEN 80
59    REM INCREASE THE TABULATING ELEMENT FOR N SETS BY ONE
60    LET T[N]=T[N]+1
70    GOTO 40
80    PRINT "NO. OF TV'S","NO. OF FAMILIES"
89    REM NOW PRINT THE NUMBER OF SETS AND THE NUMBER OF FAMILIES
90    FOR I=1 TO 4
100   PRINT I,T[I]
110   NEXT I
498   REM EACH ITEM OF DATA IS THE NUMBER OF TV'S IN ONE FAMILY
500   DATA 1,3,4,1,2,1,3,1,1,2,4,1,3,1,2,4,1,3,1,1,1,4,1,3,2,
      2,1,2
510   DATA 2,1,3,3,2,2,1,1,1,2,2,3,4,4,2,4,1,4,2,4,2,1,2,1
520   DATA -1
999   END
RUN
TV'S

NO. OF TV'S    NO. OF FAMILIES
 1                20
 2                15
 3                8
 4                9

DONE
```

There are some more things that we can do with TV'S. We might have the computer count the number of families or count the total number of television sets. These figures may be computed as the data is being read. There can be a counting statement LET C = C + 1 somewhere between lines 50 and 70, and there can be a summing statement in the same part of the program. LET S = S + N will total the number of sets. Then as long as we have the total number of sets and the total number of families, we might just as well compute the average number of sets per family. These are left as exercises.

Tabulating Several Items

With just a few modifications TV'S can be extended to handle data pertaining to several different things.

Suppose in taking a census, we ask not only how many television sets the family has, but also how many cars, homes, and bathrooms. All that is necessary is to have four counting lists instead of one. We need one list for each item being counted. In lines 10, 20, and 30 we initialize four lists at 0 for up to eight items in any one category. This could be more or less for any particular problem. We check for dummy data in line 50 and then update the four lists in lines 60 through 90. In the printing routine, I determines the element number in each list and so is the number of items in each list. T[I] is the number of families that have I television sets, C[I] is the number of families that have I cars, etc. See program TCHB.

From the results we see that there were nine families with one car, seven families with two television sets, etc. We could also do more data processing in TCHB. We could find the average number of cars per family, etc.

Tabulating Yes–No Answers

We are not limited to numerical quantities. Suppose you were to question each of your classmates about courses they want to take. If you ask, "Do you want to take chemistry?" and the answer is "no," you can call that 0, and similarly call "yes" 1. Let us ask people if they want to take the following courses: chemistry, physics, French, Spanish, calculus. If someone says he wants to take chemistry, French, and Spanish, his data will be: 1, 0, 1, 1, 0. We can use one list to count all courses. The first element of the list will count people who want to take chemistry, the second will count people who want to take French, etc. Before reading any data, we will have to initialize each element of the list at 0. Then after reading the first person's data, we want the list to be 1, 0, 1, 1, 0, which can be done by adding the number representing yes or no to the number already in that location of the list. We can get the computer to read the data in groups of five by using a loop FØR R = 1 TØ 5, with the READ statement and the tabulating statement inside. The real works of the program will be the tabulating statement

LET C[R] = C[R] + K

where R is the loop available and goes from 1 to 5 for each person's data. If R = 1, the course is chemistry; if R = 2, the course is physics, etc. Where K is

```
TCHB

10   FØR I=1 TØ 8
20   LET T[I]=C[I]=H[I]=B[I]=0
30   NEXT I
31   REM ALL TABULATING LISTS ARE INITIALIZED AT ZERØ
40   READ T,C,H,B
49   REM CHECK FØR DUMMY DATA
50   IF T=-1 THEN 110
59   REM 60 TØ 90 ENTER THE LATEST DATA IN THE FØUR LISTS.
60   LET T[T]=T[T]+1
70   LET C[C]=C[C]+1
80   LET H[H]=H[H]+1
90   LET B[B]=B[B]+1
100  GØ TØ 40
109  REM   HERE THE HEADINGS ARE PRINTED
110  PRINT "NUMBER,TV'S, CARS, HØMES,BATHS"
119  REM HERE THE RESULTS ARE PRINTED
120  FØR I=1 TØ 8
130  PRINT I;T[I];C[I];H[I];B[I]
140  NEXT I
349  REM EACH GRØUP ØF FØUR NUMBERS IS FØR ØNE FAMILY- T,C,H,B
350  DATA 1,1,1,1,2,1,1,2,3,2,1,2,4,3,2,8,4,2,1,5
355  DATA 2,1,1,3,1,1,1,3,2,1,1,2,1,1,1,1,2,1,1,1
360  DATA 2,2,2,6,1,1,1,4,3,4,2,6,1,2,1,2,2,2,2,8
365  DATA 2,1,1,2,-1,0,0,0
400  END
RUN
TCHB

NUMBER,TV'S, CARS, HØMES,BATHS
  1      5      9     12    3
  2      7      5      4    5
  3      2      1      0    2
  4      2      1      0    1
  5      0      0      0    1
  6      0      0      0    2
  7      0      0      0    0
  8      0      0      0    2

DØNE
```

0 this person does not want to take the course, and where K is 1 he does. So when K = 0, the tabulating statement adds 0 to the previous value in the C list, which does not change the number there. This is what we want for the person who does not want to take the course. However, if K = 1, then the tabulating statement adds 1 to the previous value of the entry in the C list, which is exactly what we want the computer to do for a person wanting to take the course. Again the dummy data is −1.

From CØURS1, we can easily see that seven people want to take chemistry, five people want to take physics, etc.

One last thing we might try to consider in this section is getting larger amounts of data in a program similar to CØURS1. Suppose you want to see what results might look like for say 500 people. Well, you could ask 500 people and then type out all that data. Or you could generate random data, with the understanding that the results will be random and may not simulate the real situation. However, knowing that the numbers will be random will help you spot serious errors if there are any. For 500 people and random data, each course should draw about 250 yeses. If the results show 96 or 600 yeses

```
COURS1

10    FOR I=1 TO 5
20    LET C[I]=0
30    NEXT I
40    FOR R=1 TO 5
50    READ K
60    IF K=-1 THEN 100
70    LET C[R]=C[R]+K
80    NEXT R
90    GOTO 40
100   PRINT "CHEMISTRY","PHYSICS","FRENCH","SPANISH","CALCULUS"
110   FOR I=1 TO 5
120   PRINT C[I],
130   NEXT I
990   REM DATA IS IN ORDER CHEMISTRY PHYSICS FRENCH SPANISH
      CALCULUS
995   REM    '1' MEANS YES   '0' MEANS NO
1000  DATA 1,0,1,1,0,0,0,1,1,0,1,1,1,1,1,1,0,0,1,1,0,1,1,0,0,1
1010  DATA 0,1,1,0,1,0,0,0,1,0,1,1,0,1,0,1,1,0,0,1,1,0,0,0,1
1020  DATA 0,0,1,0,1,1,0,1,0,0
1100  DATA -1
9999  END
RUN
COURS1

CHEMISTRY      PHYSICS      FRENCH      SPANISH      CALCULUS
7              5            7           6            6


DONE
```

in some course, then you must search for the error. One nice thing about using random data is that you do not have any data to type in. So in CØURS1 we may eliminate lines 1000, 1010, 1020, and 1100. Now the REM statements are not quite relevant. Line 60 can be deleted as we are not testing for dummy data and line 50 is deleted as we are not going to read data anymore. Line 90 will be taken care of by putting in a loop 1 to 500 to simulate 500 people. To get random numbers 0 or 1 we need INT(2 ° RND(1)). The initializing, the tabulating, and the printing of CØURS1 can be used in the new program CØURS2, where the results are reasonably close to 250.

SUMMARY

We have seen lists used to analyze data from questionnaire-type questions having numerical or yes–no type answers. The tabulating may be done using one or several lists depending on the problem itself. Random numbers may be used to try out such programs with many numbers. The random nature of these numbers may help to spot serious program errors, which might not show up with small amounts of data unless you check the totals by hand.

PROBLEMS FOR SEC. 5-1

1) Modify program TV'S to total the number of television sets and the number of families, and find the average number of sets per family rounded off to the nearest hundredth.

```
CØURS2

10   FØR I=1 TØ 5
20   LET C(I)=0
30   NEXT I
33   REM THIS LØØP SIMULATES 500 PEØPLE
35   FØR X=1 TØ 500
40   FØR R=1 TØ 5
42   REM   THIS LØØP LØØKS AT FIVE CØURSES FØR EACH PERSØN
48   REM    PICK A RANDØM NUMBER ZERØ ØR ØNE
50   LET K=INT(2*RND(1))
70   LET C(R)=C(R)+K
78   REM   NEXT CØURSE
80   NEXT R
88   REM    NEXT PERSØN
90   NEXT X
100   PRINT "CHEMISTRY","PHYSICS","FRENCH","SPANISH","CALCULUS"
110   FØR I=1 TØ 5
120   PRINT C(I),
130   NEXT I
9999   END
RUN
CØURS2
```

CHEMISTRY	PHYSICS	FRENCH	SPANISH	CALCULUS
253	257	237	249	256

DØNE

2) Modify program CØURS1 to find the number of people who want to take chemistry and physics.

3) Modify CØURS2 to generate twice as many yeses as nos.

4) Modify CØURS1 to find the number of people who want to take physics but not calculus.

√ 5) Consider a questionnaire in which there are 14 questions which call for yes, no, or other answers. Let 1 be yes, 2 be no, and 3 be other. Set up three separate lists for yes, no, and other. Generate 25 sets of 14 numbers 1, 2, or 3 and find the number of each type of answer for each question number. Print the results in decipherable form.

6) Modify CØURS2 to generate yes-to-no answers in a ratio of 3 to 4.

5-2   ARRAYS

So far we have only been able to store numbers in a simple variable or in a list. There will be situations where we will want to store more numbers than is convenient in a list. While we have seen that we can use several lists very effectively, BASIC provides a two-dimensional list for such situations. It may be called an *array*. You may think of an array as being similar to a checkerboard. Instead of the familiar single subscript we have been using for lists, we will need double subscripts; one for rows and the other for columns. (As with lists, computers vary. Some will allow 0 subscripts, others begin with 1.) For an array designated as A, A[1, 1] is the number in the upper lefthand corner. (In some cases, it will be A[0, 0].) A[1, 2] indicates the number in row 1 and column 2; A[5, 8] indicates the number in row 5 and column 8, etc. In other words, the first subscript indicates the row starting at the top and the second subscript indicates the column starting at the left. Thus, A[R, C] indicates the number in row R and column C.

An array is just a set of numbers arranged in columns and rows, This perfectly matches the printed result in program TCHB in Sec. 5-1. We may use each column of an array in the same manner that we used each list in that program, and we can use each row to keep track of the number of families having that number of the item being tabulated. But before we tackle TCHB in an array, we should see a little more how arrays operate.

Very often we will use a nested loop, with one loop taking the computer through the columns and the other loop going through the rows. The structure of an array is shown in Table 5-1. For students without 0 subscripts, consider the dashed outline to exclude the 0 row and 0 column. For students who have 0 subscripts, consider the dashed outline to suggest that it is optional whether or not you use them at this time.

TABLE 5-1. ARRAY STRUCTURE.

[0, 0]	[0, 1]	[0, 2]	[0, 3]	[0, 4]	[0, 5]
[1, 0]	[1, 1]	[1, 2]	[1, 3]	[1, 4]	[1, 5]
[2, 0]	[2, 1]	[2, 2]	[2, 3]	[2, 4]	[2, 5]
[3, 0]	[3, 1]	[3, 2]	[3, 3]	[3, 4]	[3, 5]

ARRAY1

```
9   REM   INITIALIZE A AT ONE
10  LET A=1
19  REM    ROWS GO FROM 1 TO 3
20  FOR R=1 TO 3
29  REM    COLUMNS GO FROM 1 TO 5
30  FOR C=1 TO 5
40  LET T[R,C]=A
50  LET A=A+1
59  REM  NEXT COLUMN
60  NEXT C
69  REM  NEXT ROW
70  NEXT R
80  PRINT "AT THIS POINT THE ARRAY IS FILLED"
999  END
RUN
ARRAY1

AT THIS POINT THE ARRAY IS FILLED

DONE
```

It is time for another demonstration program. In ARRAY1 we simply fill a 3-row by 5-column array with integers 1 through 15 going first across the page and then down, just as we read the printed page. In this program we have called the array T. Any letter of the alphabet may be used. However, do not use the same letter to name both a list and an array in the same program. This is because the computer treats a list as an array with just one column or one row, depending on the computer.

We have filled the array just as the printed message states. However, as was noted in Chap. 1, in order for the work of the computer to be useful, we must eventually get back from the computer some printed results. Note that we say eventually. The more advanced we get in programming, the more we will do things that are not immediately printed. Nonetheless, just to restore your faith in the computer, let us ask it to print some values from the array we just created. After line 80 we will insert a variety of printing

```
ARRAY2

9   REM INITALIZE A AT ØNE
10   LET A=1
19   REM    RØWS GØ FRØM 1 TØ 3
20   FØR R=1 TØ 3
29   REM    CØLUMNS GØ FRØM 1 TØ 5
30   FØR C=1 TØ 5
40   LET T[R,C]=A
50   LET A=A+1
59   REM   NEXT CØLUMN
60   NEXT C
69   REM   NEXT RØW
70   NEXT R
80   PRINT "AT THIS PØINT THE ARRAY IS FILLED"
85   PRINT
89   REM LET'S PRINT T[3,4]
90   PRINT "T[3,4] ="; T[3,4]
100   PRINT
110   PRINT "WHØ LIVES AT [2,5]?"; T[2,5]; "LIVES THERE"
120   PRINT
130   PRINT "LET'S LØØK AT THE ENTIRE ARRAY"
139   REM   INCREMENT RØWS
140   FØR R=1 TØ 3
149   REM   INCREMENT CØLUMNS
150   FØR C=1 TØ 5
160   PRINT T[R,C];
170   NEXT C
175   PRINT
176   PRINT
180   NEXT R
999   END
RUN
ARRAY2

AT THIS PØINT THE ARRAY IS FILLED

T[3,4] = 14

WHØ LIVES AT [2,5]? 10   LIVES THERE

LET'S LØØK AT THE ENTIRE ARRAY
  1     2     3     4     5

  6     7     8     9     10

 11    12    13    14    15

DØNE
```

with labels and comments much as we did earlier in the introduction to lists. See ARRAY2.

The elements of an array constitute variables just as do the elements of a list. We may operate on any element or elements in the array we choose. Consider ARRAY3.

```
ARRAY3

10   LET A=1
20   FOR R=1 TO 3
30   FOR C=1 TO 5
40   LET A[R,C]=A
50   LET A=A+1
60   NEXT C
70   NEXT R
90   PRINT "WE PRINT THE ORIGINAL ARRAY"
100  GOSUB 900
110  PRINT "WE CAN MULTIPLY EVERY ELEMENT IN THE 4TH COLUMN
     BY 6"
120  FOR R=1 TO 3
130  LET A[R,4]=A[R,4]*6
140  NEXT R
150  GOSUB 900
160  PRINT "WE CAN SUBTRACT THE 3RD ROW FROM THE 2ND ROW"
170  PRINT "AND PUT THE RESULT IN THE 3RD ROW"
180  FOR C=1 TO 5
190  LET A[3,C]=A[2,C]-A[3,C]
200  NEXT C
210  GOSUB 900
880  STOP
890  REM ****PRINTING SUBROUTINE IS HERE****
900  FOR R=1 TO 3
910  FOR C=1 TO 5
920  PRINT A[R,C];
930  NEXT C
940  PRINT
950  PRINT
960  NEXT R
970  RETURN
999  END
RUN
ARRAY3


WE PRINT THE ORIGINAL ARRAY
 1       2       3       4       5

 6       7       8       9       10

 11      12      13      14      15

WE CAN MULTIPLY EVERY ELEMENT IN THE 4TH COLUMN BY 6
 1       2       3       24      5

 6       7       8       54      10

 11      12      13      84      15

WE CAN SUBTRACT THE 3RD ROW FROM THE 2ND ROW
AND PUT THE RESULT IN THE 3RD ROW
 1       2       3       24      5

 6       7       8       54      10

 -5      -5      -5      -30     -5


DONE
```

We can even change the size of the array during a program. In ARRAY4 we begin with the original 3 by 5 array of ARRAY3 and tack on an extra row to enter the sums of the entries in the first three columns. Notice that in both ARRAY3 and ARRAY4 we are able to use GØSUB to save writing the printing routines more than once.

You should begin to see that we have exactly the same control over the contents of an array that we do over the contents of a list.

Now let us look again at our census program TCHB. There we used an 8-row by 5-column array in which the first column simply contained the row number and the other four columns each contained tabulated results for a different item. We may now put the READ statement in a loop going from 2 to 5 and let the loop variable determine the column in which the tabulation takes place. The other features of the program are procedures that we have used before. See TCHB+.

```
ARRAY 4

10   LET A=1
20   FØR R=1 TØ 3
30   FØR C=1 TØ 5
40   LET A[R,C]=A
50   LET A=A+1
60   NEXT C
70   NEXT R
80   PRINT "HERE IS THE ØRIGINAL ARRAY!"
100  FØR R=1 TØ 3
110  FØR C=1 TØ 5
120  PRINT A[R,C];
130  NEXT C
140  PRINT
150  PRINT
160  NEXT·R
168  REM SET ALL ELEMENTS IN THE 4TH RØW TØ ZERØ
170  FØR I=1 TØ 5
180  LET A[4,I]=0
190  NEXT I
200  PRINT "NØW WE HAVE THE 4 BY 5 ARRAY;"
210  GØSUB 500
219  REM THIS RØUTINE ADDS CØLUMNS AND PUTS THE SUM IN THE 4TH
     RØW
220  FØR C=1 TØ 5
230  FØR R=1 TØ 3
240  LET A[4,C]=A[4,C]+A[R,C]
250  NEXT R
260  NEXT C
270  PRINT "THE FØURTH RØW CONTAINS THE SUMS ØF THE FIRST 3
     RØWS."
280  GØSUB 500
490  STØP
498  REM **THIS IS THE PRINTING RØUTINE FØR THE 4 BY 5 ARRAY**
500  FØR R=1 TØ 4
510  FØR C=1 TØ 5
520  PRINT A[R,C];
530  NEXT C
540  PRINT
550  PRINT
560  NEXT R
570  RETURN
999  END
```

```
RUN
ARRAY 4


HERE IS THE ORIGINAL ARRAY!
 1      2      3      4      5

 6      7      8      9     10

11     12     13     14     15


NOW WE HAVE THE 4 BY 5 ARRAY;
 1      2      3      4      5

 6      7      8      9     10

11     12     13     14     15

 0      0      0      0      0


THE FOURTH ROW CONTAINS THE SUMS OF THE FIRST 3 ROWS.
 1      2      3      4      5

 6      7      8      9     10

11     12     13     14     15

18     21     24     27     30


DONE



TCHB+

10   FOR R=1 TO 8
14   REM   HERE THE ROW NUMBER IS ENTERED IN THE FIRST COLUMN
15   LET S[R,1]=R
20   FOR C=2 TO 5
30   LET S[R,C]=0
40   NEXT C
50   NEXT R
68   REM WE ARE ENTERING FIGURES IN COLUMNS 2 THROUGH 5 ONLY
70   FOR C=2 TO 5
80   READ N
85   IF N=-1 THEN 110
88   REM  N DETERMINES THE ROW NUMBER WHICH KEEPS TRACK OF N
     ITEMS
90   LET S[N,C]=S[N,C]+1
100  NEXT C
105  GOTO 70
110  PRINT "NUMBER, TV'S, CARS, HOMES, BATHS"
119  REM   HERE THE RESULTS ARE PRINTED
120  FOR R=1 TO 8
130  FOR C=1 TO 5
140  PRINT S[R,C];
150  NEXT C
155  PRINT
160  NEXT R
349  REM EACH GROUP OF FOUR NUMBERS IS FOR ONE FAMILY- T,C,H,B
350  DATA 1,1,1,1,2,1,1,2,3,2,1,2,4,3,2,8,4,2,1,5
355  DATA 2,1,1,3,1,1,1,3,2,1,1,2,1,1,1,1,2,1,1,1
360  DATA 2,2,2,6,1,1,1,4,3,4,2,6,1,2,1,2,2,2,2,8
365  DATA 2,1,1,2,-1,0,0,0
400  END
```

```
RUN
TCHB+

NUMBER, TV'S, CARS, HOMES, BATHS
    1      5     9     12     3
    2      7     5      4     5
    3      2     1      0     2
    4      2     1      0     1
    5      0     0      0     1
    6      0     0      0     2
    7      0     0      0     0
    8      0     0      0     2

DONE
```

SUMMARY

We may now use a powerful extension of the list concept, the array. An array may be thought of as an arrangement of numbers in which there are rows and columns. Numbers in an array may be accessed by designating the location by a double subscript such as H[3, 7] for the number in array named H which is located in the row numbered 3 and the column numbered 7. As you may have guessed, you will not need a DIMension statement as long as you do not exceed a subscript of [10, 10].

PROBLEMS FOR SEC. 5-2

1) Print an array with 3 rows and 6 columns filled with 0's.

2) Print an array with 6 rows and 3 columns filled with 1's.

3) Set up an array with 4 rows and 9 columns and fill it with random numbers from −999 to +999. Print the array.

4) Fill the addresses along the top left to bottom right diagonal of a square 7 by 7 array with 1's and all other locations with 0's and print the result.

5) Fill two arrays of the same dimensions with random integers and print each array. Then fill a third array with the sums of the corresponding entries from the first two and print the result.

6) Fill two arrays of the same dimensions with random integers and print each array. Then fill one of these two arrays with the sums of the corresponding entries from each array and print the result.

7) Fill a 3 by 7 array with the integers 0 through 20. Print that array. Then multiply each entry by the sum of the row number and the column number and print the result.

8) Fill a 4 by 7 array with random integers from −500 to +500 and print the result. Then multiply each entry by 2 and print that result. Insert the printing routine using GOSUB.

9) Fill a 10 by 10 array with the addition table.

10) Fill a 10 by 10 array with the multiplication table.

11) Fill a 5 by 5 array with the addition table mod 5. Then have the computer generate addition problems with a random number function and find the sum by accessing the appropriate entry in the additon array.

12) Do problem 11) for the multiplication table mod 5.

✓ 13) Consider a questionnaire containing 10 questions with yes, no, or other as the three possible answers. Generate random data and print the results in a 10 by 4 array. Use the first column for the question number and the other three for yes, no, or other. Have the computer generate 50 questionnaires.

5-3 A MORE DETAILED QUESTIONNAIRE ANALYSIS

Consider a questionnaire submitted to four categories of people: male—21 or over, male—under 21, female—21 or over, and female—under 21. On this questionnaire there are 15 questions calling for yes–no answers. Our task is to present a tabulated summary of the data collected. We can provide sample data for say 10 people for the purpose of getting a first test RUN. Let us refer to this first problem and the program as SURVEY. The flowchart for SURVEY is drawn in Fig. 5-2.

The first computer problem we run into is, how do we get 15 rows in an array? The answer is that we may dimension an array much the same as we dimensioned lists. In the array DIM (DIMension) statement, we must specify

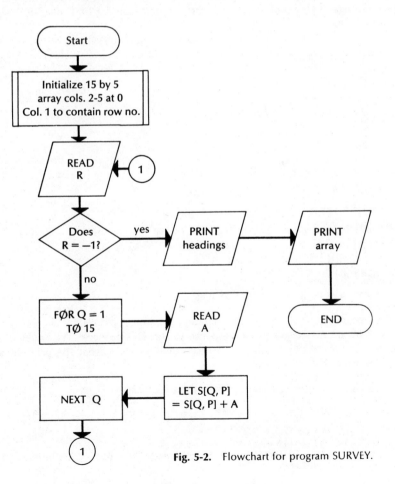

Fig. 5-2. Flowchart for program SURVEY.

two dimensions: one for rows and one for columns. We want an array with 15 rows and 5 columns (4 for categories and 1 for the question numbers). DIM S[15, 5] will provide just such an array.

DIM (TWO-DIMENSIONAL)
DIM A[R, C] sets up an array designated as A with highest column number C and highest row number R. The statement is required if either R or C exceeds 10. Some computers require explicit integers, others allow variables in DIM statements.

In our questionnaire problem, there are three things that we must keep track of: 1) the category of the respondent, 2) the question number, and 3) the response. We may organize the data and results according to Table 5-2.

TABLE 5-2.   CHART TO ORGANIZE SURVEY.

Array		Code in
Column Number	Use	DATA Line
1	Question number	Position in line
2	Male 21 or over	2
3	Male under 21	3
4	Female 21 or over	4
5	Female under 21	5

It will be easier to organize the data, if we reserve an entire data line for each person. Then we can put the category code (2 through 5) in the first location and the response (0 or 1) in the next 15 locations. A DATA line will look like this:

XXX   DATA 4, 1, 0, 1, 1, 1, 0, 0, 1, 1, 0, 1, 0, 1, 0, 1

where the 4 indicates that the respondent is female and 21 or over, and the 1's and 0's mean yes and no in response to the 15 questions. We could count the number of people in advance or use dummy data so that the printing can be done after all data is read.

```
SURVEY

9   REM  DIM S[15,5] SETS UP AN ARRAY WITH 'HIGHEST' LOCATION
       [15,5]
10   DIM S[15,5]
20   FOR R=1 TO 15
28   REM LINE 30 ENTERS THE ROW NUMBER IN THE FIRST COLUMN
30   LET S[R,1]=R
```

```
40    FOR C=2 TO 5
48    REM LINE 50 SETS THE LAST 4 COLUMNS AT ZERO
50    LET S[R,C]=0
60    NEXT C
70    NEXT R
78    REM 80 READS THE CATEGORY FOR THE NEXT PERSON IN THE SURVEY
80    READ P
90    IF P=-1 THEN 200
98    REM Q GOES THROUGH THE 15 QUESTIONS
100   FOR Q=1 TO 15
110   READ A
120   LET S[Q,P]=S[Q,P]+A
130   NEXT Q
138   REM LINE 140 SENDS THE COMPUTER BACK TO READ ANOTHER LINE
      OF DATA
140   GOTO 80
198   REM THE PRINTING BEGINS HERE
200   PRINT "QUEST MALE   MALE   FEMALEFEMALE"
210   PRINT "NUMBER 21+   UNDER   21+    UNDER"
220   FOR R=1 TO 15
230   FOR C=1 TO 5
250   PRINT S[R,C];
260   NEXT C
270   PRINT
280   NEXT R
498   REM  ***A LINE LIKE 500 MAY HELP TO LINEUP THE DATA LINES
499   REM  IN TYPING***
500   REM   1,1,1,1,1,1,1,1,1,1,1,1,1,1,1,1
501   DATA  4,1,0,1,1,1,0,0,1,1,0,1,0,1,0,1
502   DATA  4,1,0,0,0,0,1,1,0,1,1,0,0,0,1,1
503   DATA  3,1,1,1,1,0,0,1,0,1,0,0,1,1,0,0
504   DATA  5,1,1,1,0,0,0,1,0,0,0,1,1,1,1,0
505   DATA  2,1,1,1,0,0,1,0,1,0,0,1,1,1,1,0
506   DATA  5,0,0,1,0,1,0,0,0,1,1,1,0,0,1,1
507   DATA  5,0,0,0,1,1,1,0,1,0,1,0,1,0,0,1
508   DATA  2,0,0,1,1,0,0,1,1,0,1,0,1,0,0,1
509   DATA  4,1,1,1,1,1,1,1,0,0,0,1,0,1,0,0
510   DATA  2,1,1,0,0,1,0,1,0,0,0,0,1,1,1,1
900   DATA  -1
999   END
RUN
SURVEY

QUEST MALE   MALE   FEMALEFEMALE
NUMBER 21+   UNDER   21+    UNDER
 1     2      1       3      1
 2     2      1       1      1
 3     2      1       2      2
 4     1      1       2      1
 5     1      0       2      2
 6     1      0       2      1
 7     2      1       2      1
 8     2      0       1      1
 9     0      1       2      1
10     1      0       1      2
11     1      0       2      2
12     3      1       0      2
13     2      1       2      1
14     2      0       1      2
15     2      0       2      2

DONE
```

Notice in SURVEY that while there are four categories in the original problem, there are five additional categories generated by the conditions of the problem. They are male, female, under 21, 21 or over, and total. We may further process the tabulated results after line 140 in SURVEY by totaling up the appropriate columns to get these latest categories tabulated. Of course, we will have to change the DIM statement to DIM S[15, 10]. This is done in SRVEY1. Study lines 145 through 190 carefully to assure yourself that the correct values are being tabulated there.

There are many other results that we might try to find. There are other

```
SRVEY1

10    DIM S[15,10]
20    FOR R=1 TO 15
28    REM LINE 30 ENTERS THE ROW NUMBER IN THE FIRST COLUMN
30    LET S[R,1]=R
40    FOR C=2 TO 10
48    REM LINE 50 SETS THE LAST 9 COLUMNS AT ZERO
50    LET S[R,C]=0
60    NEXT C
70    NEXT R
78    REM 80 READS THE CATEGORY FOR THE NEXT PERSON IN THE SURVEY
80    READ P
90    IF P=-1 THEN 145
98    REM Q GOES THROUGH THE 15 QUESTIONS
100   FOR Q=1 TO 15
110   READ A
120   LET S[Q,P]=S[Q,P]+A
130   NEXT Q
138   REM LINE 140 SENDS THE COMPUTER BACK TO READ ANOTHER LINE
      OF DATA
140   GOTO 80
145   FOR R=1 TO 15
150   LET S[R,6]=S[R,2]+S[R,3]
160   LET S[R,7]=S[R,4]+S[R,5]
170   LET S[R,8]=S[R,3]+S[R,5]
180   LET S[R,9]=S[R,2]+S[R,4]
185   LET S[R,10]=S[R,6]+S[R,7]
190   NEXT R
198   REM THE PRINTING BEGINS HERE
200   PRINT "QUEST MALE   MALE   FEMALEFEMALE"
210   PRINT "NUMBER 21+   UNDER  21+   UNDER MALE  FEMALE UNDER
      21+";
211   PRINT "  TOTAL"
220   FOR R=1 TO 15
230   FOR C=1 TO 10
250   PRINT S[R,C];
260   NEXT C
270   PRINT
280   NEXT R
498   REM ***A LINE LIKE 500 MAY HELP TO LINEUP THE DATA LINES
499   REM IN TYPING***
500   REM   1,1,1,1,1,1,1,1,1,1,1,1,1,1,1,1,1
501   DATA 4,1,0,1,1,1,0,0,1,1,0,1,0,1,0,1
502   DATA 4,1,0,0,0,0,1,1,0,1,1,0,0,0,1,1
503   DATA 3,1,1,1,1,0,0,1,0,1,0,0,1,1,0,0
504   DATA 5,1,1,1,0,0,0,1,0,0,0,1,1,1,1,0
505   DATA 2,1,1,1,0,0,1,0,1,0,0,1,1,1,0,1
506   DATA 5,0,0,1,0,1,0,0,0,1,1,1,0,0,1,1
507   DATA 5,0,0,0,1,1,1,0,1,0,1,0,1,0,0,1
508   DATA 2,0,0,1,1,0,0,1,1,0,1,0,1,0,0,1
509   DATA 4,1,1,1,1,1,1,1,0,0,0,1,0,1,0,0
510   DATA 2,1,1,0,0,1,0,1,0,0,0,0,1,1,1,1
900   DATA -1
999   END
```

```
RUN
SRVEY1

QUEST MALE   MALE  FEMALEFEMALE
NUMBER 21+   UNDER  21+   UNDER MALE   FEMALE UNDER 21+   TOTAL
  1     2     1      3      1     3      4      2     5      7
  2     2     1      1      1     3      2      2     3      5
  3     2     1      2      2     3      4      3     4      7
  4     1     1      2      1     2      3      2     3      5
  5     1     0      2      2     1      4      2     3      5
  6     1     0      2      1     1      3      1     3      4
  7     2     1      2      1     3      3      2     4      6
  8     2     0      1      1     2      2      1     3      4
  9     0     1      2      1     1      3      2     2      4
 10     1     0      1      2     1      3      2     2      4
 11     1     0      2      2     1      4      2     3      5
 12     3     1      0      2     4      2      3     3      6
 13     2     1      2      1     3      3      2     4      6
 14     2     0      1      2     2      3      2     3      5
 15     2     0      2      2     2      4      2     4      6

DONE
```

totals that could be tabulated. At the time P is read, we could total the number of people in each of the original four categories and enter these totals in row 16. Then we could compute averages. There are numerous ratios that we could evaluate. We could have the computer generate random data to get larger numbers in the printed result. That would require random integers 2 through 5 for P in line 80 and random 0 or 1 in line 110 for the yes–no responses.

SUMMARY

We see that the two-dimensional array permits tremendous flexibility. We may determine its size exactly. The array serves as a vast storage area for large amounts of data or tabulated results. We may process the contents of an array and enter results in other parts of the same array with tremendous maneuverability.

The DIM statement may be used to specify subscripts greater than 10 in the two-dimensional array much as it was used for lists.

PROBLEMS FOR SEC. 5-3

1) Modify SURVEY to handle 75 questionnaires with random data.

2) Modify SRVEY1 to tabulate the totals discussed with that program in the 16th row of the S array.

3) Modify SURVEY to handle yes, no, and other as possible answers. Create three arrays: one for yes, a second for no, and a third for other responses. Use random data and 50 questionnaires.

4) Modify SRVEY1 to generate random data for 50 questionnaires.

5) Modify SRVEY1 to tabulate the results as percentages of the total number of yes responses. Do not create a second array.

6) Fill an array with the multiplication table up to 12 × 12, and print the last three rows.

√ 7) In a 12 by 12 array enter all 1's in the upper left to lower right diagonal and the left-most column, and all 0's elsewhere. Then beginning in the third row, second column, enter the sum of the entry in the same column of the row immediately above and in the column one to the left and the row immediately above, through the 12th row, 11th column. Print the result.

CHAPTER 6

Specific Applications

6-1 EUCLIDEAN ALGORITHM

In Chap. 4 when we first reduced common fractions to lowest terms, even though the computer did the work, it was done the hard way.

For two integers N and D,

$$N/D = I + R/D$$

or $$N = I \cdot D + R$$

where I is the integer quotient and R is the remainder. If we successively divide the remainder into the previous divisor until the remainder is 0, the last divisor is the greatest common factor. This will always happen, even for mutually prime pairs, as the last divisor will be 1.

Let us see what happens for 13398 and 7854.

$$N = I \cdot D + R$$

$13398 = (1)[7854] + 5544$	(6-1)
$7854 = (1)[5544] + 2310$	(6-2)
$5544 = (2)[2310] + 924$	(6-3)
$2310 = (2)[924] + 462$	(6-4)
$924 = (2)[462] + 0$	(6-5)

According to Euclid the greatest common factor of 13398 and 7854 is 462, because 462 was the divisor when the remainder was 0. Indeed $13398 = 29 \cdot 462$ and $7854 = 17 \cdot 462$. That took only five tries. How many would it have taken using the old method? Now all we have to do is figure out why it works.

Look carefully at Eq. (6-5). 924 is divisible by 462 because the remainder is 0 and 0 is divisible by any nonzero number. This 0 remainder is the key to the entire proposition. Now look at Eq. (6-4). Since 924 is divisible by 462, so is (2)[924] + 462, which makes 2310 divisible by 462. Now look at Eq. (6-3).

Since 2310 and 924 are both divisible by 462, so is 5544. This makes 7854 divisible by 462, which in turn makes 13398 divisible by 462, which is the original contention. The argument we have just presented is hardly a proof of the Euclidean algorithm, but it should be convincing.

Now, how do we get the computer to carry out this process? First, from Eqs. (6-1) through (6-5) we should see that we have simply taken the old divisor D and made it the dividend and the old remainder R and made it the divisor. So we will get the computer to LET N = D and LET D = R after we look at the remainder to see if it is 0. If the remainder is 0, we direct the computer to print the last divisor as it is the greatest common factor.

Now we should be able to draw the flowchart (Fig. 6-1) and write the program CØMFAC.

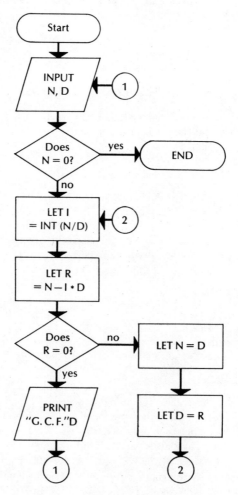

Fig. 6-1. Flowchart for using Euclidean algorithm for program CØMFAC.

```
CØMFAC

10   PRINT "N, D";
20   INPUT N, D
25   IF N=0 THEN 120
28   REM   FIND THE INTEGER QUØTIENT
30   LET I=INT(N/D)
38   REM   FIND THE REMAINDER
40   LET R=N-I*D
48   REM   IF THE REMAINDER IS ZERØ THEN D IS THE G, C.F.
50   IF R=0 THEN 90
58   REM   R WAS NØT ZERØ, SØ WE ITERATE
60   LET N=D
70   LET D=R
80   GØTØ 30
90   PRINT "G.C.F. ="; D
100  PRINT
110  GØTØ 10
120  END
RUN
CØMFAC

N, D?13398, 922251
G.C.F. = 33

N, D?741279, 922251
G.C.F. = 33

N, D?13398, 7854
G.C.F. = 462

N, D?991, 199
G.C.F. = 1

N, D?272851, 246156
G.C.F. = 281

N, D?0, 0

DØNE
```

PROBLEMS FOR SEC. 6-1

1) Write a program to add fractions given the numerators and denominators. Print the sum reduced to lowest terms.

2) Do problem 1) for multiplication.

√ 3) INPUT two pairs of coordinates. Have the computer find the slope and the Y-intercept of the straight line containing the points and print the results as rational numbers reduced to lowest terms. If the result is negative, have the numerator be the negative number.

4) As a project, write a program to factor quadratic expressions with integer coefficients. Be sure to allow for 0 coefficients and factor out greatest common factors of all three coefficients.

6-2   CHANGE BASE

In this section we are going to develop a program to convert base-10 numbers to base-2 numbers. You will recall that for base-2, only the digits 0 and 1 are permitted and each digit represents a power of 2 instead of 10.

One of the widespread uses for base-2 numbers is in computers themselves. This is because in base-2, all numbers may be expressed by a set of switches with 0 being *off* and 1 being *on*.

One difficulty that we quickly encounter is that whatever the digit capacity of the computer we have access to, that number of digits provides a much smaller number in base-2 than it does in base-10. We will use up to six digits in the base-10 number for our program. In base-2 100000 is only 32 base-10 and

$$
\begin{aligned}
111111_2 = \quad & 1 * 2 ** 0 \quad & \text{or} \quad & 1 \\
+ & 1 * 2 ** 1 \quad & \text{or} \quad & + 2 \\
+ & 1 * 2 ** 2 \quad & \text{or} \quad & + 4 \\
+ & 1 * 2 ** 3 \quad & \text{or} \quad & + 8 \\
+ & 1 * 2 ** 4 \quad & \text{or} \quad & +16 \\
+ & 1 * 2 ** 5 \quad & \text{or} \quad & +32 \\
& & & \overline{63_{10}}
\end{aligned}
$$

which we could handle easily with pencil and paper. Clearly, we are going to have to work with more than six digits in base-2.

Let us assume that we can provide for as many digits as are needed. How many digits do we need to represent the base-10 number 999999 in base-2? We could write a program that would give that information, but we can also figure it out ourselves. We can begin with 2 ** 5.

$$
\begin{aligned}
2 ** 5 &= \quad 32 \\
2 ** 10 &= \quad 32 ** 2 = 1024 \\
2 ** 20 &= 1024 ** 2 = 1048576
\end{aligned}
$$

So, if we provide for up to 2 ** 20, we can handle six-digit integers with room to spare. We know how many digits we need, now we have to figure out how to make the conversion.

Let us run a sample conversion before we attempt to write the program. We use 149 base-10 here. First find the greatest integer power of 2 that is less than 149. It is 2 ** 7 or 128.

$$149/2 ** 7 = 1 + 21/2 ** 7$$

or
$$
\begin{aligned}
149 &= 1 * (2 ** 7) + 21 & \text{(6-6)} \\
21 &= 0 * (2 ** 6) + 21 & \text{(6-7)} \\
21 &= 0 * (2 ** 5) + 21 & \text{(6-8)} \\
21 &= 1 * (2 ** 4) + 5 & \text{(6-9)} \\
5 &= 0 * (2 ** 3) + 5 & \text{(6-10)} \\
5 &= 1 * (2 ** 2) + 1 & \text{(6-11)} \\
1 &= 0 * (2 ** 1) + 1 & \text{(6-12)} \\
1 &= 1 * (2 ** 0) + 0 & \text{(6-13)}
\end{aligned}
$$

By successive substitution we see that

$$149 = \quad 1 * (2 ** 7)$$
$$+ 0 * (2 ** 6)$$
$$+ 0 * (2 ** 5)$$
$$+ 1 * (2 ** 4)$$
$$+ 0 * (2 ** 3)$$
$$+ 1 * (2 ** 2)$$
$$+ 0 * (2 ** 1)$$
$$+ 1 * (2 ** 0)$$

So that

$$149_{10} = 10010101_2$$

Equation (6-6) may be written in general as

$$N = I * (2 ** E) + R$$

where N is the number, I is the integer quotient, E is the exponent on the base-2, and R is the remainder after integer division. Therefore

$$I = INT(N/(2 ** E)$$

and, solving for R we get

$$R = N - I * (2 ** E)$$

Now, looking at Eqs. (6-6) through (6-13) we see that we have an iterative process in which the new number is to be the old remainder and the exponent on the base-2 is reduced by 1 until it gets to 0. This looks like a loop in which the loop variable is the exponent on the base-2 and stops at 0. Where does it start? Earlier we decided that the greatest exponent on 2 could be 20. Now we should be able to assemble our problem into a flowchart (Fig. 6-2).

```
BASE

10    READ N
20    PRINT N;"BASE TEN =";
30    FØR E=20 TØ 0 STEP -1
40    LET I=INT(N/2↑E)
50    PRINT I;
60    LET R=N-I*2↑E
70    LET N=R
80    NEXT E
85    PRINT "BASE TWO"
86    PRINT
90    GØTØ 10
100   DATA 999999.,1,16
110   END
RUN
BASE

999999.    BASE TEN = 0    1    1    1    1    0    1    0
    0       0       0    1    0    0    0    1    1    1    1    1

    1     BASE TWO
```

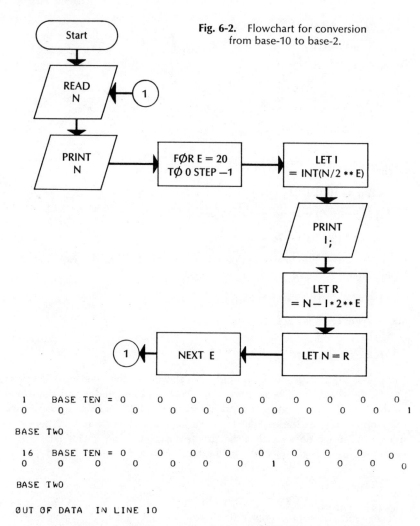

Fig. 6-2. Flowchart for conversion from base-10 to base-2.

```
1    BASE TEN = 0    0    0    0    0    0    0    0    0
0    0    0    0    0    0    0    0    0    0    0    1
BASE TWO

16   BASE TEN = 0    0    0    0    0    0    0    0    0
0    0    0    0    0    0    0    1    0    0    0    0    0
BASE TWO

ØUT ØF DATA   IN LINE 10
```

Looking carefully at the printed results in BASE, we can see that 16 base-10 does equal 00000000000000010000; however it is difficult to sort that out. Printing the variable I is controlled by semicolon spacing which will not place one-digit numbers in adjacent spaces. We can however, get the digits next to each other by printing them explicitly. If we say PRINT "1"; the next printed character will be printed in the next space. So, instead of 50 PRINT I; we insert

```
45 IF I=1 THEN 55
50 PRINT "0";
52 GØ TØ 60
55 PRINT "1";
```

and call for a RUN:

```
RUN
BASE-2

999999.     BASE TEN =011110100001000111111 BASE TWO

1      BASE TEN =000000000000000000001 BASE TWO

16    BASE TEN =000000000000000010000 BASE TWO


ØUT ØF DATA   IN LINE 10
```

By not worrying too much about the fact that we were going to require a large number of digits, we have succeeded in printing numbers with 21 digits. Quite often in programming, as in any problem-solving situation, you will solve seemingly impossible problems by emphasizing those things that you can do rather than holding back because of all the things you think that you will be unable to handle.

Let us reassemble the program as it now stands in BASE-2 and insert another set of data just to see a few more results.

```
BASE-2

10   READ N
20   PRINT N;"BASE TEN =";
30   FØR E=20 TØ 0 STEP -1
40   LET I=INT(N/2↑E)
45   IF I=1 THEN 55
50   PRINT "0";
52   GØTØ 60
55   PRINT "1";
60   LET R=N-I*2↑E
70   LET N=R
80   NEXT E
85   PRINT " BASE TWO"
86   PRINT
90   GØTØ 10
100  DATA 999999.,1,16
110  END
100 DATA 45,9875,123456
RUN
BASE-2

45    BASE TEN =000000000000000101101 BASE TWO

9875     BASE TEN =000000010011010010011 BASE TWO

123456.    BASE TEN =000011110001001000000 BASE TWO


ØUT ØF DATA   IN LINE 10
```

Of course we really are not finished with the program yet. We should eliminate the leading 0's. Then the printed results will be in more familiar form. This is left as an exercise.

PROBLEMS FOR SEC. 6-2

1) Eliminate the leading 0's in BASE-2. Be careful not to eliminate all 0's.
2) Write a program to convert base-2 numbers to base-10. It may help to put the digits of the base-2 number in a list.
3) Write a program to add two numbers in base-2.
4) Have the computer convert numbers in base-10 to base-3.
√ 5) Write a program to convert from base-10 to base-12. It is conventional to use T for 10 and E for 11 in base-12.
√ 6) Have the computer convert base-3 numbers to base-2.
√ 7) Write a program to convert base-10 numbers to any base up to 12 with the base determined from data.

6-3 LOOKING AT INTEGERS DIGIT BY DIGIT

In general, the more control we have over a number in the computer, the more complex the problems we might expect to be able to handle. So, for the purpose of learning to control a number in the computer digit by digit, let us write a program to take the digits of an integer and print them one at a time.

Consider the number 8394. The 8 means 8 thousand which may be written 8 ° 10 °° 3; the 3 means 3 hundred which may be written 3 ° 10 °° 2; the 9 means ninety which may be written 9 ° 10 °° 1; and the 4 means four which may be written 4 ° 10 °° 0. Looking at the numbers step by step,

$$8394 = 8 \text{ ° } 10 \text{ °° } 3 + 394$$
$$394 = 3 \text{ ° } 10 \text{ °° } 2 + 94$$
$$94 = 9 \text{ ° } 10 \text{ °° } 1 + 4$$
$$4 = 4 \text{ ° } 10 \text{ °° } 0 + 0$$

This is an example of the general relationship

$$N = I \text{ ° } 10 \text{ °° } E + R$$

where I is the integer quotient found by

$$I = INT(N/10 \text{ °° } E)$$

and an iterative process whereby the new N is the old R and the value of E is decreased by 1 for each iteration. Solving for R we get

$$R = N - I \text{ ° } 10 \text{ °° } E$$

All of this should begin to look familiar.

For six-digit integers the value of E will have to begin at 5 and go to 0 STEP −1. Carefully study program DIGIT and you will see that we have indeed broken integers into their separate digits. However, as always, we should look for ways to improve our programs. One change that will save a little paper

```
DIGIT

10    PRINT "INPUT ANY INTEGER";
20    INPUT N
30    IF N=0 THEN 999
40    FOR E=5 TO 0 STEP -1
50    LET I=INT(N/10↑E)
60    PRINT I
70    LET R=N-I*10↑E
80    LET N=R
90    NEXT E
100   PRINT
110   GOTO 10
999   END
RUN
DIGIT

INPUT ANY INTEGER?123456
 1
 2
 3
 4
 5
 6

INPUT ANY INTEGER?819045
 8
 1
 9
 0
 4
 5

INPUT ANY INTEGER?53627
 0
 5
 3
 6
 2
 7

INPUT ANY INTEGER?0

DONE
```

would be to print the digits across the page with semicolon spacing. We can do that by changing line 60 to read 60 PRINT I; and call for a RUN.

```
60 PRINT I;
RUN
DIGIT

INPUT ANY INTEGER?123456
 1     2     3     4     5     6
INPUT ANY INTEGER?975432
 9     7     5     4     3     2
INPUT ANY INTEGER?53627
 0     5     3     6     2     7
INPUT ANY INTEGER?0

DONE
```

Now let us see the program with the change and try another number. (See DIGIT1.)

```
DIGIT1

10   PRINT "INPUT ANY INTEGER";
20   INPUT N
30   IF N=0 THEN 999
40   FØR E=5 TØ 0 STEP -1
50   LET I=INT(N/10↑E)
60   PRINT I;
70   LET R=N-I*10↑E
80   LET N=R
90   NEXT E
100   PRINT
110   GØTØ 10
999   END
RUN
DIGIT1

INPUT ANY INTEGER?666666
  6     6     6     6     6     6
INPUT ANY INTEGER?0

DØNE
```

One last consideration is that we might want to eliminate the leading 0's. We leave this as an exercise.

PROBLEMS FOR SEC. 6-3

1) Eliminate the leading 0's in DIGIT. Be careful not to eliminate all zeroes.

2) Test integers for divisibility by 3 by summing the digits.

3) Construct the integer formed by reversing the order of the digits in an INPUT integer. Print the result as an integer.

√ 4) Test integers with the integer formed by reversing the order of the digits to find the greatest common factor.

√ 5) Find all three-digit integers that are prime. Form new integers by reversing the digits and see if the new number is also prime. Print a number only if it and its reverse number is prime. There are 43 pairs of numbers, some of which will appear twice. You should pay particular attention to efficiency in this problem.

CHAPTER 7

Strings and Files

7-1 INTRODUCTION TO STRINGS

To a BASIC programmer, a string is a set of characters. We use strings every time we print a message by enclosing it in quotes in a PRINT statement. BASIC provides the ability to save strings in a special string variable, identified by using a trailing dollar sign ($). We may use A$, B$, etc., to designate string variables. Some computers allow A1$, B8$, etc., and some allow A$(R,C) to designate string arrays. The use of strings enables us to process alphabetic data, such as names and addresses, and descriptive data of all kinds.

We may work with string variables in many of the ways that we do with numeric variables. For instance, in BASIC programs we may use such statements as

```
100   LET A$ = "FIRST"
100   READ A$, B$
100   INPUT A$, B$
100   PRINT A$, B$
```

In order to READ A$, B$, we must provide a corresponding DATA statement. Some systems require all strings in DATA statements to be enclosed in quotes. Others require quotes only when the string contains a comma or 'looks like' a number. For PRINT A$, B$, the output will have "comma spacing." That is, the page will be arranged in 15-character columns. If we replace the comma with a semicolon, the two strings will be printed with no space between them.

We will use a short program named FIRST$ to demonstrate LET, READ, INPUT, and PRINT.

FIRST$

```
95    REM * FIRST STRING PRØGRAM
96    REM
100   LET A$ = "THIS IS A"
110   READ B$, C$
120   PRINT A$; " "; B$; " "; C$;
130   INPUT D$
140   PRINT
150   PRINT A$; " "; B$; " "; C$; " "; D$
155   REM
160   DATA  "PRØGRAM TØ", "DEMØNSTRATE"
170   END
RUN
FIRST$
```

THIS IS A PRØGRAM TØ DEMØNSTRATE?STRINGS

THIS IS A PRØGRAM TØ DEMØNSTRATE STRINGS

BASIC allows us to compare strings for order in accordance with a sequence known as ASCII (American Standard Code for Information Interchange). For strictly alphabetic strings, this code will alphabetize in the conventional order. ASCII places the digits 0 through 9 ahead of the letters of the alphabet. We can easily write a short program to demonstrate order comparison. See ORD$.

ØRD$

```
95    REM * CØMPARES STRINGS FØR ØRDER
100   PRINT
110   PRINT "A$";
120   INPUT A$
130     IF A$ = "STØP" THEN 240
140   PRINT "B$";
150   INPUT B$
160     IF A$ < B$ THEN 220
170     IF A$ = B$ THEN 200
180   PRINT A$; " IS GREATER THAN "; B$
190   GØTØ 100
195   REM
200   PRINT A$; " IS EQUAL TØ "; B$
210   GØTØ 100
215   REM
220   PRINT A$; " IS LESS THAN "; B$
230   GØTØ 100
240   END
RUN
ØRD$
```

```
A$?WHAT'S THIS
B$?WHAT'S THAT
WHAT'S THIS IS GREATER THAN WHAT'S THAT

A$?WHAT'S THIS
B$?WHAT'S WHAT
WHAT'S THIS IS LESS THAN WHAT'S WHAT

A$?WHAT'S WHAT
B$?WHAT'S WHAT
WHAT'S WHAT IS EQUAL TØ WHAT'S WHAT

A$?STØP
```

In the handling of strings, we find that different computers have significantly different BASIC language definitions. For example, on one computer, the statement 100 PRINT A$(4) will cause the computer to output the character string stored in string variable A$, beginning with the fourth character, whereas on another, the same statement will cause the computer to output the fourth string of the string list A$. It is because of these differences that we present two distinctly different schemes for handling strings in the next two sections.

7-2 STRINGS—THE SUBSTRING SCHEME°

In the substring scheme, strings may be considered as a complete entity by referring to A$, B$, etc., or we may consider segments of A$ by using one or two subscripts. A$(I) specifies the segment beginning with the Ith character and continuing to the end of the string. A$(I,J) [some computers using this scheme may require A$(I:J)] specifies the segment from the Ith character through the Jth character inclusive, provided I $\le$ J. If I = J, then A$(I,J) is a single character. This scheme does not provide for string arrays. (It has been extended on some computers, however, by using A$(I;J,K), where the I designates which string in the single dimension array is referred to and the J,K pair designates the segment from the Jth through the Kth character.)

As with arrays, it is necessary to specify the capacity of any string variable we intend to use (for more than one character) in a DIMension statement, Thus, 100 DIM A$(10),B$(16),C(2,11) provides for up to 10 characters in A$, up to 16 characters in B$, and two rows and 11 columns in a numeric array C. The C dimensioning is included here merely to demonstrate that string and array dimensioning may be intermixed in a single statement. The LEN( ) function is provided to count the number of characters actually stored in a string. LEN(Z$) takes on the value of the number of characters stored in string variable Z$.

In program SEG$1, note the dimensioning in line 100, the use of the LEN( ) function in lines 140 and 150, and the printing of segments in line 160.

```
SEG$1

95   REM * DEMØNSTRATES STRING SUBSCRIPTS
100  DIM A$[8]
110  READ A$
120  IF A$="STØP" THEN 210
130  PRINT "A$=";A$
140  PRINT "LEN(A$)=";LEN(A$)
150  FØR I=1 TØ LEN(A$) STEP 2
160  PRINT "A$(";I;",";I+1;")=";A$[I,I+1]
170  NEXT I
180  PRINT
190  GØTØ 110
195  REM
200  DATA "ABCDEF","BASIC","STØP"
210  END
RUN
SEG$1

A$=ABCDEF
LEN(A$)= 6
A$( 1   , 2   )=AB
A$( 3   , 4   )=CD
A$( 5   , 6   )=EF
```

° The programs of this section were run on a Hewlett-Packard computer.

```
A$=BASIC
LEN(A$)= 5
A$( 1    , 2    )=BA
A$( 3    , 4    )=SI
A$( 5    , 6    )=C
```

The ability to isolate a segment of a string has many uses. We may wish to pack related information into a single string such as

100   LET D$ = "JANFEBMARAPRMAYJUNJULAUGSEPØCTNØVDEC"

Now we, may select the desired month according to its position in D$. Or, we might want to use a single string to contain the names of a group of individuals, last name first, but to print only the last name and first initial.

One common use of string segments is to format numbers in printed results. For instance, the appearance of the output produced by program SEG$1 could be improved by using string output to print I and I + 1 in line 160. See lines 110 and 160 in program SEG$2. Notice the compact appearance of the printed result there.

```
SEG$2

95   REM * PRINTING A SINGLE DIGIT NUMERIC
96   REM   USING STRING ØUTPUT
100  DIM A$[8],D$[9]
110  LET D$="123456789"
120  READ A$
130  IF A$="STØP" THEN 210
140  PRINT "A$=";A$
150  FØR I=1 TØ LEN(A$) STEP 2
160  PRINT "A$(";D$[I,I];",";D$[I+1,I+1];")=";A$[I,I+1]
170  NEXT I
180  PRINT
190  GØTØ 110
195  REM
200  DATA "ABCDEF","BASIC","STØP"
210  END
RUN
SEG$2

A$=ABCDEF
A$(1,2)=AB
A$(3,4)=CD
A$(5,6)=EF

A$=BASIC
A$(1,2)=BA
A$(3,4)=SI
A$(5,6)=C
```

We see in SEG$2 the beginning of a technique for printing a numeric using string output. Obviously missing are the ability to print zero and the ability to handle more than one digit. We can take care of zero by using LET D$ = "0123456789", but printing numbers of more than one digit requires that we use the technique of program DIGIT in Sec. 6-3. That is, we must isolate the digits of our number one at a time. Once we have the digit to be printed stored in I, we must print D$(I + 1,I + 1) since zero is the first digit in D$. This step is taken in program DIGIT2. The numeric output is placed between # signs, and the string output is placed between $ signs.

```
DIGIT2

95    REM * PRINTING A NUMERIC ØF MØRE
96    REM   THAN ØNE DIGIT USING STRING
97    REM   ØUTPUT
100   DIM D$[10]
110   LET D$="0123456789"
120   PRINT "INPUT ANY INTEGER";
130   INPUT N
140   IF N=0 THEN 260
150   PRINT "#";N;"#"
160   PRINT "$";
170   FØR E=5 TØ 0 STEP -1
180   LET I=INT(N/10↑E)
190   PRINT D$[I+1,I+1];
200   LET R=N-I*10↑E
210   LET N=R
220   NEXT E
230   PRINT "$"
240   PRINT
250   GØTØ 120
260   END
RUN
DIGIT2

INPUT ANY INTEGER?93617
# 93617.       #
$093617$

INPUT ANY INTEGER?0
```

It is left as an exercise to eliminate the printing of the leading zero in the output of DIGIT2.

SUMMARY

We have used strings to store nonnumeric data. Any string may be considered in its entirety, or any segment may be isolated using subscripts. A$(I,J) designates the substring from the Ith to the Jth characters, inclusive. By placing the ten digits in a dummy string, we gain complete control over the printing of numerics by using string output.

PROBLEMS FOR SEC. 7-2

1) Write a program to print the characters of a string in reverse order.

2) Eliminate leading zeros in the output of DIGIT2. Be careful not to eliminate all zeros.

3) Write a program to arrange the characters of a string in order using the technique of program ARANG5 of Sec. 4-4.

4) Use string formatting to print the output in problem 7 of Sec. 6-2.

5) Write a program to convert a string integer to a numeric.

√ 6) Write a program to convert a numeric input to a string output if the numeric input is allowed to contain a decimal point and be negative.

7-3   THE STRING ARRAY SCHEME*

In the string array scheme, A$(I) names the string stored in the position numbered I of a string single-dimensioned array, and A$(I,J) names the string stored in row I and column J of a string two-dimensional array. As with arrays used elsewhere, a DIMension statement is required if we intend to have either subscription exceed 10. The maximum number of characters which may be stored in any one array position varies from computer to computer but ranges from 6 to the thousands.

We may do many things with string arrays that we do with numeric arrays. We may READ, PRINT, INPUT, assign, and compare for order elements of the array. We may even be able to use the statement LET A$ = "XYZ" + "ATV" to assign "XYZATV" to A$.

```
DAYS01

100   DIM W$(7)
105
108   REM * READ DAYS ØF THE WEEK
110   FØR I = 1 TØ 7
120      READ W$(I)
130   NEXT I
135
138   REM * PRINT DAYS ØF THE WEEK
140   FØR I = 1 TØ 7
150      PRINT I; W$(I)
160   NEXT I
165
168   REM * DATA
170   DATA   SUNDAY, MØNDAY, TUESDAY, WEDNESDAY
180   DATA   THURSDAY, FRIDAY, SATURDAY
190   END
RUN

 1  SUNDAY
 2  MØNDAY
 3  TUESDAY
 4  WEDNESDAY
 5  THURSDAY
 6  FRIDAY
 7  SATURDAY
```

Suppose we wish to work with the days of the week. We can easily read the names of the days of the week into an array. Then these names can be printed later as labels whenever needed, as shown in program DAYS01.

It is useful to be able to manipulate data in string variables. We might want to know the number of characters in one of them, for example. There are two ways to find out. One is to use the LEN function. LEN(A$) returns the number of characters in A$. Another is to use the CHANGE statement. CHANGE A$ TØ A stores the number of characters in A$ in A(O), converts each of the characters in the string A$ to a numeric equivalent code, and then stores that numeric in a corresponding position of the one-dimensional A array. The code used for this is ASCII (American Standard Code for Information Interchange). CHANGE A TØ A$ makes the conversion in the opposite direction. This can

---

* The programs of this section were run on the General Electric Information Services time sharing system.

```
CHANGE
98    REM * DEMØNSTRATE CHANGE STATEMENT
100   DIM A(30),B(1)
110   PRINT "STRING";
120   INPUT A$          •
130   CHANGE A$ TØ A
140   PRINT LEN(A$); "CHARACTERS IN '"; A$; "'"
150   PRINT
160   LET B(0) = 1
170   PRINT "CHAR ASCII CØDE"
180   FØR I = 1 TØ A(0)
190      LET B(1) = A(I)
200      CHANGE B TØ B$
210      PRINT "'"; B$; "'  "; A(I)
220   NEXT I
230   END
RUN

STRING? TRY THIS
 8 CHARACTERS IN 'TRY THIS'

CHAR ASCII CØDE
'T'    84
'R'    82
'Y'    89
' '    32
'T'    84
'H'    72
'I'    73
'S'    83
```

probably best be demonstrated with a program. See especially lines 130 and 200 of program CHANGE.

Notice that it required four statements to extract the Ith character of A$. In program CHANGE, we used statements 130, 160, 190, and 200 to do this. The EXT$ function is available for just this purpose. EXT$(A$,I,J) extracts the group of characters beginning with I and ending with J for string A$. Some computers use SEG$ for this. Using EXT$, program CHANGE becomes CHANGF.

```
CHANGF
98    REM * DEMØNSTRATE CHANGE STATEMENT
100   DIM A(30)
110   PRINT "STRING";
120   INPUT A$
130   CHANGE A$ TØ A
140   PRINT LEN(A$); "CHARACTERS IN '"; A$; "'"
150   PRINT
170   PRINT "CHAR ASCII CØDE"
180   FØR I = 1 TØ A(0)
210      PRINT "'"; EXT$(A$,I,I); "'  "; A(I)
220   NEXT I
230   END
RUN

STRING? #!&+:]
 6 CHARACTERS IN '#!&+:]'

CHAR ASCII CØDE
'#'    35
'!'    33
'&'    38
'+'    43
':'    58
']'    93
```

We may form strings from the characters of strings in some rearranged sequence. We might print a string backwards or with the characters in alphabetic order. In order to arrange the characters of a string in alphabetic order, we can simply provide a one-dimensional array with the corresponding ASCII code numerics in increasing order. Program ORDER$ does exactly this.

```
ØRDER$

100   DIM A(100)
110   PRINT "A$";
120   INPUT A$
130   PRINT
140   CHANGE A$ TØ A
150   FØR I = 1 TØ A(0) - 1
160      FØR J = I + 1 TØ A(0)
170            IF A(I) <= A(J) THEN 210
175   REM * EXCHANGE ØUT ØF ØRDER CØDES
180            LET S = A(I)
190            LET A(I) = A(J)
200            LET A(J) = S
210      NEXT J
220   NEXT I
230   CHANGE A TØ A$
240   PRINT A$
250   END
RUN

A$? WHAT IF I CAN'T THINK ØF SØMETHING?

     '?AACEFFGHHHIIIIKMNNNØØSTTTTW
```

SUMMARY

Whenever subscripted array string variables may be used, A$(I,J) specifies the string stored in row I, column J. We may use CHANGE A$ TØ A to convert the characters in the string variable A$ to the equivalent ASCII code numerics in corresponding positions of the A array. We may also reverse this process by using CHANGE A TØ A$. We also find the number of characters in A$ stored in A(O). Alternatively, we may use the LEN function. We may extract a group of characters with the EXT$(A$,I,J) function. This may be implemented as SEG$.

We may assign, PRINT, INPUT, and READ string variables in much the same way that we handle these operations with numeric variables. Strings may be placed in DATA statements, and string arrays must be DIMensioned if a subscript is to exceed 10.

PROBLEMS FOR SEC. 7-3

1) Write a program to print the characters of a string in reverse order.

2) Write a progam to accept string input, and tabulate the number of times each character appears.

3) Write a program to alphabetize the strings of a single-dimension string array.

4) Write a program to produce the following output, using the days of the week as stored in W$ in program DAYS01.

```
S  M  T  W  T  F  S
U  0  U  E  H  R  A
N  N  E  D  U  I  T
D  D  S  N  R  D  U
A  A  D  E  S  A  R
Y  Y  A  S  D  Y  D
      Y  D  A     A
         A  Y     Y
         Y
```

5) Modify program ORDER$ to eliminate duplicates.

6) Write a program to produce the following output, using the days of the week as stored in W$ in program DAYS01.

7-4 INTRODUCTION TO DATA FILES

So far in our programming work all of the data used by our programs has been entered through DATA statements, INPUT statements, or LET statements. Consequently, we have had to store the data as part of the program or type the data directly at the keyboard of our terminal. This works out all right for small amounts of data that we wish to process just once. But, if we have large amounts of data or we expect to carry out several processes on our data, then we need to separate the data from the program. We can do this by using data files.

A data file is simply a storage space in the computer where we store data, much as a program may be stored in a storage space. (In fact, in some computers, files and programs are indistinguishable until we type certain commands. Obviously, we cannot RUN a data file.) By designating a separate storage space for data, we gain many capabilities. We may now store much larger amounts of data than we could possibly store in the data statements of a program. We may alter the data to accommodate the results of program calculations. We may rearrange the data according to program specifications. The possibilities are limited only by our ability to think of problems to solve.

Most computer processing done today utilizes data files. Data files are used for inventory, bookkeeping, and data processing of all kinds. Just considering the data handled by the Internal Revenue Service and the Census Bureau, the use of data files can be seen as a very complex business indeed. So we will attempt here to present only some rudiments of files processing in BASIC.

As we said earlier, a file is a storage space accessible to the computer. This space may be used to store programs and data, which may be accessed during program execution. One of the features of these files that makes them mysterious is that they are invisible. But then, so are programs during execution. However, it is now possible to carry out tremendous amounts of useful computer work without the need for printing at the terminal, although it is good programming practice to provide some printed output to help keep track of what the computer has done. After we have seen several examples, we will gain confidence that the computer is really performing the expected operations.

The fundamental concept is that we may write or print data into a file and that we may retrieve that data under program control. Several versions of program statements are used to achieve these purposes. The next two sections explain the use of files as defined by two different systems. We have chosen Hewlett-Packard and General Electric versions of BASIC for this.

7-5   HEWLETT-PACKARD FILES

Just to get an idea about how data gets into files and how file data is accessed, let's look at two short programs. The first is a program to enter some numbers into a file. See program PRINT.

```
PRINT

90    REM * FIRST FILE DEMONSTRATION
100   FILES TEST
110   FOR I=1 TO 4
115   READ X
120   PRINT #1;X
130   NEXT I
140   DATA 3,17,11,31
150   END
RUN
PRINT
```

This is the very first program we have run which does something useful without any printed output. (As a general rule, however, it is good practice to have programs produce some meaningful printed output at the terminal.) Statements 100 and 120 introduce the first two file handling statements. Statement 100 is called the FILES statement. It is the statement which makes the file whose name is TEST available to the program. Statement 120 instructs the computer to print data into the film instead of onto the paper in the terminal. In that statement, the #1 specifies the first file named in the files statement. We may be able to name eight or more files, separated by commas. In addition, some computers allow us to replace any file originally named during program execution by using the ASSIGN statement. In the PRINT # statement, everything past the semicolon is printed into the file. We may list several data items here, and strings and numerics may be intermixed.

In order to allocate the file space in the first place, we used the OPEN command. OPEN–TEST, 15 designates a file space, called *TEST*, that contains 15 segments called *records* or *sectors*. Typically, a sector is large enough to store 32 numbers, or about 128 alphameric characters. More recent Hewlett-Packard computers allow the option of specifying record size through the CREATE command. On such a machine, CREATE TEST, 15,106 provides 15 records, each allowing up to 53 numerics, or about 212 alphameric characters. (106, 212, and 319 are storage efficient numbers to use in the CEATE command.)

In counting space for strings, we must add two to the number of characters for each string and add one if there is an odd number of characters. Thus three characters require the same storage space as four.

Now let's examine a program to read the contents of our file TEST.

```
READ

90   REM * PRØGRAM TØ READ NUMBERS FRØM A FILE
100   FILES TEST
110   READ #1;Y
120   PRINT Y;
130   GØTØ 110
140   END
RUN
READ

   3      17     11     31
END-ØF-FILE/END ØF RECØRD   IN LINE 110
```

The printed output produced by program READ should convince us that those numbers really came from a computer file as they do not appear anywhere in the program itself. We also got an error message which is exactly analogous to the ØUT ØF DATA IN LINE n message we have seen before.

There are several ways to avoid terminating with this error. One is to keep track of the number of entries in the file; another is to place an item of artificial data at the end of the real data just as we did in DATA statements in programs. However, BASIC provides a special statement just for this purpose. It is the IF END statement. See line 105 of program READ01.

```
READO1

90   REM * PRØGRAM READ WITH IF END 'TRAP'
100   FILES TEST
105   IF   END #1 THEN 140
110   READ #1;Y
120   PRINT Y;
130   GØTØ 110
140   END
RUN
READO1

   3      17     11     31
```

Statement 105 caused the computer to "remember" that if at any time we ask it to read beyond the data, it is to then execute line 140 as the next statement. In our case, that causes the program execution to terminate through the END statement.

The IF END "trap" may also be used to find the end of data in a file so that we may begin at that point to print additional data into it. Program PRINT1 does exactly this.

```
PRINT1

90   REM * PRINT WITH IF END 'TRAP'
100   FILES TEST
110   IF   END #1 THEN 140
120   READ #1;X
130   GØTØ 120
140   FØR I=1 TØ 3
```

```
150   READ X
160   PRINT #1;X
170   PRINT X;
180   NEXT I
190   DATA 19,2,6
200   END
RUN
PRINT1

  19    2      6
```

Note that PRINT1 will also print numbers into an empty file. Consequently, we can eliminate the need for program PRINT. Now we run program READ01 to verify for us that the file now contains numbers printed into it in separate runs of two programs.

```
RUN
READO1

  3     17    11    31    19    2     6
```

When we used file TEST above, we simply printed numbers one after another into the file without any concern for exactly where in the file those numbers were placed. Used in this way, file TEST is called a *serial file*. However, we could have directed the computer to print each of those numbers on a different record of the file. We need the following expanded file PRINT statement for this purpose:

$$999 \quad \text{PRINT} \#1,R;X$$

This statement allows us to specify that the data following the semicolon is to be printed in the Rth record of file #1. See line 130 of program PRINT2.

```
PRINT2

90    REM * PRINT TO RECORD R IN A FILE
100   FILES TEST
110   FOR R=1 TO 4
120   READ X
130   PRINT #1,R;X
140   PRINT X;
150   NEXT R
160   DATA 3,17,11,31
170   END
RUN
PRINT2

  3     17    11    31
```

Now to read the Rth value we needn't read through all R items. We may read it directly with the statement,

$$999 \quad \text{READ} \#1,R;X$$

Since this structure allows us to select at random any starting point in the file, we refer to the file as a *random access file*. See program READ02.

READ02

```
90    REM * DEMØNSTRATE RANDØM ACCESS
100   FILES TEST
110   PRINT "ITEM #";
120   INPUT R
130   IF R=0 THEN 170
140   READ #1,R;X
150   PRINT X
160   GØTØ 110
170   END
RUN
READ02

ITEM #?4
 31
ITEM #?1
 3
ITEM #?0
```

One of the uses of data files is to rearrange data and store it in rearranged form. For example, let's enter the names of seven people along with their dates of birth and death in file TEST, one person to a record, and arrange them in alphabetical order using the technique of program ARANGE in Sec. 3-4.

Program ENTERA reads the data from DATA statements and prints it in the first seven records of the file.

ENTERA

```
90    REM * FILE PRINT ØNE TØ A RECØRD
100   DIM N$[72]
110   FILES TEST
120   FØR I=1 TØ 7
130   READ N$,A,B
140   PRINT #1,I;N$,A,B
150   NEXT I
160   DATA "JØNES, JØHN PAUL",1747,1792
170   DATA "ANTHØNY, SUSAN B.",1820,1906
180   DATA "WASHINGTØN, BØØKER T.",1859,1915
190   DATA "BELL, ALEXANDER GRAHAM",1847,1922
200   DATA "EDISØN, THØMAS ALVA",1847,1931
210   DATA "FØRD, HENRY",1863,1947
220   DATA "BLØØMER, AMELIA JENKS",1818,1894
230   END
RUN
ENTERA
```

Program READA reads from file TEST and prints at the terminal.

READA

```
90    REM * READ NAMES FRØM A FILE
100   DIM N$[72]
110   FILES TEST
120   PRINT "  DØB           NAME"
130   FØR I=1 TØ 7
140   READ #1,I;N$,A,B
150   PRINT A;N$
160   NEXT I
170   END
RUN
READA
```

```
DØB        NAME
1747       JØNES, JØHN PAUL
1820       ANTHØNY, SUSAN B.
1859       WASHINGTØN, BØØKER T.
1847       BELL, ALEXANDER GRAHAM
1847       EDISØN, ·THØMAS ALVA
1863       FØRD, HENRY
1818       BLØØMER, AMELIA JENKS
```

Program ORDERA arranges the data in the file alphabetically. Note that line 190 is required so that when the comparison for order is made in line 160 after an. exchange has taken place, A$ stores the appropriate string. This is necessary because data is stored in two places—in the file and in the variables of the program. It is the programmer's job to keep these two storage areas coordinated.

```
ØRDERA

90   REM * ALPHABETIZE NAMES IN A FILE
100    DIM A$[72],B$[72]
110    FILES TEST
120    FØR I=1 TØ 6
130    READ #1,I;A$,A,A1
140    FØR J=I+1 TØ 7
150    READ #1,J;B$,B,B1
160    IF A$ <= B$ THEN 200
170    PRINT #1,I;B$,B,B1
180    PRINT #1,J;A$,A,A1
190    READ #1,I;A$,A,A1
200    NEXT J
210    NEXT I
220    PRINT "FILE ALPHABETIZED"
230    END
RUN
ØRDERA

FILE ALPHABETIZED
```

And once again we run READA to see that the data is properly arranged in the file.

```
RUN
READA

DØB        NAME
1820       ANTHØNY, SUSAN B.
1847       BELL, ALEXANDER GRAHAM
1818       BLØØMER, AMELIA JENKS
1847       EDISØN, THØMAS ALVA
1863       FØRD, HENRY
1747       JØNES, JØHN PAUL
1859       WASHINGTØN, BØØKER T.
```

SUMMARY

The FILES statement is used to make files accessible to a program. We may be able to replace the files named during execution using the ASSIGN statement. We may print data into a file using PRINT #N;A,B,C$ to print in the next available space serially. Or we may use PRINT #N,R;A,B,C$ to specify that the printing be at the beginning of record R. This approach is referred to as *random access*. We have the same options in the file READ statement. READ #N;A,B,C$ reads the next available data serially and READ #N,R;A,B,C$ reads at record R. The IF END statement allows us to determine when we are reading past the end of data in the file or are trying to read or print past the physical boundaries of the file itself.

PROBLEMS FOR SEC. 7-5

1) Use the IF END "trap" to avoid reading empty records or past the physical end of the file in program READ02.

2) Modify ENTERA so that it will accept varying numbers of names and can be used to add names to a file without "losing" data.

3) Modify READA to read any number of names.

4) Modify ORDERA to handle any number of names.

5) Modify ORDERA to arrange the data in increasing order of date of birth.

6) Write a program to print the names in file TEST at the terminal in alphabetical order without altering the arrangement in the file itself.

7) Write a program to print the names from file TEST in order of increasing age at death without altering the arrangement within the file itself.

8) Since strings and numbers may be intermixed in a file and an attempt to read one when the other is next will result in an error condition, it is desirable to be able to distinguish between them. The TYP( ) function is provided for this purpose. TYP(N) takes on a value of one if the next item in the file is a numeric, two if the next item is a string, three if the next item is the end of file, and, if N is negative, four if the next item is end of record. The absolute value of N is the position of the file in the files statement. In order to get positioned at the beginning of a record without reading data, we can READ #N,R. Using the TYP( ) function and the positioning READ statement, write a program to read the unknown contents of a file and print them record by record at the terminal.

7-6   GENERAL ELECTRIC FILES

The files we are concerned with in this section are referred to as *external files* since they store data externally to any programs. Files are generally characterized in two ways: the *access type* and the *data storage type*.

Data in files may be accessed sequentially or at random. Sequential access is similar to the way in which DATA statements of a program are accessed. Random access is similar to the way in which the elements of an array are accessed. As long as we know the exact position of a data item in a file, we may access it directly.

The data contained in a file may be stored either as ASCII character codes or as the binary representations of ASCII character codes and the numbers being stored. We do not need to be concerned with the details of this distinction when writing BASIC programs. We need only identify the slight differences in program statement syntax required. ASCII files may be accessed only sequentially whereas binary files may be accessed either sequentially or at random.

ASCII Files

ASCII files behave in many ways just like the DATA statements of a program. The data must be read sequentially, beginning with the first data item in the file. There is no way to access data at random points. The file may be filled from the keyboard exactly as DATA statements of a program are typed, but omitting the word DATA. The file may be listed at the keyboard with the LISt command, just as programs may be listed. Lines may be corrected in a file by retyping them. Lines may be removed by typing the line number followed by a carriage return. In order to make a file available for future use, it must be SAVed, just as a program must.

Perhaps the best way to learn about files is to study an example. Let's type an ASCII file containing test score data for a class. Suppose we consider a class of only five people and enter their test scores on six tests.

File SCØRE has been typed at the keyboard and SAVed as described earlier. We list the file here:

```
LIST

SCØRE

100 MARK UNDERWØØD,65,83,92,77,68,79
110 SUSAN STALBERG,73,88,82,77,69,79
120 EDGAR ANGLEMAN,74,86,73,79,80,73
130 ALTHEA LARGE,91,92,90,99,92,90
140 GERTRUDE SMITH,71,86,87,90,83,92
```

Now, to gain some file handling experience, let's make our first program merely print the contents of the file under program control rather than use the LIST command. This approach makes it possible to print labels and arrange the data in an easy-to-read form. See program READTEST.

```
READTEST

94   REM * READ FRØM A FILE AND PRINT ON THE TERMINAL
100  FILES SCØRE
110  PRINT "NAME","TEST1 TEST2 TEST3 TEST4 TEST5 TEST6"
130  READ #1, N$
150  PRINT N$; TAB(15);
160  FØR I = 1 TØ 6
170     READ #1, X
190     PRINT X; "  ";
200  NEXT I
210  PRINT
230     IF MØRE #1 THEN 130
260  END
RUN

NAME           TEST1 TEST2 TEST3 TEST4 TEST5 TEST6
MARK UNDERWØØD  65    83    92    77    68    79
SUSAN STALBERG  73    88    82    77    69    79
EDGAR ANGLEMAN  74    86    78    79    80    78
ALTHEA LARGE    91    92    90    99    92    90
GERTRUDE SMITH  71    86    87    90    88    92
```

In program READTEST, there are just four statements of a file-handling nature. The statement 100 FILES SCØRE makes the file available to the pro-

gram. The file must exist to execute the program. The statement 130 READ
#1, N$ is like a DATA READ statement except that the "#1" appears to notify
the computer to read from the first file named in the FILES statement. We may
name up to eight files there by separating them with semicolons. Statement 160
is another file read statement. A statement 999   READ #N, A,B,X$,T would
read three numerics and one string from the Nth-named file in the FILES statement. The statement 230   IF MØRE #1 THEN 130 has the ability to "look
ahead" in the file to "see" if there is more data in the file. If there is more data,
the computer is transfered to line 130; if not, then control passes to the next line.

Now that we are able to read the file, let's perform the necessary operations
to find each student average and the class average. We will require two variables to store running totals. In program AVERAGE, T2 is the running total
for the class, and T1 is the student running total.

```
AVERAGE

94    REM * CALCULATE AVERAGES FROM A FILE
100   FILES SCØRE
110   PRINT "NAME","TEST1 TEST2 TEST3 TEST4 TEST5 TEST6 AVERAGE"
120   LET T1=0
130   READ #1, N$
140   LET T2 = 0
150   PRINT N$; TAB(15);
160   FØR I = 1 TØ 6
170       READ #1, X
180       LET T2 = T2 + X
190       PRINT X; "  ";
200   NEXT I
210   PRINT T2/6
220   LET T1 = T1 + T2
230       IF MØRE #1 THEN 130
240   PRINT
250   PRINT "CLASS AVERAGE = "T1/30
260   END
RUN
```

NAME	TEST1	TEST2	TEST3	TEST4	TEST5	TEST6	AVERAGE
MARK UNDERWØØD	65	83	92	77	68	79	77.3333
SUSAN STALBERG	73	88	82	77	69	79	78
EDGAR ANGLEMAN	74	86	78	79	80	78	79.1667
ALTHEA LARGE	91	92	90	99	92	90	92.3333
GERTRUDE SMITH	71	86	87	90	88	92	85.6667

CLASS AVERAGE = 82.5

Now that we know how to read an ASCII file under program control, let's
see how to write data into such a file under program control. Suppose that we
consolidate the data in file SCØRE, retaining just the names and averages to
write into a new file, SCØRE1. To do this, we begin by naming both files in
the FILES statement. We may enter data into an ASCII file with the WRITE
#N statement. However, before writing into the file, it must be prepared for
writing with the SCRATCH #N statement. SCRATCH #N sets a pointer to
the beginning of the Nth-named file and prepares it for writing. In program
WRITEAVG, we print each name at the terminal just to show the progress
of execution during the program run. For large amounts of data, we might
simply print the number of names moved. See lines 110 and 140 of program
WRITEAVG.

```
WRITEAVG

94    REM * READ SCORE - WRITE SCORE1
100   FILES SCORE; SCORE1
110   SCRATCH #2
120   READ #1, N$,X1,X2,X3,X4,X5,X6
130   PRINT N$
140   WRITE #2, N$; (X1+X2+X3+X4+X5+X6)/6
150     IF MORE #1 THEN 120
160   END
RUN

MARK UNDERWOOD
SUSAN STALBERG
EDGAR ANGLEMAN
ALTHEA LARGE
GERTRUDE SMITH
```

Since this is an ASCII file, we may LISt it at the keyboard as follows:

```
SCORE1

100 MARK UNDERWOOD, 77.3333 ,
110 SUSAN STALBERG, 78 ,
120 EDGAR ANGLEMAN, 79.1667 ,
130 ALTHEA LARGE, 92.3333 ,
140 GERTRUDE SMITH, 85.6667 ,
```

Additional files statements include APPEND #N, which sets a pointer to the end of data in a file and prepares the file for the write mode in a way similar to that of the SCRATCH #N statement, and RESTORE #N, which sets a pointer to the beginning of the file and prepares it for the read mode so that we may read the data in a file more than once in a single execution of a program.

Binary Files

Binary files may be used only under program control. They may be either sequential or random access. Sequential binary files are treated for programming purposes exactly like ASCII files except that where pound signs (#) appear for an ASCII file, a colon (:) is used for a binary file.

Random Access Files

Random access files may be segmented into blocks of storage called *records*. We may dictate the size of each record and the number of records in a file when we create it, much as we dimension a two-dimensional array. The record size is measured in words of storage. The word requirements for data are as follows:

One word per numeric
One word per four string characters, or fraction thereof
One word per string for internal computer control

The exact arrangement of data within a file is completely the programmer's responsibility. We must know exactly where data is to be found and what it means. The situation is no different from data handling within an array except that once data is in a file, it seems more invisible.

For our first example, let's simply write three rows of six numbers each into a binary file with one program and then select some of them for printing at the keyboard with another program. The storage requirements amount to just three records, each containing six words. We obtain such a file with the CREate command, as follows:

CRE NUMB,(RAN(6,3))

See program RND.

```
RND

94    REM * LOAD RANDOM NUMBERS INTO A BINARY FILE
100   FILES NUMB
110   FOR I = 1 TO 3
120      FOR J = 1 TO 6
130         LET X = RND(X)
140         WRITE :1, X
150         PRINT X;
160      NEXT J
170      PRINT
180   NEXT I
190   END
RUN
```

```
0.98385    0.362274    0.250535    0.338074    0.250009    0.342306
0.676737   0.820017    0.290332    0.68319     0.373523    0.853779
0.151996   0.975866    0.811924    0.448439    0.139038    0.847165
```

Notice that we are able to fill the file without regard to position in the file because we are exactly filling each record as we go. This is not always the case.

To select locations at random within the file, we need the SETW statement. SETW N TØ X places a pointer in file N to the Xth word in the file without regard to file dimensions. Thus, in our file of six words per record, the ninth word is the third word on the second record. To think in terms of records and words within a record, we need a formula to determine the value of X. For the Cth word in record R where there are W words per record, the value of X is W*(R−1) + C. Now let's write a short program to find selected positions in file NUMB. See program PICK. Notice that the RESTØRE statement is not required for random access files. RESTØRE:N is equivalent to SETW N TØ 1.

```
PICK

94    REM * SELECT A NUMBER FROM A FILE AT RANDOM
100   FILES NUMB
110   PRINT "ROW,COL";
120   INPUT R,K
130      IF R = 0 THEN 190
140   SETW 1 TO 6*(R-1) + K
150   READ :1, A
160   PRINT "FOUND"; A
170   PRINT
180   GOTO 110
190   END
RUN

ROW,COL? 2,3
FOUND 0.290332
```

```
RØW,CØL? 3,6
FØUND 0.847165

RØW,CØL? 0,0
```

For our final example we will use a binary file to arrange the student data from our ASCII file SCØRE1 in order of increasing test average. We must write the necessary data into a binary file, arrange it, and then print the results. This can be done with three different programs or with a single program. We will use a single program here. See ØRDERAUG.

To determine the size records required, we must know the number of characters in the name strings. We find a maximum of 14 characters. We should go to at least 16 since that is the next multiple of four. In practice, to make such a file generally useful, we would probably go even higher. Allowing for 16 characters, we need four words for storage of string data, plus one word for control, plus one word for the numeric. For this problem, a file with five records containing six words per record is sufficient. We get that with CRE SCØRE2,(RAN(6,5)).

```
ØRDERAVG

100    FILES SCØRE1; SCØRE2
104    REM * WRITE DATA INTØ BINARY FILE
110    FØR I = 1 TØ 5
120        READ #1, N$,A1
130        SETW 2 TØ 6*(I-1) + 1
140        WRITE :2, N$,A1
150    NEXT I
154    REM * NOW ARRANGE THE DATA ACCORDING TO AVERAGES
160    FØR I = 1 TØ 4
170        FØR J = I + 1 TØ 5
180            SETW 2 TØ 6*(I-1) + 1
190            READ :2, N$,A1
200            SETW 2 TØ 6*(J-1) + 1
210            READ :2, M$,B1
220                IF A1 <= B1 THEN 270
230            SETW 2 TØ 6*(I-1) + 1
240            WRITE :2, M$,B1
250            SETW 2 TØ 6*(J-1) + 1
260            WRITE :2, N$,A1
270        NEXT J
280    NEXT I
284    REM * AND NOW PRINT THE RESULTS
290    PRINT " NAME","AVERAGE"
300    PRINT
310    FØR I = 1 TC 5
320        SETW 2 TØ 6*(I-1) + 1
330        READ :2, N$,A1
340        PRINT N$,A1
350    NEXT I
360    END
RUN


    NAME            AVERAGE

MARK UNDERWOOD      77.3333
SUSAN STALBERG      73
EDGAR ANGLEMAN      79.1667
GERTRUDE SMITH      85.6667
ALTHEA LARGE        92.3333
```

SUMMARY

The FILES statement is used to make files accessible to a program. The files of this section are of two types: ASCII and BINARY. ASCII files are sequential and may be accessed from the keyboard or through a program. Binary files may be either sequential or random access and may be accessed only through a program. We may use READ #N, WRITE #N, SCRATCH #N, APPEND #N or RESTORE #N to handle data in an ASCII file. For sequential binary files, all of the above statement types may be used by replacing the pound signs (#) with colons (:). For random access files, we have the additional statement SETW N TØ X which sets a pointer at the Xth word of a file in preparation for the next READ or WRITE statement. A file is made random access in the CREate command.

PROBLEMS FOR SEC. 7-6

1) Type a few inventory items with quantity and price data into an ASCII file. Write a program to print the value of each item and the total value of inventory at the terminal.

2) Write a program to print a list of an unknown number of names in an ASCII file at the terminal in alphabetic order. Use RESTORE #N and repeated reading of the file for this purpose. Assume that there are no duplicates.

3) Consider a random access file containing five words per record and six records filled with numbers. Write a program to find the largest number in each record and the largest number in each "column."

4) You are presented with a random access file with a set of ten names in it; each name was entered first name first, followed by a space, followed by last name. Since this ordering is difficult to alphabetize, you are to replace each entry in the file rearranged so that the last name is first, followed by a comma, a space, and the first name. You know that each string is to be allocated eight words of storage.

5) (*Project*) Print some names into a random access file. Place a list of pointers to those names in an ASCII file so that if the pointers are read sequentially from the ASCII file and used to access the names in the random access file with the SETW statement, the names will be accessed in alphabetic order. Use the ASCII file to print the names in alphabetic order.

CHAPTER 8

The Quadratic Function

We define a *quadratic function* as a real function of the form

$$f(X) = AX^2 + BX + C \tag{8-1}$$

where A does not equal 0.

8-1 ZEROS

Often in mathematics we would like to find the zeros of a quadratic function. For some sets of coefficients, we may factor the expression on the right in Eq. (8-1) and set each factor equal to 0. This would be the method to use for $f(X) = X^2 + 3X + 2$. We would find zeros as follows:

$$X^2 + 3X + 2 = 0$$

Factoring,

$$(X + 1)(X + 2) = 0$$

and $(X + 1) = 0$ or $(X + 2) = 0$

So $X = -1$ or $X = -2$

and the truth set is $\{-2, -1\}$.

However, in general for nonfactorable as well as factorable quadratic expressions on the right in Eq. (8-1), we may use the quadratic formula, which may be derived by the method of completing the square. The zeros of $f(X) = AX^2 + BX + C$ are

$$X1 = \frac{-B + \sqrt{B^2 - 4AC}}{2A}$$

$$X2 = \frac{-B - \sqrt{B^2 - 4AC}}{2A}$$

Since we are going to insert these equations into a program we will write

ZZZ   LET X1 = (−B + SQR(B °° 2 − 4 ° A ° C))/(2 ° A)

and

ZZZ + 10   LET X2 = (−B − SQR(B °° 2 − 4 ° A ° C))/(2 ° A)

Now all we need is some data and some printing instructions (see QUAD1), which seems to work well enough. You will want to modify QUAD1 to account for nonreal zeros. You may want to just print a message or you may go ahead and compute the nonreal values. As the program stands though, if B °° 2 − 4 ° A ° C is negative, the computer will at best print an error message and at worst it will terminate the RUN.

```
QUAD1

 5   PRINT " A      B      C      ","X1","X2"
10   READ A,B,C
15   IF A=0 THEN 99
20   LET X1=(-B+SQR(B↑2-4*A*C))/(2*A)
30   LET X2=(-B-SQR(B↑2-4*A*C))/(2*A)
40   PRINT A;B;C,X1,X2
45   GOTO 10
50   DATA 1,3,2
60   DATA 1,2,-3,2,4,-6,6,13,6,5,-7,2
70   DATA 0,0,0
99   END
RUN
QUAD1
```

A	B	C	X1	X2
1	3	2	-1	-2
1	2	-3	1	-3
2	4	-6	1	-3
6	13	6	-.666667	-1.5
5	-7	2	1	.4

DONE

8-2 AXIS OF SYMMETRY AND TURNING POINT

The graph of a quadratic function is called a *parabola*. In examining the graph of a quadratic function we often want to know where the axis of symmetry is and where the turning point is. By completing the square on the right

$$f(X) = AX^2 + BX + C$$

$$f(X) = A\left[X^2 + \frac{B}{A}X + \frac{B^2}{4A^2} - \frac{B^2}{4A^2} \right] + C$$

$$f(X) = A\left[X^2 + \frac{B}{A}X + \frac{B^2}{4A^2} \right] - \frac{B^2}{4A} + C$$

we get

$$f(X) = A\left[X + \frac{B}{2A} \right]^2 + \frac{4AC - B^2}{4A}$$

Now, when $X = -B/2A$, $X + B/2A = 0$. The value of $f(X)$ is minimum if A is positive and maximum if A is negative, and the value of $f(-B/2A)$ is $(4AC - B^2)/4A$. Thus the coordinates of the turning point are

$$\left(-\frac{B}{2A} , \frac{4AC - B^2}{4A} \right)$$

You should know, too, that the line whose equation is $X = -B/2A$ is called the *axis of symmetry*. We should now be able to write a program to print three items of information: 1) the maximum or minimum status of the parabola, 2) the equation of the axis of symmetry, and 3) the coordinates of the turning point. Let us collect things into a flowchart (see Fig. 8-1), and write program QUAD2.

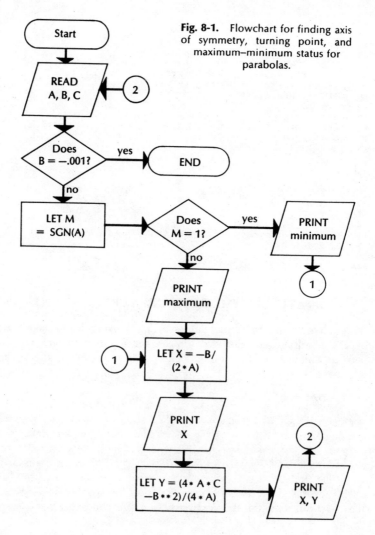

Fig. 8-1. Flowchart for finding axis of symmetry, turning point, and maximum–minimum status for parabolas.

QUAD2

```
10    READ A,B,C
15    IF B=-.001 THEN 9999
20    PRINT A;B;C
25    IF A <> 0 THEN 30
26    PRINT "A=0 THE EXPRESSIØN IS NØT QUADRATIC"
27    GØTØ 20
28    REM    DETERMINE   MAX. ØR MIN.
30    LET M=SGN(A)
40    IF M=1 THEN 70
50    PRINT "MAXIMUM PARABØLA"
60    GØTØ 80
70    PRINT "MINIMUM PARABØLA"
78    REM   FIND THE AXIS ØF SYMMETRY
80    LET X=-B/(2*A)
90    PRINT "AXIS ØF SYMMETRY IS   X ="; X
98    REM    FIND THE EXTREME VALUE
100   LET Y=(4*A*C-B↑2)/(4*A)
110   PRINT "THE TURNING PØINT IS   (";X;",";Y;")"
115   PRINT
120   GØTØ 10
150   DATA 1,3,2,1,2,-3,6,13,6
155   DATA -3,5,11
160   DATA 4,-.001,1
9999  END
RUN
QUAD2
```

```
   1      3      2
MINIMUM PARABØLA
AXIS ØF SYMMETRY IS   X =-1.5
THE TURNING PØINT IS  (-1.5           ,-.25          )

   1      2     -3
MINIMUM PARABØLA
AXIS ØF SYMMETRY IS   X =-1
THE TURNING PØINT IS  (-1      ,-4    )

   6     13      6
MINIMUM PARABØLA
AXIS ØF SYMMETRY IS   X =-1.08333
THE TURNING PØINT IS  (-1.08333      ,-1.04167     )

  -3      5     11
MAXIMUM PARABØLA
AXIS ØF SYMMETRY IS   X = .833333
THE TURNING PØINT IS  ( .833333      , 13.0833      )
```

DØNE

8-3 PLOTTING THE PARABOLA

One last consideration for the parabola is to plot its graph. This works well right on the terminal itself. We may use the spaces across the carriage as one axis and the paper lengthwise as the other axis. Since the line feed is automatically set on the terminal, the X-axis should run perpendicular to the carriage and the Y-axis should run across the page. This means that one line represents one unit on the X-axis and one space represents one unit on the Y-axis. This is rotated 90 degrees clockwise from the conventional system.

Let us start out with the simplest possible graph and see what refinements will be required. We will first graph $Y = X ** 2$. We will put " "; in a loop to get the printing head to the point that we want plotted. Any printed character may be used to represent the plotted points. The range you select will depend on the width of the carriage on your terminal. Selecting the domain for X as -7 to $+7$ we will require a range of 0 to 49.

When $X = -7$, we want the printing head to step out 48 spaces, then print a character, and then RETURN. Now we want X to go to -6 and the printing head will have to step out only 35 spaces, print a character, and RETURN. As this process is repeated, it too will be put in a loop with X going from -7 to $+7$ incrementing by 1. It will be convenient to define a function here, not as a saving now, but to fit in with later plotting problems. Before writing the program PLØT1, let us draw a flowchart (see Fig. 8-2). Notice that we intend printing the spaces followed by a semicolon and the plotted points also followed by a semicolon. After the point has been plotted, we do not want the printing head to step the rest of the way across the carriage as that would be a waste of computer time for this particular plot. So line 62 is used to return the printing head to the left margin. We should observe that the procedure we are developing is not especially efficient in the first place, and so should be used sparingly.

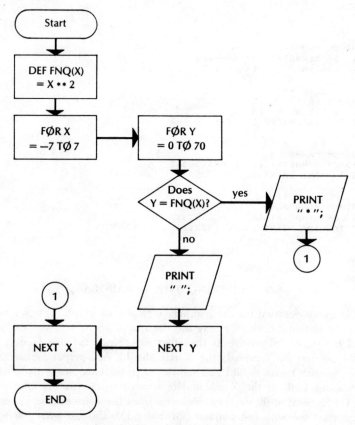

Fig. 8-2.   Flowchart to plot $Y = X ** 2$.

```
PLØT1

30    DEF FNQ(X)=X†2
60    FØR X=-7 TØ 7
62    PRINT
88    REM    LINE 90 HAS THE EFFECT ØF NUMBERING THE SPACES
89    REM ACRØSS THE PAGE 0 TØ 70
90    FØR Y=0 TØ 70
120   IF Y=FNQ(X) THEN 210
148   REM   IF Y DØES NØT EQUAL FNQ(X) THEN PRINT A BLANK SPACE
150   PRINT " ";
180   NEXT Y
210   PRINT "*";
212   REM  PLØT THE PØINT AND GØ TØ NEXT X
240   NEXT X
270   END
RUN
PLØT1
```

```
                                                                *
                                             *
                                       *
                            *
                  *
           *
        *
      *
     *
      *
         *
            *
                 *
                      *
                               *
                                         *
```

```
DØNE
```

PLØT1 was not bad for our first try. If we are going to plot other parabolas, we will have to make a provision for values of Y less than 0. So we may change line 90 to read 90 FØR Y = −M TØ 70 − M, where M is the number of spaces to the left of 0, and then we can put M on INPUT:

```
90   FØR Y= -M TØ 70-M
5 INPUT M
4 PRINT "INPUT THE NUMBER ØF SPACES DESIRED TØ THE LEFT ØF ZERØ";
88
89
6 PRINT
RUN
PLØT2
```

```
INPUT THE NUMBER ØF SPACES DESIRED TØ THE LEFT ØF ZERØ?10
                                                                *
                                             *
                                       *
                            *
                  *
           *
        *
      *
     *
      *
         *
            *
                 *
                      *
                               *
                                         *
```

```
DØNE
```

We have indeed graphed Y = X ** 2; however, the graph is not clearly defined because there are no axes to specify the coordinate system. Let us build up the coordinate system by first putting in the origin by plotting a 0 there. Immediately, we are faced with a decision. If the graph contains the origin, do we want the plotted point or the origin designation? Since the absence of the plotted point for X = 0 would indicate that it should have been plotted at the origin, let us plot the 0 at the origin as first priority. So, before anything gets done for a particular value of X, we ask if the value of Y is 0. If it is, we next look for the point at which X is also 0. At (0, 0) we print 0. Having printed 0, we next look to see if FNQ(X) is greater than 0. If it is, we send the printing head on across the page.

```
92  IF Y <> 0 THEN 120
94 IF X <> 0 THEN 120
95 REM    IF THE COMPUTER GETS THROUGH HERE THE
96 REM PRINTING HEAD IS AT THE ORIGIN
98 PRINT "0";
100   IF FNQ(X)>0 THEN 180
102   REM IF  FNQ(X) > 0 GO FIND WHERE IT IS
103   REM OTHERWISE GET THE NEXT VALUE OF X
106 GOTO 240

RUN
PLOT3

INPUT THE NUMBER OF SPACES DESIRED TO THE LEFT OF ZERO?6
```

```
                                                      *
                                              *
                                    *
                          *
                  *
              *
          *
      0
        *
          *
              *
                  *
                          *
                                    *
                                              *
                                                      *

    DONE
```

As long as we have the X-axis located, we might just as well put it in the graph. All that is necessary is to have a PRINT instruction whenever Y = 0 but X does not.

```
94 IF X=0 THEN 98
95 PRINT "!";
96 GOTO 100
RUN
PLOT4
```

INPUT THE NUMBER ØF SPACES DESIRED TØ THE LEFT ØF ZERØ?9

```
        ↑                              *
        ↑                    *
        ↑              *
        ↑         *
        ↑     *
        ↑  *
        ↑*
        0
        ↑*
        ↑  *
        ↑     *
        ↑         *
        ↑              *
        ↑                    *
        ↑                         *
DØNE
```

Finally, we may put in a Y-axis. Let us settle for having the Y-axis along the leading side of the graph. By putting the Y-axis there, we will be able to print the scale without interfering with the graph itself. For the particular graph we have been plotting a range from 0 to 50 is reasonable.

```
 8   PRINT "    ";
10   FØR X=0 TØ 50 STEP 10
12   PRINT "     ";X;
14   NEXT X
15   PRINT
16   FØR X=1 TØ 70
18   IF X/10=INT(X/10) THEN 24
20   PRINT "-";
22   GØTØ 26
24   PRINT "↑";
26   NEXT X
RUN
PLØT5
```

INPUT THE NUMBER ØF SPACES DESIRED TØ THE LEFT ØF ZERØ?9

```
          0         10        20        30        40        50
---------↑---------↑---------↑---------↑---------↑---------↑
          ↑                                        *
          ↑                              *
          ↑                    *
          ↑              *
          ↑         *
          ↑     *
          ↑  *
          0
          ↑*
          ↑     *
          ↑         *
          ↑              *
          ↑                    *
          ↑                         *
          ↑                                   *
DONE
```

At this point, the program is scattered all over the place and some of the line numbers are very close together. So we renumber beginning with line 10 and print the entire program in PLØT5.

```
PLØT5

10   PRINT "INPUT THE NUMBER ØF SPACES DESIRED TØ THE LEFT ØF
     ZERØ";
20   INPUT M
30   PRINT
40   PRINT "      ";
50   FØR X=0 TØ 50 STEP 10
60   PRINT "      ";X;
70   NEXT X
80   PRINT
90   FØR X=1 TØ 70
100  IF X/10=INT(X/10) THEN 130
110  PRINT "-";
120  GØTØ 140
130  PRINT "!";
140  NEXT X
150  DEF FNQ(X)=X↑2
160  FØR X=-7 TØ 7
170  PRINT
180  FØR Y=-M TØ 70-M
190  IF Y <> 0 THEN 280
200  IF X=0 THEN 230
210  PRINT "!";
220  GØTØ 240
230  PRINT "O";
240  IF FNQ(X)>0 THEN 310
250  REM IF   FNQ(X) > 0 GØ FIND WHERE IT IS
260  REM ØTHERWISE GET THE NEXT VALUE ØF X
270  GØTØ 340
280  IF Y=FNQ(X) THEN 320
290  REM  IF Y DØES NØT EQUAL FNQ(X) THEN PRINT A BLANK SPACE
300  PRINT " ";
310  NEXT Y
320  PRINT "*";
330  REM  PLØT THE PØINT AND GØ TØ NEXT X
340  NEXT X
350  END
```

There are still several considerations regarding this program for plotting. For instance, as the program is written, it will not plot the X-axis if the Y value is less than 0. The scale is fixed. There is provision for only one function to be plotted. Also, consider what happens if the value of Y is not an integer. All of these comments suggest areas in which the program could be improved. Let us insert a different function and call for one last RUN of PLØT5.

```
150 DEF FNQ(X)=(X-2)↑2+3
160 FØR X=-5 TØ 8
RUN
PLØT5
```

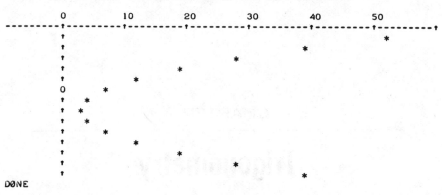

```
INPUT THE NUMBER ØF SPACES DESIRED TØ THE LEFT ØF ZERØ?9
```

DØNE

SUMMARY FOR CHAP. 8

There are several things that can be done with the quadratic function on a computer: 1) we can calculate the zeros; 2) we can find the various constants that specify the appearance of the graph; 3) and we can even use the terminal itself to plot a graph of the function. Of course the graphing program may be used to plot other functions as well.

PROBLEMS FOR CHAP. 8

1) Write a program that finds the results of QUAD1, but prints rational zeros as fractions reduced to lowest terms.

2) Modify QUAD1 to compute nonreal zeros.

3) The Y-coordinate of the turning point of a parabola may also be found by evaluating $f(-B/(2 * A))$. Rewrite QUAD2 by defining a function.

4) For sets of coefficients in data lines, have the computer print coordinate pairs (X, Y) for a reasonable range.

5) Modify PLØT5 to permit the X-axis to be printed for Y-coordinates less than 0. Also provide for the point to be plotted where the graph crosses the X-axis.

CHAPTER 9

Trigonometry

9-1 INTRODUCTION TO SIN(X), CØS(X), AND TAN(X)

We choose to define the circular functions in terms of a point (X, Y) plotted in a rectangular coordinate system. Consider the point (X, Y). It is at a distance R from the origin. We may find R from X and Y by using the *Pythagorean theorem:*

$$R = \sqrt{X^2 + Y^2}$$

It is conventional to use Greek letters for angles. However, since computer terminals do not provide them, we may use any letters we wish. Let us use G to measure the angle whose initial side is the non-negative portion of the X-axis and whose terminal side is the ray that has its endpoint at the origin and contains the point (X, Y). See Fig. 9-1.

From Fig. 9-1 we define three circular functions as follows:

$$\cos G = X/R$$
$$\sin G = Y/R$$
$$\tan G = Y/X$$

where cos stands for cosine, sin stands for sine, and tan stands for tangent.

In BASIC it is required that the angles be measured in radians. 1 radian may be defined as the central angle subtended by an arc length of R on the circumference of a circle of radius R. Since the circumference of a circle of radius R is $2\pi R$, we see that

$$2\pi \text{ radians} = 360 \text{ degrees}$$
$$\pi \text{ radians} = 180 \text{ degrees}$$
$$1 \text{ radian} = 180/\pi \text{ degrees}$$
$$\pi/180 \text{ radians} = 1 \text{ degree}$$

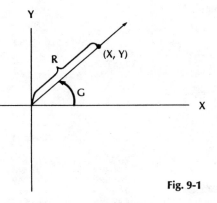

Fig. 9-1

Although some time-share systems provide the special computer functions RAD(X) and DEG(X) to convert from degrees to radians and from radians to degrees, respectively, you should be prepared to make the required conversions.

The usually available computer trigonometric functions are SIN(X), CØS(X), and TAN(X). They are used in much the same way that all other computer functions are used. Just be sure that the argument of the function is in radians.

In mathematics, it is customary to define three additional circular functions as follows:

$$\sec G = R/X \qquad \text{or} \qquad \sec G = 1/\cos G$$
$$\csc G = R/Y \qquad \text{or} \qquad \csc G = 1/\sin G$$
$$\cot G = X/Y \qquad \text{or} \qquad \cot G = 1/\tan G$$

where sec stands for secant, csc stands for cosecant, and cot stands for cotangent. Some computers provide these three functions in addition to the earlier three, but we may always use the appropriate reciprocal. As always, should an expression become too cumbersome, we have the option of defining a program function using DEF.

Let us get the computer to print a small table of values of sin, cos, and tan for 0 to 80 degrees in intervals of 10 degrees. We stop short of 90 degrees to avoid having an undefined value for the tangent of 90 degrees. To write program TRIG1, we will have to convert degrees to radians, so we multiply by $\pi/180$.

9-2 RIGHT TRIANGLES AND ARCTANGENT

Taking the graph of Fig. 9-1 and dropping the perpendicular from (X, Y) in the first quadrant to the X-axis we get Fig. 9-2. We have formed a right triangle in which the length of the hypotenuse is R, the length of the base is X, and the length of the altitude is Y. Redrawing the triangle without the coordinate system, we get triangle ABC with the trigonometric ratios as in Fig. 9-3.

```
TRIG1

5   PRINT "SINE","CØSINE","TANGENT","RADIANS","DEGREES"
9   REM  WE CØMPUTE A CØNVERSIØN CØNSTANT
10   LET C=3.14159/180
20   FØR G=0 TØ 80 STEP 10
30   PRINT SIN(G*C),CØS(G*C),TAN(G*C),G*C, G
40   NEXT G
50   END
RUN
TRIG1
```

SINE	CØSINE	TANGENT	RADIANS	DEGREES
0	1.	0	0	0
.173648	.984808	.176327	.174533	10
.34202	.939692	.36397	.349066	20
.5	.866025	.57735	.523599	30
.642788	.766044	.8391	.698132	40
.766044	.642788	1.19175	.872665	50
.866025	.5	1.73205	1.0472	60
.939692	.34202	2.74748	1.22173	70
.984808	.173648	5.67129	1.39626	80

```
DØNE
```

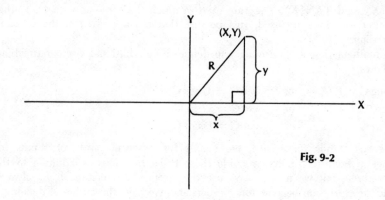

Fig. 9-2

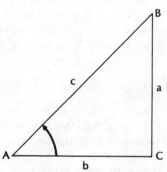

$\cos \angle A = b/c$

$\sin \angle A = a/c$

$\tan \angle A = a/b$

Fig. 9-3

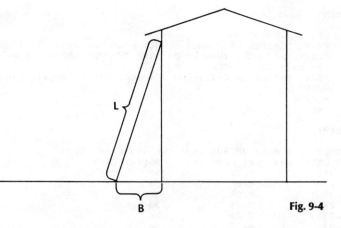

Fig. 9-4

We also know from geometry that ∠A and ∠B are complements, i.e., their sum is 90 degrees or $\pi/2$ radians.

Let us solve a problem: George has a 36-ft ladder which he is going to use to paint his father's house. He believes that the angle formed by the ladder and the side of the house should be not less than 14 degrees and not more than 15 degrees. He needs to know how far out from the house to place the foot of the ladder. See Fig. 9-4.

We may use either SIN(G) = B/L or CØS(90 − G) = B/L. Let us choose the sin function and solve for B:

   B = L ° SIN(G)

We will have to convert degrees to radians. This is the purpose of line 10 in program LADER.

```
LADER

10   LET C=3.14159/180
20   LET L=36
30   PRINT "36' LADDER BASE MUST BE ØUT FRØM THE HØUSE IN FEET"
40   PRINT "NØT LESS THAN","NØT MØRE THAN"
50   PRINT L*SIN(C*14),L*SIN(C*15)
60   END
RUN
LADER

36' LADDER BASE MUST BE ØUT FRØM THE HØUSE IN FEET
NØT LESS THAN    NØT MØRE THAN
  8.70918          9.31748

DØNE
```

We really do not need more than hundredths, so let us round off. Also, since George may want to change the length of the ladder to reach different heights, let the ladder length go from 36 ft to 20 ft. See LADER1.

```
LADER1

10   LET C=3.14159/180
30   PRINT "LADDER BASE MUST BE ØUT FRØM THE HØUSE IN FEET"
40   PRINT "NØT LESS THAN","NØT MØRE THAN","LADDER LENGTH"
45   FØR L=36 TØ 20 STEP -2
50   PRINT INT(L*SIN(C*14)*100+.5)/100,INT(L*SIN(C*15)*100+.5)/100,
51   PRINT L
55   NEXT L
60   END
RUN
LADER1
```

```
LADDER BASE MUST BE ØUT FRØM THE HØUSE IN FEET
NØT LESS THAN    NØT MØRE THAN    LADDER LENGTH
    8.71             9.32              36
    8.23             8.8               34
    7.74             8.28              32
    7.26             7.76              30
    6.77             7.25              28
    6.29             6.73              26
    5.81             6.21              24
    5.32             5.69              22
    4.84             5.18              20

DØNE
```

ATN(X)

Suppose we know the lengths of the sides of a right triangle and we need to know the angles. If we are using printed tables in a book, we may look up the angle whose sin, cos, or tan is known. Not so with the computer. An additional computer function is required for this. ATN(X) is the function usually available, though some systems will provide others as well. ATN(X) computes the angle whose tangent is X. If

$$TAN(G) = X$$

then

$$ATN(X) = G$$

where ATN stands for arctangent and G is in radians.

Fig. 9-5

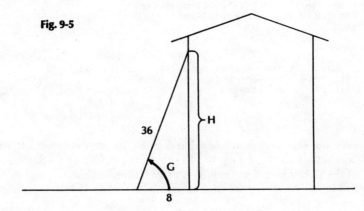

Suppose we lean a 36-ft ladder against a building with the base 8 ft out and we would like to know the angle formed by the ground and the ladder, as in Fig. 9-5. We can say

TAN(G) = H/8

which means

ATN(H/8) = G
H = SQR(36 ** 2 − 8 ** 2)

Therefore, G may be found in radians by

G = ATN(SQR(36 ** 2 − 8 ** 2)/8)

and the angle in degrees may be found by

LET G = G * 180/π

See LADER2.

```
LADER2

10    LET  G=ATN(SQR(36*2-8*2)/8)
15    PRINT  G; "RADIANS"
20    LET  G=G*180/3.14159
30    PRINT  G; "DEGREES"
40    END
RUN
LADER2

    1.3467        RADIANS
   77.1605        DEGREES

DONE
```

SUMMARY

We now may apply the computer to the trigonometry of the right triangle using SIN(X), COS(X), and TAN(X) to find sides when angles are known and using ATN(X) when we wish to compute angles. We must always be aware of the need to use radians for the argument of the computer trigonometric functions.

PROBLEMS FOR SEC. 9-2

1) Modify LADER2 to give the angle in degrees and minutes.
2) Modify LADER2 to give the angle in degrees, minutes, and seconds.
3) Rewrite LADER2 so that the number of radians is given in terms of π.
4) If the sides of a triangle are 10, 10, and 4, find the angles of the triangle to the nearest minute.
5) Find the angles of a 3, 4, 5 right triangle to the nearest minute.
6) Find the angles of a 5, 12, 13 right triangle to the nearest minute.

7) A right triangle has one angle 42°25′ and the side opposite that angle has a length of 10.0″. Find the other sides of the triangle.

8) Standing 1000 ft from the base of a lighthouse on level ground, the angle of elevation is 7°30′. Find the height of the lighthouse.

9-3   LAW OF SINES AND LAW OF COSINES

Law of Sines

By drawing a triangle successively with each of its vertices at the origin of a rectangular coordinate system, we may compute its area in three ways. Referring to Fig. 9-6, the area is found by

$$\text{Area} = \tfrac{1}{2}b(H1) \quad \text{or} \quad \tfrac{1}{2}a(H2) \quad \text{or} \quad \tfrac{1}{2}c(H3) \tag{9-1}$$

We should see that

$$\sin C1 = H1/a$$
$$\sin B1 = H2/c$$
$$\sin A1 = H3/b$$

Solving for the heights we get

$$H1 = a \sin C1$$
$$H2 = c \sin B1$$
$$H3 = b \sin A1$$

Substituting in Eq. (9-1) we get

$$\text{Area} = \tfrac{1}{2}b(a \sin C1) \quad \text{or} \quad \tfrac{1}{2}a(c \sin B1) \quad \text{or} \quad \tfrac{1}{2}c(b \sin A1) \tag{9-2}$$

Therefore we may find the area of any triangle by taking one half the product of two sides and the sine of the included angle.

Since the area of a triangle is unique, we may set the three expressions for area in Eq. (9-2) equal to get

$$\tfrac{1}{2}ba \sin C1 = \tfrac{1}{2}ac \sin B1 = \tfrac{1}{2}cb \sin A1$$

By clearing of fractions and dividing through by abc, we get

$$\frac{\sin C1}{c} = \frac{\sin B1}{b} = \frac{\sin A1}{a} \tag{9-3}$$

Equation (9-3) is called the *Law of Sines*. It enables us to find all parts of a triangle if we are given any two sides and the angle opposite one of them, or if we are given any two angles and any one side (provided, of course, the triangle exists).

Let us write a program to find the remaining parts of a triangle ABC given A1, B1, and a. Since the sum of the measures of the angles of a triangle is 180 degrees, we first get

$$C1 = 180° - (A1 + B1) \tag{9-4}$$

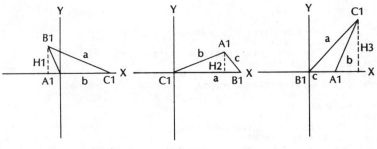

Fig. 9-6

The Law of Sines gives us

$$\frac{\sin A1}{a} = \frac{\sin B1}{b}$$

Solving for b gives

$$b = \frac{a \sin B1}{\sin A1} \qquad (9\text{-}5)$$

Similarly we get

$$c = \frac{b \sin C1}{\sin B1} \qquad (9\text{-}6)$$

And finally, the area may be found by

$$\text{Area} = \tfrac{1}{2}ab \sin C1 \qquad (9\text{-}7)$$

All we have to do is put all that into a program. We may do that almost directly from Eqs. (9-4)–(9-7). These four equations appear in order in lines 60, 70, 80, and 90 of program LAWSIN.

In writing the program, we have done only slightly more work than we would do preparing to do the calculation by hand. However, we are letting the computer take the drudgery out of the actual calculation. We also have the program available to do large numbers of calculations at a later date with virtually no additional effort required. However, we continue to be totally responsible for the mathematics required.

If we reflect for a moment upon the congruence of triangles, the various congruence conditions come to mind. They are side-angle-side, angle-side-angle, side-side-side, and angle-angle-corresponding side. There are special cases for right triangles. We should see then, that if any of these four sets of measures is known, we should be able to find the remaining three parts uniquely. And so we can. We have just used LAWSIN for two angles and a nonincluded side. We should be able to handle two angles and the included side with only slight modifications of LAWSIN. However, you should see that we cannot handle side-side-side or side-angle-side with the Law of Sines. For these we need the *Law of Cosines*.

```
LAWSIN

8   REM    WE COMPUTE THE CONVERSION FACTOR
10   LET K=3.14159/180
18   REM    DEFINE TRIG FUNCTION FOR DEGREES
20   DEF FNT(G)=SIN(G*K)
28   REM    DEFINE A ROUNDING FUNCTION
30   DEF FNR(X)=INT(X*100+.5)/100
38   REM ' A1 AND B1 ARE ANGLES AND A IS A SIDE
40   READ A1,B1,A
50   IF A1=0 THEN 999
58   REM   FIND THE THIRD ANGLE
60   LET C1=180-(A1+B1)
68   REM   70 AND 80 COMPUTE THE OTHER TWO SIDES
70   LET B=A*FNT(B1)/FNT(A1)
80   LET C=B*FNT(C1)/FNT(B1)
88   REM COMPUTE AREA
90   LET A2=.5*A*B*FNT(C1)
98   REM NOW PRINT THE RESULTS
100   PRINT " "," A"," B"," C"
110   PRINT "THE ANGLES ARE",A1,B1,C1
120   PRINT "THE SIDES ARE",FNR(A),FNR(B),FNR(C)
130   PRINT "AND THE AREA IS ";FNR(A2)
140   PRINT
150   GOTO 40
500   DATA 24,51,10
510   DATA 30,60,15
520   DATA 45,45,20
530   DATA 0,0,0
999   END
RUN
LAWSIN
```

```
                     A              B              C
THE ANGLES ARE   24             51             105
THE SIDES ARE    10             19.11          23.75
AND THE AREA IS   92.28


                     A              B              C
THE ANGLES ARE   30             60             90
THE SIDES ARE    15             25.98          30
AND THE AREA IS   194.86


                     A              B              C
THE ANGLES ARE   45             45             90
THE SIDES ARE    20             20             28.28
AND THE AREA IS   200


DONE
```

Law of Cosines

For any triangle A1B1C1 we may place a vertex at the origin of a rectangular coordinate system and designate the vertices as shown in Fig. 9-7.

Using the Pythagorean theorem, we may compute a^2 by

$$a^2 = (c \cos A1 - b)^2 + (c \sin A1)^2$$

Simplifying the right side we get

$$a^2 = c^2 \cos^2 A1 - 2bc \cos A1 + b^2 + c^2 \sin^2 A1$$

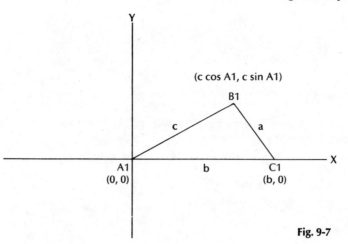

Fig. 9-7

Rearranging terms

$$a^2 = b^2 + c^2(\cos^2 A1 + \sin^2 A1) - 2bc \cos A1$$

Since $\cos^2 A1 + \sin^2 A1 = 1$, we finally get

$$a^2 = b^2 + c^2 - 2bc \cos A1 \qquad (9\text{-}8)$$

Equation (9-8) is the statement of the Law of Cosines solved for vertex A1 at the origin. Placing B1 at the origin we would get

$$b^2 = a^2 + c^2 - 2ac \cos B1 \qquad (9\text{-}9)$$

and placing C1 at the origin would produce

$$c^2 = a^2 + b^2 - 2ab \cos C1 \qquad (9\text{-}10)$$

In the form of Eqs. (9-8)–(9-10) the Law of Cosines is appropriate for handling problems in which two sides and the included angle are given. Once you obtain the third side by taking the square root of the right side of the equation, you may use the Law of Sines to obtain a second angle, or you may proceed as for the side-side-side congruence.

If we solve Eq. (9-8) for $\cos A1$, we get

$$\cos A1 = \frac{b^2 + c^2 - a^2}{2bc} \qquad (9\text{-}11)$$

So, if we are faced with a side-side-side congruence, we may easily find the value of $\cos A1$. Now our only problem is to get the value of A1 from the value of $\cos A1$. This will require the ATN(X) function. We should know that

$$\tan A1 = \frac{\sin A1}{\cos A1}$$

and for A1 between 0 and 180 degrees, $\sin A1$ is always positive. Thus,

$$\sin A1 = \sqrt{1 - \cos^2 A1} \qquad (9\text{-}12)$$

Thus

$$\tan A1 = \frac{\sqrt{1 - \cos^2 A1}}{\cos A1}$$

And so,

$$A1 = \text{ATN}\left(\frac{\sqrt{1 - \cos^2 A1}}{\cos A1}\right) \tag{9-13}$$

Now, we will be able to translate Eqs. (9-11)–(9-13) into BASIC program statements. From Eq. (9-11) we get

LET T = (B ** 2 + C ** 2 − A ** 2)/(2 * B * C)

and from Eq. (9-12) we get

LET T1 = SQR(1 − T ** 2)

and finally from Eq. (9-13),

LET A1 = ATN(T1/T)

These three statements constitute the heart of our program LAWCØS which reads three sides from data and prints all six parts of the triangle. See especially lines 50, 60, and 70.

We could have done the work of lines 90 through 120 by shuffling the data around and using lines 50 through 80 as a subroutine.

SUMMARY

This section has been devoted to solving triangles which may be uniquely determined. We have developed the Law of Sines into a program to solve the case of two angles and a nonincluded side and indicated that, with a few changes, the angle-side-angle case is solvable by the Law of Sines also.

The Law of Cosines has been used to find the angles of a triangle whose sides are known. It has been indicated that the case of side-angle-side is appropriate for the Law of Cosines also. This covers the uniquely determined cases except hypotenuse-leg. There remains the ambiguous case. If two sides and a nonincluded angle are given, there may be two, one, or no triangles possible. If solvable, such triangles are solvable by the Law of Sines. This is left to the student in the exercises.

PROBLEMS FOR SEC. 9-3

1) Write a program to solve the angle-side-angle case.

2)· Write a program to handle given two angles and a nonincluded side, and two angles and the included side. Use an item of data to determine which kind of data is provided.

3) Modify LAWCØS to use lines 50, 60, 70, and 80 as a subroutine and shuffle the data as discussed in text.

4) Write a program to solve the side-angle-side case.

5) Write a program to handle given three sides, and two sides and the included angle. Use an item of data to designate which set of data is provided.

LAWCØS

```
10   DEF FNR(X)=INT(X*100+.5)/100
15   PRINT "   "," A"," B"," C"
20   READ A,B,C
30   IF A=0 THEN 999
40   PRINT "THE SIDES ARE",A,B,C
48   REM   T IS REALLY  CØS(A1)
50   LET T=(B↑2+C↑2-A↑2)/(2*B*C)
58   REM  T1 IS REALLY SIN(A1)
60   LET T1=SQR(1-T↑2)
68   REM  A1 IS THE ANGLE INCLUDED BY SIDES B AND C
70   LET A1=ATN(T1/T)
78   REM     CØNVERT RADIANS TØ DEGREES
80   LET A1=A1*180/3.14159
88   REM   WE NØW REPEAT THE PRØCESS TØ FIND ANGLE B1
90   LET T=(A↑2+C↑2-B↑2)/(2*A*C)
100  LET T1=SQR(1-T↑2)
110  LET B1=ATN(T1/T)
120  LET B1=B1*180/3.14159
130  PRINT "THE ANGLES ARE",FNR(A1),FNR(B1),180-(FNR(A1)+FNR(B1))
140  PRINT
150  GØTØ 20
500  DATA 3,4,5,300,400,500
510  DATA 1.73205,1,2
520  DATA 2,2,3
530  DATA 0,0,0
999  END
RUN
LAWCØS
```

	A	B	C
	A	B	C
THE SIDES ARE	3	4	5
THE ANGLES ARE	36.87	53.13	90
THE SIDES ARE	300	400	500
THE ANGLES ARE	36.87	53.13	90
THE SIDES ARE	1.73205	1	2
THE ANGLES ARE	60	30	90
THE SIDES ARE	2	2	3
THE ANGLES ARE	41.41	41.41	97.18

DØNE

✓ 6) Write a program to solve the ambiguous case. Be sure to provide for no triangles, one triangle, or two triangles.

✓ 7) Rewrite problem 3) to handle degrees, minutes, and seconds.

✓ 8) Rewrite problem 4) to handle degrees, minutes, and seconds.

9) *Project:* Write a single program to process data in four uniquely determined cases. You might include the HL case.

9-4 POLAR COORDINATES

Every point in a rectangular coordinate system may be named by a unique pair of real numbers. The pair is usually designated (X, Y). If we plot a point (X, Y), we find that we may determine another ordered pair of numbers, one of which is the distance from the origin and the other is an angle measured from the positive portion of the X-axis to the ray with endpoint at the origin and containing point (X, Y). If we call the distance R and the measure of the angle G, we may designate a new ordered pair (R, G). Refer to Fig. 9-1.

Ordered pairs of this kind are called *polar coordinates.* The ray consisting of the origin and the positive portion of the X-axis is called the *polar axis* and the origin is called the *pole.* Our new coordinate system appears in Fig. 9-8. Such a coordinate system is particularly adapted to plotting periodic functions with finite upper and lower bounds.

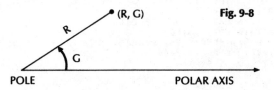

Fig. 9-8

Note that there is no one-to-one correspondence between ordered pairs and plotted points for the polar coordinate system. How do we designate the origin? (0, 0°)? How about calling it (0, 10°) or (0, −25°)? Also note that (1, 45°) and (1, 405°) name the same point. Any particular ordered pair does name a unique point, but every point may be named by an unlimited number of ordered number pairs in this polar coordinate system.

Looking at the polar equation R = cos G suggests that for some values of G we would like to allow R to take on negative values. So we extend the definition of R to permit this. The absolute value of R is the distance of the point from the pole and we define (−R, G) and (R, G + 180°) to name the same point.

Some polar equations are relatively easy to convert to rectangular form. For instance,

$$R = 2 \cos G$$

is equivalent to

$$\sqrt{X^2 + Y^2} = \frac{2X}{\sqrt{X^2 + Y^2}}$$

which is equivalent to

$$X^2 + Y^2 - 2X = 0$$

which turns out to be a circle with radius 1 and center at the point (1, 0). However, other polar equations are not so easily identifiable when converted and so are more appropriate to plot on a polar coordinate system. Consider,

$$R = 1 - 2 \cos G \tag{9-14}$$

$$R = 2 + \sin 2G \tag{9-15}$$

$$R = 1 + 2 \cos G - 3 \sin^2 G \tag{9-16}$$

No matter how you approach plotting any of these, you run into a tremendous amount of calculating.

We can easily get the coordinates of the points to plot for all three of these in the same computer program.

In program PØLAR we have simply defined a function for each of the Eqs. (9-14), (9-15), and (9-16), and put the value of the angle G in a loop to get values every 15 degrees. We are not obligated to define functions, but with converting to radians and rounding off to hundredths this seems a reasonable approach. Now if we want different functions we only need change the printing in line 10 and redefine the new functions in lines 30, 40, and 50. Of course the actual plotting is left to the student to do on polar coordinate paper.

```
PØLAR

 5   LET K=3.14159/180
10   PRINT "ANGLE","1-2COS(G)","2+SIN(2G)","1+2CØS(G)-3SIN(G)↑2"
20   DEF FNR(X)=INT(X*100+.5)/100
30   DEF FNA(X)=1-2*CØS(K*X)
40   DEF FNB(X)=2+SIN(2*K*X)
50   DEF FNC(X)=1+2*CØS(K*X)-3*SIN(K*X)↑2
60   FØR G=0 TØ 360 STEP 15
70   PRINT G,FNR(FNA(G)),FNR(FNB(G)),FNR(FNC(G))
80   NEXT G
90   END
RUN
PØLAR
```

ANGLE	1-2COS(G)	2+SIN(2G)	1+2CØS(G)-3SIN(G)↑2
0	-1	2	3
15	-.93	2.5	2.73
30	-.73	2.87	1.98
45	-.41	3	.91
60	0	2.87	-.25
75	.48	2.5	-1.28
90	1	2	-2
105	1.52	1.5	-2.32
120	2	1.13	-2.25
135	2.41	1	-1.91
150	2.73	1.13	-1.48
165	2.93	1.5	-1.13
180	3	2	-1
195	2.93	2.5	-1.13
210	2.73	2.87	-1.48
225	2.41	3	-1.91
240	2	2.87	-2.25
255	1.52	2.5	-2.32
270	1	2	-2
285	.48	1.5	-1.28
300	0	1.13	-.25
315	-.41	1	.91
330	-.73	1.13	1.98
345	-.93	1.5	2.73
360	-1	2	3

DØNE

SUMMARY

The computer is an invaluable aid to obtaining values of ordered pairs of polar coordinates for polar equations.

PROBLEMS FOR SEC. 9-4

1) Obtain polar coordinates for plotting any of the following polar equations. (It would be instructive to plot the graph as well.)

(a) $R = \cos 2G$

(b) $R = \cos 3G$

(c) $R = \cos 4G$

(d) $R = \sin 2G$

(e) $R = \sin 3G$

(f) $R \cos G = 1$

(g) $R = 1 + R \cos G$

(h) $R = \sin G + \cos G$

2) Write a program to convert from polar coordinates to rectangular coordinates for any of the polar equations in problem 1).

√ 3) Write a program to store rectangular coordinates in an array for any of the polar equations in problem 1) except (f) and (g) and then rearrange the ordered pairs in order of increasing values of X. Print the resulting set of ordered pairs. Plot the graph on rectangular coordinate paper and compare it with the plot obtained in problem 1).

CHAPTER 10

Complex Numbers

10-1 FUNDAMENTAL OPERATIONS

In the development of mathematics we find that we cannot solve the equation

$$X^2 + 1 = 0$$

if we are limited to real numbers. We want to say

$$X = \sqrt{-1} \quad \text{or} \quad X = -\sqrt{-1}$$

However, such numbers are not allowed in the real number system. So we define a new number i such that

$$i^2 = -1 \quad \text{or} \quad i = \sqrt{-1}$$

Then, if we should try to solve $X^2 + 2X + 2 = 0$ using the quadratic formula, we get

$$X = \frac{-2 \pm \sqrt{4-8}}{2} \quad \text{or} \quad X = \frac{-2 \pm \sqrt{-4}}{2}$$

and we decide to call $\sqrt{-4}$ the same number as $i\sqrt{4}$ which is 2i. So now

$$X = \frac{-2 \pm 2i}{2}$$

or $X = -1 + i$
$\qquad = -1 - i$

These two numbers are representative of complex numbers in rectangular form. In general, rectangular form is written as a + bi, where a and b are real numbers. Another number could be written c + di. Of course, the computer cannot handle a + bi because it is limited to real numbers. But we can deal with the two real numbers a and b. This means that we will be working with complex numbers in ordered pair form or (a, b) form. Since the computer terminal is limited to capital letters, we use (A, B).

For two complex numbers (A, B) and (C, D) we define equality:

$$(A, B) = (C, D)$$

if and only if

$$A = C \quad \text{and} \quad B = D \tag{10-1}$$

Their sum is found by

$$(A, B) + (C, D) = (A + C, B + D) \tag{10-2}$$

and their product is found by

$$(A, B) \cdot (C, D) = (AC - BD, AD + BC) \tag{10-3}$$

Equations (10-1), (10-2), and (10-3) are relatively straightforward considerations for a computer program. We can test a pair of real numbers for equality with another pair or we can perform the addition of Eq. (10-2) or the multiplication of Eq. (10-3). As an example, let us write a short program to add two complex numbers on INPUT. See ADDA, B.

```
ADDA,B
10   PRINT "THIS PROGRAM ADDS TWO COMPLEX NUMBERS IN A,B FORM"
20   PRINT
30   PRINT "  FIRST NUMBER";
40   INPUT A,B
50   IF A=999 THEN 999
60   PRINT " SECOND NUMBER";
70   INPUT C,D
80   PRINT "THE SUM IS (";A+C;",";B+D;")"
90   GOTO 20
999  END
RUN
ADDA,B

THIS PROGRAM ADDS TWO COMPLEX NUMBERS IN A,B FORM

  FIRST NUMBER?1,4
SECOND NUMBER?0,0
THE SUM IS ( 1     , 4    )

  FIRST NUMBER?1,5
SECOND NUMBER?3,8
THE SUM IS ( 4     , 13   )

  FIRST NUMBER?-467,902
SECOND NUMBER?56,-1234
THE SUM IS (-411   ,-332  )

  FIRST NUMBER?999,1

DONE
```

Subtraction and multiplication are also relatively straightforward. Now consider division:

$$(A, B)/(C, D) = (X, Y) \tag{10-4}$$

Equation (10-4) may be defined in terms of multiplication:

$$(A, B) = (X, Y) \, ^\circ \, (C, D)$$
$$(A, B) = (XC - YD, XD + YC)$$

By the definiton of equality for complex numbers,

$$A = XC - YD \quad \text{and} \quad B = XD + YC$$

Solving for X and Y we get

$$X = \frac{AC + BD}{C^2 + D^2} \quad \text{and} \quad Y = \frac{BC - AD}{C^2 + D^2}$$

This is a little more complicated than the other operations, but still manageable.

SUMMARY

The computer may be programmed to work with complex numbers, if we represent them as ordered pairs of real numbers. The four fundamental operations of addition, subtraction, multiplication, and division may all be done by formula.

PROBLEMS FOR SEC. 10-1

1) Write a program to give the sum, difference, product, and quotient for pairs of complex numbers assigned as data.

2) Write a program to compute and print the complex roots of quadratic equations.

3) Write a program to test the commutative properties of both addition and multiplication for five pairs of complex numbers.

4) Demonstrate that subtraction and division are not commutative.

5) Write a program to generate random complex numbers. Then test the associative property for both addition and multiplication.

√ 6) Find the reciprocal of complex numbers assigned as data.

7) Whenever we talk about ordered pairs of real numbers, the rectangular coordinate system should come to mind. Think of (A, B) as a plotted point on a graph with an A-axis and a B-axis. Write a program to find the distance from the origin of five complex numbers assigned as data.

10-2   POLAR COORDINATES

If we think of ordered pairs of real numbers as being associated with a rectangular coordinate system, we may plot a point representing (A, B) as shown in Fig. 10-1, where the distance from the B-axis is the absolute value of A and the distance from the A-axis is the absolute value of B.

Whenever we plot an ordered pair of real numbers on a rectangular coordinate system, we may associate the point with another ordered pair of real numbers. In the new pair, the first number is the distance from the origin and the second is the angle whose initial side is the positive A-axis and whose terminal side is the ray with an endpoint at the origin and containing the point

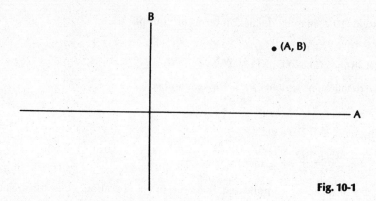

Fig. 10-1

(A, B). We use R for the distance and call it the absolute value of the complex number (A, B). R is found from (A, B) by

$$R = |(A, B)| = \sqrt{A^2 + B^2}$$

We use G for the angle. G may be found from (A, B) by

$$G = \arctan (A/B)$$

G is sometimes called the *argument of the complex number*. We may now refer to complex numbers in polar form as (R, G). This form for complex numbers is the same as the form for (X, Y) ordered pairs converted to polar form in Chap. 9, with the one exception that we prefer not to allow R to be negative for complex numbers.

So we see that for every complex number we may choose a rectangular form or polar form depending on which form is appropriate to the problem at hand. We saw in Sec. 10-1 that addition and subtraction worked out easily in (A, B) form, but that multiplication and division were more cumbersome. Let us look at multiplication in (R, G) form.

It turns out that a third form will be helpful in establishing the multiplication algorithm. From (R, G) we get that A = R cos G and B = R sin G, and similarly for (R1, G1) we get that C = R1 cos G1 and D = R1 sin G1. Using the old formula to multiply (A, B) by (C, D) we get

$$(R \cos G, R \sin G) \ (R1 \cos G1, R1 \sin G1)$$
$$= (RR1 \cos G \cos G1 - RR1 \sin G \sin G1,$$
$$RR1 \sin G \cos G1 + RR1 \cos G \sin G1)$$

After factoring, the right side becomes

$$(RR1(\cos G \cos G1 - \sin G \sin G1), RR1(\sin G \cos G1 + \cos G \sin G1))$$

$$(10\text{-}5)$$

It can be shown that

$$\cos G \cos G1 - \sin G \sin G1 = \cos (G + G1) \qquad (10\text{-}6)$$

and

$$\sin G \cos G1 + \cos G \sin G1 = \sin (G + G1) \qquad (10\text{-}7)$$

Substituting Eqs. (10-6) and (10-7) into (10-5) we get

$(RR1 \cos (G + G1), RR1 \sin (G + G1))$

which is a plotted point associated with a distance from the origin of RR1 and an angle of $G + G1$. So

$$(R, G)(R1, G1) = (RR1, G + G1) \tag{10-8}$$

This means that to multiply two complex numbers in polar form we should multiply their absolute values and add their arguments. This is less cumbersome than the method of Sec. 10-1.

It follows from Eq. (10-8) that to divide two complex numbers in polar form we divide their absolute values and subtract their arguments:

$$(R, G)/(R1, G1) = (R/R1, G - G1)$$

Again this is less cumbersome than the formula of Sec. 10-1.

Let us multiply some randomly assigned complex numbers in polar form. We generate arguments in degrees and absolute values in units 1 to 10. See MLTR, G.

```
MLTR, G

10   DEF FNC(Z)=INT(Z*RND(Z)+1)
20   FOR X=1 TO 6
30   LET R=FNC(10)
40   LET G=FNC(360)
50   LET R1=FNC(10)
60   LET G1=FNC(360)
70   PRINT "(";R;",";G;")*(";R1;",";G1;")=(";R*R1;",";G+G1;")"
80   NEXT X
90   END
RUN
MLTR, G

( 10  , 135 )*( 2  , 311 )=( 20  , 446 )
( 6   , 98  )*( 9  , 341 )=( 54  , 439 )
( 9   , 6   )*( 1  , 231 )=( 9   , 237 )
( 10  , 95  )*( 8  , 307 )=( 80  , 402 )
( 6   , 60  )*( 5  , 356 )=( 30  , 416 )
( 10  , 139 )*( 2  , 343 )=( 20  , 482 )

DONE
```

SUMMARY

Complex numbers may be represented in polar form as (R, G), where R is the absolute value and G is the angular location starting at the positive end of the A-axis on an (A, B) graph. We have seen that while addition and subtraction are easily done in (A, B) form, multiplication and division are better suited to (R, G) form. $(R, G)(R1, G1) = (RR1, G + G1)$ and $(R, G)/(R1, G1) = (R/R1, G - G1)$. To multiply in polar form, multiply absolute values and add arguments. To divide in polar form, divide absolute values and subtract arguments.

PROBLEMS FOR SEC. 10-2

1) Write a program to find the quotient of two complex numbers in polar form.
2) Write a program to print the positive integral powers of $(1, 45°)$ from 1 to 8.
3) Write a program to convert from (R, G) form to (A, B) form.
√ 4) Write a program to convert complex numbers from (A, B) form to (R, G) form. You will want to use the ATN(X) computer function here and be sure you have the angle in the correct quadrant. To check this, simply try numbers in all four quadrants.
√ 5) Write a program to take two complex numbers in (A, B) form and print their product in (R, G) form.
√ 6) Write a program to print the positive integral powers of a complex number in (A, B) form. Keep the result in (A, B) form.
√ 7) Modify MLTR, G to generate negative as well as positive numbers for angles. Print the resulting angle as a value between −360 and +360 degrees.

10-3 POWERS AND ROOTS

We have seen that for multiplying two complex numbers the polar form provides a very convenient algorithm. If we wish to square a complex number, i.e., multiply it by itself, we get

$$(R, G)^2 = (R^2, G + G) \qquad \text{or} \qquad (R^2, 2G)$$

We also see that for a positive integer n,

$$(R, G)^n = (R^n, nG) \tag{10-9}$$

It can also be shown that an nth root of (R, G) may be found by

$$(R, G)^{1/n} = (R^{1/n}, G/n) \tag{10-10}$$

where $R^{1/n}$ means $\sqrt[n]{R}$. Equations (10-9) and (10-10) constitute a portion of *De Moivre's theorem*. It can also be shown that every nonzero complex number has exactly n complex nth roots.

Let us find the four complex fourth roots of unity. By taking the square roots of the square roots of 1, we should get 1, i, −1, and −i, which in (R, G) form are $(1, 0°)$, $(1, 90°)$, $(1, 180°)$, and $(1, 270°)$. Using De Moivre's theorem,

$$(1, 0°)^{1/4} = (1^{1/4}, 0/4°) \qquad \text{or} \qquad (1, 0°)$$

However, there should be three more. Now we see that there is a tremendous advantage associated with the nonuniqueness for polar coordinates. By writing unity $(1, 0°)$ as $(1, 360°)$ we may apply Eq. (10-10) again:

$$(1, 360°)^{1/4} = (1, 90°)$$

Writing $(1, 0°)$ as $(1, 720°)$ we get

$$(1, 720°)^{1/4} = (1, 180°)$$

and finally $(1, 0°) = (1, 1080°)$ gives

$$(1, 1080°)^{1/4} = (1, 270°)$$

```
ROOTS

10    PRINT "TAKE ROOTS OF COMPLEX NUMBERS IN POLAR FORM"
20    READ R,G,N
30    PRINT "THE";N;",";N;"TH ROOTS OF (";R;",";G;") ARE:"
40    FOR X=1 TO N
50    PRINT "(";R↑(1/N);",";G/N;")"
60    LET G=G+360
70    NEXT X
80    PRINT
90    GOTO 20
100   DATA 1,0,4
110   DATA 1,0,3
120   DATA 1,45,2
130   DATA 3,90,3
140   END
RUN
ROOTS

TAKE ROOTS OF COMPLEX NUMBERS IN POLAR FORM
THE 4    , 4      TH ROOTS OF ( 1    , 0    ) ARE:
( 1.             , 0    )
( 1.             , 90   )
( 1.             , 180  )
( 1.             , 270  )

THE 3    , 3      TH ROOTS OF ( 1    , 0    ) ARE:
( 1.             , 0    )
( 1.             , 120  )
( 1.             , 240  )

THE 2    , 2      TH ROOTS OF ( 1    , 45   ) ARE:
( 1.             , 22.5       )
( 1.             , 202.5      )

THE 3    , 3      TH ROOTS OF ( 3    , 90   ) ARE:
( 1.44225        , 30   )
( 1.44225        , 150  )
( 1.44225        , 270  )


OUT OF DATA  IN LINE 20
```

as expected. Suppose we add 360 degrees again. Then $G = 1440°$ and $1440(1/4) = 360°$ which we have already in $(1, 0°)$. Finding roots of complex numbers in polar form becomes a very straightforward computer program. See ROOTS.

PROBLEMS FOR SEC. 10-3

1) In program ROOTS have the computer convert the roots to (A, B) form.

√ 2) Write a program to find the n complex nth roots of complex numbers in (A, B) form and print the results in (A, B) form.

√ 3) In program ROOTS print the roots in both (A, B) and polar form.

CHAPTER 11

Polynomials

11-1 FUNDAMENTAL OPERATIONS

We define a real polynomial in X as an expression that can be written in the form

$$A_N X^N + A_{N-1} X^{N-1} + \cdots + A_2 X^2 + A_1 X + A_0$$

where N is a non-negative integer, X is a complex number, and the A_N are constant real coefficients. The following are examples of polynomials in X:

$$5 \qquad X - 3 \qquad X^8 + 3X^5 - X + 1 \qquad X^2 + 3X - 4$$

For the polynomial 5, note that $5 = 5X^0$ so the polynomial consists of the term A_0, which is 5. The number 0 is considered a polynomial. All real polynomials except the zero polynomials have degree i where $A_i X^i$ is the term of the polynomial with the greatest value of i for A_i not equal to 0. Polynomials may be used to describe many physical problems. For instance, the trajectory of a projectile is described by a second-degree polynomial.

We may perform operations on polynomials much as we perform operations on explicit numbers. You have had considerable experience adding and subtracting such expressions. You have often multiplied two binomials of the form $(AX + B)(CX + D)$. One of the problems in Chap. 1 was to perform just that multiplication by computer. We now develop a program to multiply two polynomials.

Multiplication

Clearly we will perform operations on the computer by working with the coefficients and being careful to line things up properly. This means being very much aware of missing terms and inserting zero coefficients where necessary. Let us begin with an example, say $(2X + 7)(3X^2 + 11X - 5)$. By hand we get

$$3X^2 + 11X - 5$$
$$2X + 7$$
$$\overline{21X^2 + 77X - 35}$$
$$6X^3 + 22X^2 - 10X$$
$$\overline{6X^3 + 43X^2 + 67X - 35}$$

where all the X^N were known in advance and do not depend on the coefficients. So the problem could have been done in the following manner:

$$3 + 11 - 5$$
$$2 + 7$$
$$\overline{21 + 77 - 35}$$
$$6 + 22 - 10$$
$$\overline{6 + 43 + 67 - 35}$$
(11-1)

The program can be set up by putting 3, 11, and -5 in one computer list, 2 and 7 in another, and making provision for putting 6, 43, 67, and -35 in a third list. We may find the organization to be a little easier by thinking of the computation in Eq. (11-1) as being set up in columns numbered from right to left. (If your computer permits 0 subscripts in a list, you may use that to good advantage here by starting with 0.)

3	2	1	0	Column numbers
4	3	2	1	Column numbers
		3	+11	− 5
			2	+ 7
		21	+77	−35
	6	+22	−10	
	6	+43	+67	−35

We observe that when we multiply two numbers in column 1, we put the result in column 1; when we multiply a number from column 1 by a number from column 3, we put the result in column 3; and when we multiply a number in column 2 by a number in column 3 we put the result in column 4. This suggests that multiplying a number in column I by a number in column J calls for the result to go in column $(I + J - 1)$. [If 0 is allowed, then the result goes in column $(I + J)$.] So, if we store the two polynomials being multiplied in an F list and an S list and the product in a P list, our computer program will have an instruction to store $F[1] \circ S[J]$ in $P[I + J - 1]$. We must also provide for subtotals. Thus the program statement will be

XXX   LET $P[I + J - 1] = P[I + J - 1] + F[I] \circ S[J]$

where we initialize the P list at 0. Program TRI $\circ$ BI multiplies the two polynomials of our example.

It will be left as an exercise to modify TRI $\circ$ BI to multiply pairs of polynomials of various degrees.

```
TRI*BI

8    REM LINES 10 THRØUGH 40 READ AND PRINT THE FIRST PØLYNØMIAL
10   FØR X=3 TØ 1 STEP -1
20   READ F[X]
30   PRINT F[X];
40   NEXT X
50   PRINT "TIMES  ";
58   REM LINES 60 THRØUGH 90 READ AND PRINT THE SECØND PØLYNØMIAL
60   FØR Y=2 TØ 1 STEP -1
70   READ S[Y]
80   PRINT S[Y];
90   NEXT Y
98   REM 100 THRØUGH 120 SET THE RESULT LIST AT ALL ZERØS
100  FØR W=1 TØ 4
110  LET P[W]=0
120  NEXT W
128  REM LINES 130 THRØUGH 170 DØ THE ACTUAL MULTIPLYING
130  FØR I=1 TØ 3
140  FØR J=1 TØ 2
150  LET P[I+J-1]=P[I+J-1]+F[I]*S[J]
160  NEXT J
170  NEXT I
180  PRINT "YIELDS  ";
188  REM AND NØW WE PRINT THE 'ANSWER LIST'
190  FØR Z=4 TØ 1 STEP -1
200  PRINT P[Z];
210  NEXT Z
218  REM THE FIRST THREE NUMBERS REPRESENT 3X+2+11X-5
219  REM THE NEXT TWØ NUMBERS REPRESENT 2X+7
220  DATA 3,11,-5,2,7
230  END
RUN
TRI*BI

 3     11   -5   TIMES   2    7    YIELDS   6    43    67   -35
DØNE
```

Division

When working with polynomials we often wish to perform the operation of division. It is especially frequent that we wish to divide by a polynomial of the form $X - R$ where R is a constant. Let us divide $2X^3 - 3X^2 - 10X + 3$ by $X - 3$ and see what can be done to computerize the operation. As with multiplication, we will end up considering only the coefficients. First we do the division by hand:

$$
\begin{array}{r}
2X^2 + 3X - 1 \\
X - 3 \overline{)\,2X^3 - 3X^2 - 10X + 3} \\
\underline{2X^3 - 6X^2} \\
3X^2 - 10X \\
\underline{3X^2 - 9X} \\
-X + 3 \\
\underline{-X + 3}
\end{array}
$$

Every term in the computation that will be written twice in every problem appears in bold face. Now if we simply decide not to write things twice and at the same time compress the problem vertically, we get

$$\begin{array}{r}
2X^2 + 3X - 1 \\
X - 3)\overline{2X^3 - 3X^2 - 10X + 3} \\
-6X^2 - 9X + 3 \\
\hline
3X^2 - X
\end{array}$$

We saw that for multiplication, as long as everything was lined up correctly, we could eliminate all the X's. Also note that we are dividing only by binomials of the form $X - R$, so the coefficient of X will always be 1. Let us not even write it. Now we have the division in the following form:

$$\begin{array}{r}
2 + 3 - 1 \\
-3)\overline{2 - 3 - 10 + 3} \\
-6 - 9 + 3 \\
\hline
3 - 1
\end{array}$$

Since the coefficient of X in the divisor is always 1, the coefficient of each term in the quotient will always be the same as the coefficient of the leading term of the expression into which we divide the X term. Thus it is no accident that we see $3 - 1$ in the bottom row as well as in the answer. So, if we agree to simply insert the leading coefficient of the polynomial into which we are dividing $X - R$ in front of the bottom row of figures, we will always have the coefficients of the quotient polynomial and we would not need the top row. We now have reduced the problem to an iteration involving "multiply and subtract" repeatedly, and the division looks like

$$\begin{array}{r}
-3)\overline{2 - 3 - 10 + 3} \\
-6 - 9 + 3 \\
\hline
2 + 3 - 1
\end{array}$$

which we got by the following set of steps: 1) copy down the first coefficient of the original polynomial 2; 2) multiply 2 by -3 to get -6 and write it down under the second term of the original polynomial; 3) subtract to get 3, multiply 3 by -3 to get -9; 4) write it down beneath the next term to the right and subtract to get -1; 5) multiply -1 by -3 to get $+3$ and write it down beneath the next term; 6) subtract to get 0 and we have a 0 remainder. So we see that $2 + 3 - 1$ is interpreted as $2X^2 + 3X - 1$.

Since subtracting a number may be accomplished by multiplying the number to be subtracted by -1 and adding, we may convert "multiply and subtract" to "multiply and add" if we multiply the -3 by -1 to get 3. Or for $X - R$ we just use R. Let us complete the development of this algorithm by inserting the 0 in the last column to the right to indicate a remainder of 0.

$$\begin{array}{r}
3)\overline{2 - 3 - 10 + 3} \\
6 + 9 - 3 \\
\hline
2 + 3 - 1 + 0
\end{array}$$

Dividing $3X^4 - 2X^2 + 5X - 2$ by $X + 2$ results in

$$\begin{array}{r}
-2)\overline{3 + 0 - 2 + 5 - 2} \\
-6 + 12 - 20 + 30 \\
\hline
3 - 6 + 10 - 15 + 28
\end{array}$$

yielding a quotient of $3X^3 - 6X^2 + 10X - 15$ and a remainder of 28.

Division by the algorithm we have just developed is usually called *synthetic division*. Since this is essentially an iterative process, we should be able to get the computer to perform division in this way. We put the original polynomial in a P list and the quotient polynomial in a Q list. Let us store the division constant in R. For every division problem of the kind we are working with here, the first coefficient in the quotient polynomial is the same as the first coefficient in the dividend polynomial. So we need a line in the program which says LET Q[4] = P[4]. See line 70 in program SYNDIV.

```
SYNDIV

5   PRINT "SYNTHETIC DIVISION:"
8   REM  READ THE DIVISOR
10  READ R
18  REM  READ AND PRINT ORIGINAL POLYNOMIAL IN LINES 20 THRU 50
20  FOR N=4 TO 1 STEP -1
30  READ P[N]
40  PRINT P[N];
50  NEXT N
60  PRINT "DIVIDED BY X -";R;"YIELDS"
68  REM FIRST QUOTIENT COEFFICIENT EQUALS FIRST
69  REM COEFFICIENT OF ORIGINAL POLYNOMIAL
70  LET Q[4]=P[4]
80  PRINT Q[4];
90  FOR X=3 TO 1 STEP -1
98  REM  "MULTIPLY AND ADD"
100 LET Q[X]=P[X]+Q[X+1]*R
110 PRINT Q[X];
120 NEXT X
130 DATA 3,2,-3,-10,3
140 END
RUN
SYNDIV

SYNTHETIC DIVISION:
 2    -3    -10    3    DIVIDED BY X - 3    YIELDS
 2     3    -1     0

DONE
```

In SYNDIV, 2   3   −1   0 is to be interpreted as $2X^2 + 3X - 1$ with a remainder of 0. Let us try another:

```
130 DATA 2,3,-1,4,-5
RUN
SYNDIV

SYNTHETIC DIVISION:
 3    -1    4    -5    DIVIDED BY X - 2    YIELDS
 3     5   14    23

DONE
```

The 3   5   14   23 is to be interpreted as $3X^2 + 5X + 14$ with a remainder of 23.

SUMMARY

You should be able to add and subtract polynomials easily using computer lists. We have written an elementary program for multiplication of two polynomials, and we have written a program to perform synthetic division using X − R as the divisor.

PROBLEMS FOR SEC. 11-1

1) Write a program to find the sum of two polynomials assigned as data. Be sure to avoid printing leading zero coefficients when adding pairs similar to $3X^4 + 6X − 4$ and $− 3X^4 + 5X^3 − 3X + 1$.

2) Do problem 1) for subtraction.

3) Write a single program to add or subtract pairs of polynomials as determined by an item of data. (Example: use $S = 1$ for add and $S = 0$ for subtract.)

4) Prepare a program to multiply two polynomials of varying degrees.

5) Write a program to multiply three polynomials.

6) Generate pairs of random polynomials of random degree and multiply them. Print the original polynomials and the product. Be sure to allow negative coefficients.

√ 7) Extend SYNDIV to divide X − R into polynomials of any degree. Also have the computer print the remainders with a message to the effect that the remainder equals whatever it comes out to.

√ 8) Write a program to print the first 11 integral powers of $(X + 1)$.

√ 9) Write a program to divide any polynomial by any polynomial of equal or lesser degree. Suggestion: get data from problem 6.

11-2   INTEGRAL ZEROS

It is common practice to abbreviate any polynomial and call it $P_{(X)}$ for a polynomial in X (read as P of X). We often look at the polynomial equation

$$Y = P_{(X)}$$

and its graph. The values of X for which $Y = 0$ are called the *zeros of the function*. You have solved many quadratic functions in which there were always two zeros. Sometimes they were equal, sometimes integral, sometimes real, and sometimes complex. It can be shown that every Nth-degree polynomial equation has exactly N complex zeros. Before we actually look for any zeros of $Y = P_{(X)}$ we need to have some theorems available.

Remainder Theorem

According to the *Remainder theorem*, if a polynomial is divided by X − Z, then the remainder is the value of the polynomial when Z is substituted for X. Dividing $P_{(X)}$ by $(X − Z)$ we get

$$\frac{P_{(X)}}{(X − Z)} = Q_{(X)} + \frac{R}{(X − Z)}$$

where $Q_{(X)}$ is the quotient polynomial. Multiplying through by $(X − Z)$ we get

$$P_{(X)} = Q_{(X)} \cdot (X - Z) + R$$

and we can see that if we substitute Z for X, then $X - Z = 0$ and

$$P_{(Z)} = R \tag{11-2}$$

Looking at SYNDIV we see that substituting 3 for X in $2X^3 - 3X^2 - 10X + 3$ gives $54 - 27 - 30 + 3$ or 0, confirming that $P_{(3)} = 0$, which is the remainder after dividing by $X - 3$. We also see that substituting 2 for X in $3X^3 - X^2 + 4X - 5$ gives $24 - 4 + 8 - 5$ or 23, confirming that $P_{(2)} = 23$, which is the remainder after dividing by $X - 2$.

Factor Theorem

The *Factor theorem* states very simply that if the value of R in Eq. (11-2) is 0, then $X - Z$ is a factor of $P_{(X)}$. Looking at SYNDIV again, we see that $X - 3$ is a factor of $2X^3 - 3X^2 - 10X + 3$ while $X - 2$ is not a factor of $3X^3 - X^2 + 4X - 5$. Now all we have to do is find a value of Z so that $P_{(Z)} = 0$ and Z is a zero of the function.

Search for Integral Zeros

What integers do we try for Z to test $P_{(Z)}$ for 0? We have assumed that there are N complex zeros. Let us call them $Z_N, Z_{N-1}, \ldots, Z_2, Z_1$. It can be shown that

$$(X - Z_N)(X - Z_{N-1}) \cdots (X - Z_2)(X - Z_1)$$
$$= A_N X^N + A_{N-1} X^{N-1} + \cdots + A_1 X + A_0$$

Multiplying the left side out we should see that the only constant term in the product is $(-Z_N)(-Z_{N-1}) \cdots (-Z_2)(-Z_1)$ which simplifies to $(-1)^N (Z_N)(Z_{N-1}) \cdots (Z_2)(Z_1)$ and must equal the constant term in the product polynomial which is A_0. And so it follows that if a polynomial has any integral zeros, they must be factors of the constant term A_0. That is not to say that all integral factors of A_0 are zeros of the polynomial.

This should provide sufficient basis for writing a computer program to find the integral zeros of a polynomial function. We can define a computer function and test for $FNP(X) = 0$ for all integral factors of the constant term. If we continue to enter the coefficients of polynomials in computer lists as we have been doing, then we know that the constant term will always be P[1]. For our first program, let us define our function using the list entries as coefficients in a DEF statement and look at only third-degree polynomials.

One feature of the program that requires comment is the finding of numbers to test for factors. These numbers must be in the interval $-P[1]$ to $P[1]$ including the end numbers. Well, if P[1] is negative, we want to step -1 and if P[1] is positive, we want to step $+1$. This is a perfect place to use SGN(P[1]). See line 80 of program INTZER. It would be useful to print that there are no integral zeros if that turns out to be the case. In order to do that, we need a switch which is off initially and which we turn on only if we find at least one zero. Then after we test all possible factors of P[1], we test to see if the switch is on. If it is, we read more data. If the switch is off, there were no zeros, so we print a message and then read more data. See the flowchart in Fig. 11-1.

INTZER works well for polynomials of the same degree; but suppose we have polynomials of several different degrees we wish to study using the same program? Well, we could define a different function for each degree or we could define a function of the highest degree we anticipate and fill in with leading zeros. But suppose we want up to ninth or tenth degree? The function would not fit on one line on some terminals. We could define two functions

```
INTZER

10    DEF FNP(X)=P[4]*X↑3+P[3]*X↑2+P[2]*X+P[1]
20    PRINT
22    PRINT
25    FØR S=4 TØ 1 STEP -1
30    READ P[S]
40    PRINT P[S];
50    NEXT S
60    PRINT "INTEGRAL ZERØ(S):  ";
68    REM   TURN SWITCH ØFF
70    LET K=0
78    REM   STUDY LINE 80 CAREFULLY!
80    FØR X=-P[1] TØ P[1] STEP SGN(P[1])
88    REM LINE 90 PREVENTS AN ERRØR MESSAGE CAUSED BY
89    REM DIVIDING BY ZERØ
90    IF X=0 THEN 140
98    REM IS X A FACTØR ØF P[1]?
100   IF P[1]/X <> INT(P[1]/X) THEN 140
108   REM IS THE REMAINDER ZERØ?
110   IF FNP(X) <> 0 THEN 140
118   REM IF THE CØMPUTER GETS THRØUGH HERE, THE
119   REM VALUE ØF X IS A ZERØ ØF THE FUNCTIØN
120   PRINT X;
128   REM TURN THE SWITCH ØN - WE HAVE A ZERØ
130   LET K=1
140   NEXT X
150   IF K=1 THEN 20
160   PRINT "NØNE FØUND";
165   GØTØ 20
170   DATA 1,-2,-11,12
180   DATA 1,1,-5,-2
190   DATA 1,-2,3,-4
200   DATA 2,-3,-10,3
210   END
RUN
INTZER


1    -2    -11    12    INTEGRAL ZERØ(S):  -3    1    4

1     1    -5    -2    INTEGRAL ZERØ(S):  2

1    -2     3    -4    INTEGRAL ZERØ(S):  NØNE FØUND

2    -3    -10    3    INTEGRAL ZERØ(S):  3


ØUT ØF DATA  IN LINE 30
```

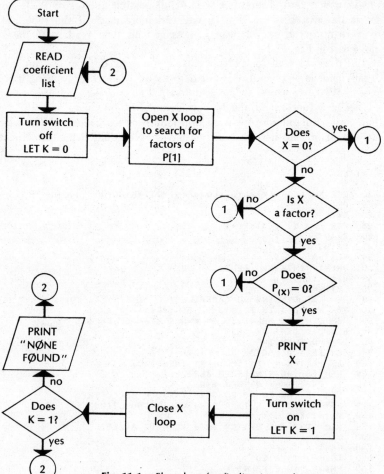

Fig. 11-1.   Flowchart for finding integral zeros of polynomial.

and add them. But then we have large numbers of leading zeros to worry about. All of these complications may be eliminated by using a subroutine to define a function instead of a DEF statement. Notice that evaluating an Nth-degree polynomial is equivalent to summing up N + 1 terms which look like $A_i X^i$ where i goes from N to 0. If you have 0 subscripts, this is perfect. For those of us without 0 subscripts, we must use a term similar to P[I] ° X °° (I − 1), where the value of I goes from N to 1 for N equal to one more than the degree of the polynomial.

We may now define a polynomial function in a five-line subroutine for any degree with no further complications and no fuss over leading zeros and such:

```
500   LET P = 0
510   FØR I = N TØ 1 STEP −1
```

520 LET P = P + P[I] ° X °° (I − 1)
530 NEXT I
540 RETURN

Let us insert GØSUB 500 after line 100 in INTZER, insert line 23 READ N, where N is the number of terms in the polynomial, and change line 25 to read FØR S = N TØ 1 STEP −1. See IZERØ1.

This program will handle up to ninth-degree polynomials. (Tenth, if you have 0 subscripts.) If we want to work with polynomials of greater degree, all we need is a DIM statement to specify a longer list for P.

SUMMARY

We have seen that by combining the Remainder theorem, the Factor theorem, and the fact that the product of all zeros multiplied by $(-1)^N$, where N is the degree of the polynomial, gives the constant term, we are able to find all integral zeros. We simply test all integral factors of the constant term to see if the remainder is 0. If the remainder is 0, then we have a zero of the polynomial. If it is not 0, then we do not have a zero of the polynomial. We have two alternative methods of evaluating a polynomial for a specified value of X: one is to use a DEF statement, and the other is to write a subroutine to sum up terms.

PROBLEMS FOR SEC. 11-2

1) For each of the polynomials to follow: (a) find an integral zero, (b) use synthetic division to find the resulting factor after dividing by $(X - Z)$, and (c) search for zeros of the depressed polynomial. Repeat until all integral zeros are found and then print the remaining polynomial.

$10X^3 - 71X^2 - 76X + 32$

$6X^8 - 32X^7 - 23X^6 - 3X^5 - 12X^4 - 36X^3 - X^2 + 8X - 12$

$8X^5 - 18X^4 - 8X^3 - 32X^2 + 2X + 3$

$2X^4 + 5X^3 - 31X^2 - 21X + 45$

2) Generate random integers in sets of three. Have the computer print the polynomial having those three integers as zeros. Be sure to get some negative integers.

3) Do problem 2) for sets of four integers.

4) In IZERØ1 have the computer determine if $P_{(X)}$ is within two units of 0 for each factor of the constant term.

5) Prepare a table of ordered pairs $(X, P_{(X)})$ such as would be appropriate for plotting points. Sketch a graph on graph paper. How would you estimate nonintegral zeros?

11-3   REAL ZEROS

It can be shown that for a polynomial, if $P_{(X_1)} > 0$ and $P_{(X_2)} < 0$, then there is a value of X between X_1 and X_2 such that $P_{(X)} = 0$. This is called the *Location Principle*. In graphical terms, the Location Principle may be stated as

```
IZERO1

20    PRINT
22    PRINT
23    READ N
25    FOR S=N TO 1 STEP -1
30    READ P[S]
40    PRINT P[S];
50    NEXT S
55    PRINT
60    PRINT "INTEGRAL ZERO(S):   ";
68    REM   TURN SWITCH OFF
70    LET K=0
78    REM   STUDY LINE 80 CAREFULLY!
80    FOR X=-P[1] TO P[1] STEP SGN(P[1])
88    REM LINE 90 PREVENTS AN ERROR MESSAGE CAUSED BY
89    REM DIVIDING BY ZERO
90    IF X=0 THEN 140
98    REM IS X A FACTOR OF P[1]?
100   IF P[1]/X <> INT(P[1]/X) THEN 140
105   GOSUB 500
108   REM IS THE REMAINDER ZERO?
110   IF P <> 0 THEN 140
118   REM IF THE COMPUTER GETS THROUGH HERE, THE
119   REM VALUE OF X IS A ZERO OF THE FUNCTION
120   PRINT X;
128   REM TURN THE SWITCH ON - WE HAVE A ZERO
130   LET K=1
140   NEXT X
150   IF K=1 THEN 20
160   PRINT "NONE FOUND";
165   GOTO 20
170   DATA 4,1,-2,-11,12
180   DATA 4,1,1,-5,-2
190   DATA 4,1,-2,3,-4
200   DATA 5,2,-1,-11,11,-2
210   DATA 7,2,-5,-6,9,9,-39,36
490   REM SUBROUTINE 500 THROUGH 540 TAKES THE PLACE OF A
491   REM DEF STATEMENT AND EVALUATES A POLYNOMIAL OF
492   REM OF DEGREE N-1.
500   LET P=0
510   FOR I=N TO 1 STEP -1
520   LET P=P+P[I]*X↑(I-1)
530   NEXT I
540   RETURN
999   END
RUN
IZERO1


1    -2    -11    12
INTEGRAL ZERO(S):  -3     1     4

1     1    -5    -2
INTEGRAL ZERO(S):   2

1    -2     3    -4
INTEGRAL ZERO(S):   NONE FOUND

2    -1    -11    11    -2
INTEGRAL ZERO(S):   2

2    -5    -6     9     9    -39    36
INTEGRAL ZERO(S):   3


OUT OF DATA  IN LINE 23
```

follows: If point $(X_1, P_{(X_1)})$ and point $(X_2, P_{(X_2)})$ are on opposite sides of the X-axis, then the graph must cross the X-axis between $(X_1, 0)$ and $(X_2, 0)$.

We may now search for real zeros by finding intervals in which the graph crosses the X-axis. In order to find out if the value of the function is positive for one value of X and negative for another, we may simply test the product. If the product is negative, they are of opposite sign. If the product is positive, then they are of the same sign and we are not concerned with those values of X. Since we anticipate more than one zero, let us make a provision for putting the information in a list. For that, we need a counter. It seems reasonable to list the left number of the interval. As long as we know the increment, we should be able to see the right number of the interval. It is usual to start looking for real zeros in an increment of one unit. Let us prepare a flowchart for this problem and call the program REAL. See Fig. 11-2.

Thus, we have found that the three zeros of $12X^3 - 64X^2 + 17X + 195$ fall in the three intervals -2 to -1, 2 to 3, and 3 to 4. That is fine to know, but we generally prefer more precision than that. So, we should try to improve on

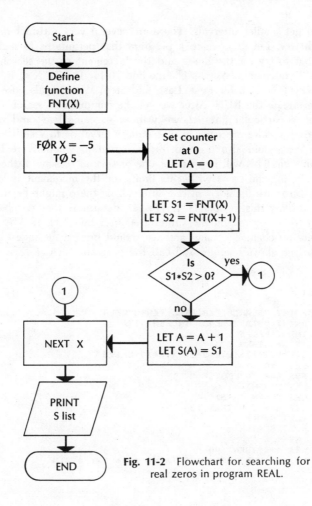

Fig. 11-2 Flowchart for searching for real zeros in program REAL.

```
REAL

50    DEF FNT(X)=12*X↑3-64*X↑2+17*X+195
60    LET A=0
70    FØR X=-5 TØ 5
80    LET S1=FNT(X)
90    LET S2=FNT(X+1)
100   IF S1*S2>0 THEN 130
110   LET A=A+1
120   LET S[A]=X
130   NEXT X
190   PRINT "INTERVAL(S) BEGIN AT:"
200   FØR I=1 TØ A
210   PRINT S[I];
220   NEXT I
270   END
RUN
REAL

INTERVAL(S) BEGIN AT:
-2    2    3
DØNE
```

REAL to get smaller intervals. There are several very satisfactory procedures one might try. Let us develop a program that permits us to make decisions about what to try for the limits and the increment of the search. That calls for INPUT statements. We can change line 70 to 70 FØR X = F TØ L STEP S and INPUT F, L, S for First, Last, and Step. We may also use S = 0 as a flag to terminate the RUN. After we get the computer to search for a change of sign in a particular interval, we want it to come back and permit us to either look for more precision in that same interval or to search in a different interval. We should also provide for the situation where there has been no change in sign. This will happen for one of several reasons. Either the search is not including the zeros within its limits, or the increment is large enough that two zeros are included in one interval, or there might be no real zeros. We will discuss this in Sec. 11-4. We can determine that no change of sign has been found by testing the value of A after line 130. If A is still 0, then there were no changes of sign and we should print a message to that effect. We make the above changes and call the program REAL1.

```
REAL 1

10    PRINT "SEARCH FØR REAL ZERØS ØF A PØLYNØMIAL"
20    PRINT "START, END, INCREMENT";
30    INPUT F,L,S
40    IF S=0 THEN 270
50    DEF FNT(X)=12*X↑3-64*X↑2+17*X+195
60    LET A=0
70    FØR X=F TØ L STEP S
80    LET S1=FNT(X)
90    LET S2=FNT(X+S)
100   IF S1*S2>0 THEN 130
110   LET A=A+1
120   LET S[A]=X
130   NEXT X
140   IF A>0 THEN 190
150   PRINT "NØ INTERVALS FØUND **** TRY AGAIN "
```

```
160   PRINT "WITH EITHER GREATER LIMITS ØR SMALLER INCREMENT"
170   PRINT
180   GØTØ 20
190   PRINT "INTERVAL(S) BEGIN AT:"
200   FØR I=1 TØ A
210   PRINT S[I];
220   NEXT I
230   PRINT
240   PRINT
250   PRINT "NØW ";
260   GØTØ 20
270   END
RUN
REAL1

SEARCH FØR REAL ZERØS ØF A PØLYNØMIAL
START, END, INCREMENT?-5,5,1
INTERVAL(S) BEGIN AT:
-2     2     3

NØW START, END, INCREMENT?-3,-2,.1
NØ INTERVALS FØUND **** TRY AGAIN
WITH EITHER GREATER LIMITS'ØR SMALLER INCREMENT

START, END, INCREMENT?-2,-1,.1
INTERVAL(S) BEGIN AT:
-1.5

NØW START, END, INCREMENT?-1.5,-1.4,.01
INTERVAL(S) BEGIN AT:
-1.45

NØW START, END, INCREMENT?2,3,.1
INTERVAL(S) BEGIN AT:
 2.8

NØW START, END, INCREMENT?1,2,0

DØNE
```

Since we are using INPUT often in this program, we should pick limits and increments carefully. We should also be prepared to make up our mind quickly. Some of the things we should not try are −50 to 50 STEP .01, or 50 to −50 STEP 1. A little care should avoid such blunders.

Let us define a new function and obtain another RUN.

```
50 DEF FNT(X)=X↑3+49.1809*X↑2+2.67761*X-15223.8
RUN
REAL2

SEARCH FØR REAL ZERØS ØF A PØLYNØMIAL
START, END, INCREMENT?-10,10,1
NØ INTERVALS FØUND **** TRY AGAIN
WITH EITHER GREATER LIMITS ØR SMALLER INCREMENT

START, END, INCREMENT?-100,100,5
INTERVAL(S) BEGIN AT:
-40    -30    15

NØW START, END, INCREMENT?-40,-35,.1
INTERVAL(S) BEGIN AT:
-39.3
```

```
NØW START, END, INCREMENT?-39.3,-39.2,.01
INTERVAL(S) BEGIN AT:
-39.22

NØW START, END, INCREMENT?15,20,.1
INTERVAL(S) BEGIN AT:
 15.3

NØW START, END, INCREMENT?15.3,15.4,.01
INTERVAL(S) BEGIN AT:
 15.33

NØW START, END, INCREMENT?0,0,0

DØNE
```

One of the contingencies that we have not accounted for in REAL1 is the possibility that the polynomial has integral zeros. As the program stands, if S1 or S2 equals 0, then the value of X used for S1 will be identified as the number at the beginning of the interval in which a real zero will be found. It will be left as an exercise to identify a zero more explicitly if S1 or S2 does equal 0.

SUMMARY

We have used the Location Principle to find intervals within which real zeros are expected to occur. It should be noted that the Location Principle may be applied to any continuous function and is not limited to polynomial functions.

PROBLEMS FOR SEC. 11-3

1) Modify REAL1 so that if the value picked for X in line 70 gives either S1 or S2 equal to 0, we get a message and the value of the zero printed.

2) In program REAL1, after the computer has found the initial intervals for all real zeros, we do not want the computer to search the entire intervals specified in subsequent searches in the X-loop. We want the computer to print immediately after finding the change in sign without searching the rest of the interval. Incorporate this into the program.

3) Modify REAL1 to read data for more than one polynomial. You may use some dummy value for S in line 30 as a signal to read the next set of data.

√ 4) Write a program to search for real zeros by first finding the unit intervals and then using linear interpolation until FNT(X) is within 10^{-4} of zero. You may want to specify less or greater precision.

11-4   COMPLEX ZEROS

The simplest real polynomial for which we may find complex zeros is the second-degree polynomial $A_2X^2 + A_1X + A_0$. We may use the general quadratic formula

$$X = \frac{-A_1 \pm \sqrt{A_1^2 - 4A_2A_0}}{2A_2}$$

(11-3)

Letting the radicand equal D we get

$$D = A_1{}^2 - 4A_2A_0$$

D is called the *discriminant* of the quadratic expression. We can see that if D is negative, the zeros are nonreal. We can rewrite Eq. (11-3) as

$$X = \frac{-A_1}{2A_2} \pm \frac{\sqrt{D}}{2A_2}$$

and finally, considering X as being associated with two numbers A and B, we let

$$A = \frac{-A_1}{2A_2} \quad \text{and} \quad B = \frac{\sqrt{|D|}}{2A_2}$$

If D is greater than or equal to 0, the real zeros are

$$X1 = A + B \quad \text{and} \quad X2 = A - B \tag{11-4}$$

But if D is less than 0, we get the nonreal zeros

$$X1 = (A, B) \quad \text{and} \quad X2 = (A, -B) \tag{11-5}$$

So, in our computer program we compute D, A, and B. Then we test D. If D is negative, we print as in Eq. (11-5) and if D is not negative, we print as in Eq. (11-4). See Fig. 11-3 for the flowchart. We call the program CØMP-1.

It turns out that there is no convenient general procedure for finding non-real zeros for polynomials of higher degree than two. But for any polynomial that has exactly two nonreal zeros, we may find the real zeros first, then for each real zero Z we may divide out the corresponding X − Z using synthetic division and if after all division is carried out the result is a second-degree polynomial, we may apply the technique of program CØMP-1. We demonstrate this procedure by an elementary example: Find all zeros of the following polynomials, given that each has at least one integral zero:

$$X^3 + 2X^2 - X - 2$$
$$X^3 - X^2 - 48$$
$$X^3 - 1$$
$$X^3 + 1$$
$$X^3 - X^2 + X - 1$$
$$6X^3 - 77X^2 - 189X - 90$$

This is of course a special case, but it should help us develop a more general approach. Since we have a third-degree polynomial with one integral zero, we may take program INTZER to find the integral zero Z and then use program SYNDIV to divide the given polynomial by X − Z. The polynomial we get is called a *depressed polynomial*. We know that in this problem each depressed polynomial will be a second-degree polynomial. So we may then use program CØMP-1. In each of these earlier programs the polynomials were all represented with the same variable P list. So all that will have to be changed is the various READ statements and the variable in which the integral zero in INTZER is called X, while in SYNDIV the corresponding number was stored in R. Thus the need for line 170 in program ALLZER. We also changed

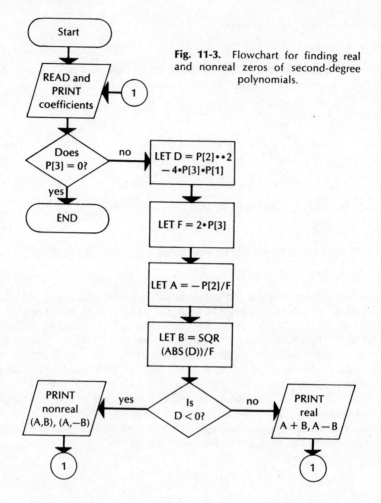

Fig. 11-3. Flowchart for finding real and nonreal zeros of second-degree polynomials.

```
CØMP-1

10   PRINT
20   READ P[3],P[2],P[1]
30   IF P[3]=0 THEN 170
40   PRINT P[3];P[2];P[1]
50   LET D=P[2]↑2-4*P[3]*P[1]
60   LET F=2*P[3]
70   LET A=-P[2]/F
80   LET B=SQR(ABS(D))/F
90   IF D<0 THEN 130
100  PRINT "REAL ZERØS:"
110  PRINT A+B;"AND    ";A-B
120  GØTØ 10
130  PRINT "NØN-REAL ZERØS:"
140  PRINT "(";A;",";B;") AND (";A;",";-B;")"
150  GØTØ 10
160  DATA 1,2,3,1,-3,2,1,3,2,1,3,13,-1,2,-3,1,3,12,0,0,0
170  END
```

```
RUN
COMP-1


  1     2     3
NON-REAL ZEROS:
(-1     , 1.41421     ) AND (-1      ,-1.41421      )

  1    -3     2
REAL ZEROS:
  2     AND    1

  1     3     2
REAL ZEROS:
 -1     AND   -2

  1     3     13
NON-REAL ZEROS:
(-1.5        , 3.27872     ) AND (-1.5         ,-3.27872      )

 -1     2    -3
NON-REAL ZEROS:
( 1     ,-1.41421     ) AND ( 1      , 1.41421      )

  1     3     12
NON-REAL ZEROS:
(-1.5        , 3.1225      ) AND (-1.5         ,-3.1225       )


DONE



ALLZER

8    REM   INTZER BEGINS HERE    (WE HAVE REMOVED THE REM STATEMENTS)
9    REM   SEE THE PROGRAM FOR REM STATEMENTS
10   DEF FNP(X)=P[4]*X↑3+P[3]*X↑2+P[2]*X+P[1]
20   PRINT
30   PRINT
40   FOR S=4 TO 1 STEP -1
50   READ P[S]
60   IF P[S]=.0101 THEN 430
70   PRINT P[S];
80   NEXT S
90   PRINT "INTEGRAL ZERO:   ";
100   FOR X=-P[1] TO P[1] STEP SGN(P[1])
110   IF X=0 THEN 160
120   IF P[1]/X <> INT(P[1]/X) THEN 160
130   IF FNP(X) <> 0 THEN 160
140   PRINT X
150   GOTO 170
160   NEXT X
164  REM   INTZER ENDS HERE ***   SYNDIV BEGINS HERE
170   LET R=X
180   PRINT "SYNTHETIC DIVISION BY   X -";R;"YIELDS:"
190   PRINT P[4];
200   FOR X=3 TO 1 STEP -1
210   LET P[X]=P[X]+P[X+1]*R
220   IF X>1 THEN 240
230   PRINT "REMAINDER =";
240   PRINT P[X];
250   NEXT X
252  REM SYNDIV ENDS HERE
258  REM   HERE WE MOVE EACH ENTRY IN THE P LIST
259  REM    TO THE LOCATION ONE SUBSCRIPT LOWER
```

```
260    FØR X=1 TØ 3
270    LET P[X]=P[X+1]
280    NEXT X
290    PRINT
298    REM CØMP-1 BEGINS HERE
300    LET D=P[2]↑2-4*P[3]*P[1]
310    LET F=2*P[3]
320    LET A=-P[2]/F
330    LET B=SQR(ABS(D))/F
340    IF D<0 THEN 380
350    PRINT "REAL ZERØS:"
360    PRINT A+B;"AND    ";A-B
370    GØTØ 20
380    PRINT "NØN-REAL ZERØS:"
390    PRINT "(";A;",";B;") AND (";A;",";-B;")"
400    GØTØ 20
405    DATA 1,2,-1,-2
410    DATA 1,-1,0,-48,1,0,0,-1,1,0,0,1,1,-1,1,-1
415    DATA 6,-77,-189,-90
420    DATA .0101
430    END

RUN
ALLZER


1     2     -1     -2    INTEGRAL ZERØ:     1
SYNTHETIC DIVISIØN BY    X - 1     YIELDS:
1     3     2     REMAINDER = 0
REAL ZERØS:
-1     AND     -2


1     -1     0     -48    INTEGRAL ZERØ:     4
SYNTHETIC DIVISIØN BY    X - 4     YIELDS:
1     3     12     REMAINDER = 0
NØN-REAL ZERØS:
(-1.5          , 3.1225     ) AND (-1.5          ,-3.1225      )


1     0     0     -1    INTEGRAL ZERØ:     1
SYNTHETIC DIVISIØN BY    X - 1     YIELDS:
1     1     1     REMAINDER = 0
NØN-REAL ZERØS:
(-.5          , .866025     ) AND (-.5          ,-.866025      )


1     0     0     1    INTEGRAL ZERØ:     -1
SYNTHETIC DIVISIØN BY    X --1     YIELDS:
1     -1     1     REMAINDER = 0
NØN-REAL ZERØS:
( .5          , .866025     ) AND ( .5          ,-.866025      )


1     -1     1     -1    INTEGRAL ZERØ:     1
SYNTHETIC DIVISIØN BY    X - 1     YIELDS:
1     0     1     REMAINDER = 0
NØN-REAL ZERØS:
( 0     , 1     ) AND ( 0     ,-1      )


6     -77     -189     -90    INTEGRAL ZERØ:     15
SYNTHETIC DIVISIØN BY    X - 15     YIELDS:
6     13     6     REMAINDER = 0
REAL ZERØS:
-.666667     AND     -1.5

DØNE
```

the way in which the quotient was stored in SYNDIV. It turns out that the quotient polynomial can be stored right back in the P list instead of creating the new Q list. This is done in line 210 of ALLZER. Then in order to avoid changing the subscripts in CØMP-1 it seems reasonable to simply take the quotient polynomial, which also stores the remainder in the lowest subscripted location, and move every entry into the location one subscript lower. Instead of having the quotient polynomial in P[4], P[3], and P[2], we are putting the quotient polynomial in P[3], P[2], and P[1], which exactly fits program CØMP-1. This is done in lines 260, 270, and 280.

As always, some interesting problems have been left for you to solve. For instance, suppose we have third-degree polynomials with two nonreal zeros and a real zero that is not an integer, or what about higher degree polynomials? These considerations are left as exercises in the problems set for Sec. 11-4.

Descartes' Rule of Signs

We may define the *variation* in a sequence of numbers as the number of changes in sign found by comparing successive pairs of adjacent numbers. For example, for the sequence 1, 3, 4, −8, 2, the value of V is 2. There is no change for 1 to 3 or 3 to 4. There is one change for 4 to −8 and for −8 to 2. If zeros appear in the sequence, we drop them. The sequence −2, 8, 0, 5, −3, 6 becomes −2, 8, 5, −3, 6 in order to determine the number of variations which is 3.

Descartes' Rule of Signs says that for

$$A_N X^N + A_{N-1} X^{N-1} + \cdots + A_1 X + A_0$$

the number of positive zeros depends on the number of variations in the sequence

$$A_N, A_{N-1}, \ldots, A_1, A_0$$

in the following manner. If V is the number of variations, then the number of positive zeros is either V or V − 2 or V − 4, etc., but not less than 0. This may be written V − 2I, where I is a positive integer.

It turns out that we may find a corresponding number for negative zeros by finding positive zeros for $P_{(-X)}$. Substituting −X for X will change the sign of all terms which have an odd exponent on X. So if $P_{(X)} = -4X^5 - 3X^4 + 5X^3 - 2X^2 + X - 3$, the value of V is 4 and there must be 4 or 2 or 0 positive zeros. Now we find $P_{(-X)} = +4X^5 - 3X^4 - 5X^3 - 2X^2 - X - 3$, and V is 1. So there must be exactly one negative zero.

This is something we can get the computer to do for us. We may read the coefficients into the first row of a P array and change the sign of the coefficients of the terms with odd exponents on X and put the new coefficient list in the second row of the P array. Then we may look for changes in sign and provide two counters: one for the first row keeping track of changes of sign for the positive zeros, and the other for the second row counting sign changes for the negative zeros. These are V1 for the positive zeros and V2 for the negative zeros in program DESCRT.

```
DESCRT

10    READ N
15    IF N=0 THEN 999
20    FØR X=N TØ 1 STEP -1
30    READ P[1,X]
40    PRINT P[1,X];
48    REM ENTER THE SAME CØEFFICIENT IN THE SAME CØLUMN
49    REM ØF THE SECØND RØW
50    LET P[2,X]=P[1,X]
58    REM IF THE EXPØNENT ØN X IS ØDD THEN CHANGE THE SIGN
60    IF (X+1)/2=INT((X+1)/2) THEN 80
70    LET P[2,X]=-P[2,X]
80    NEXT X
90    PRINT
100   PRINT N-1;"CØMPLEX ZERØS"
200   LET V1=V2=0
210   FØR X=N-1 TØ 1 STEP -1
218   REM LØØK AT PØSITIVE ZERØS
220   IF P[1,X]*P[1,X+1]>0 THEN 240
230   LET V1=V1+1
238   REM LØØK AT NEGATIVE ZERØS
240   IF P[2,X]*P[2,X+1]>0 THEN 260
250   LET V2=V2+1
260   NEXT X
300   PRINT V1;"MAX PØSITIVE"
310   PRINT V2;"MAX NEGATIVE"
320   PRINT
340   GØTØ 10
500   DATA 4,6,103,201,90
510   DATA 5,1,3,4,-8,2
520   DATA 6,-4,-3,5,-2,1,-3
600   DATA 0
999   END
RUN
DESCRT

6      103    201    90
3      CØMPLEX ZERØS
0      MAX PØSITIVE
3      MAX NEGATIVE

1      3      4      -8     2
4      CØMPLEX ZERØS
2      MAX PØSITIVE
2      MAX NEGATIVE

-4     -3     5      -2     1      -3
5      CØMPLEX ZERØS
4      MAX PØSITIVE
1      MAX NEGATIVE

DØNE
```

You might reasonably ask, just what have we done that could not be done quicker by hand. Well, maybe not much, but look at 6   103   201   90 in DESCRT. If we run these coefficients through INTZER, the computer tests $P[1]/X$ 180 times (from -90 to 90 skipping 0). We may now use DESCRT and change the limits on the test loop in INTZER to test no positive values of X. So the computer will now test a maximum of 90 values of X. We could take this one step further and use the fact that the maximum number of negative zeros is three to transfer out of the loop after the third value is found if they all are integral.

There is more to Descartes' Rule of Signs than appears in program DESCRT. The rule states that zero coefficients are to be dropped. DESCRT does not provide for that. You will find that when zero coefficients appear, we may consider polynomials such as

$$P_{(x)} = 3X^4 + 2X^3 - 5X^2 - 7$$

V1 for positive zeros gives us 1. The coefficients for $P_{(-x)}$ are 3, -2, -5, -7, and V2 is 1. Since there are no 0 zeros, there are a total of two real zeros. Since there are 4 complex zeros, we find that there are two nonreal zeros for $P_{(x)}$.

SUMMARY

Once again we have used polynomial coefficients stored in a computer list. This time we find all zeros whenever no more than two zeros are nonintegral. In addition, we have used Descartes' Rule of Signs to obtain the possible numbers of positive and negative zeros and outlined a procedure for determining the possible numbers of nonreal zeros.

PROBLEMS FOR SEC. 11-4

1) Modify DESCRT to permit zero coefficients. Read all coefficients into a P list and then eliminate the zero coefficients as you enter them into a two-row array.

2) Modify ALLZER to handle polynomials of degree greater than three which have for degree D at least $D - 2$ integral zeros.

√ 3) Write a program to generate polynomials of random degree D which are guaranteed to have exactly $D - 2$ integral zeros and two nonreal zeros.

4) *Project:* Modify your program in problem 2) to handle $D - 2$ real zeros using linear interpolation until $P_{(x)}$ is within .001 of 0. (You may want to change the tolerance.)

5) *Project:* Use DESCRT to modify ALLZER to reduce the number of tests for polynomials similar to $6X^3 + 103X^2 + 201X + 90$.

CHAPTER 12

MAT Instructions in BASIC

12-1 INTRODUCTION TO MAT INSTRUCTIONS

MAT instructions are BASIC statements which allow us to manipulate entire arrays in the computer without being required to do it entry by entry. This capability will enable us to write shorter programs, using arrays, than we have been able to write thus far.

We have had to assign values of array entries one at a time. We have been putting LET A[I, J] = or READ A[I, J] in a nested loop for assignment and then in order to print the array, we have been putting PRINT A[I, J]; in another nested loop. In order to print out a 3 by 4 array consisting of −1's, we

```
MAT-1

8   REM   LINES 10 TØ 50 'ASSIGN VALUES
10   FØR R=1 TØ 3
20   FØR C=1 TØ 4
30   LET A[R,C]=-1
40   NEXT C
50   NEXT R
98   REM LINES 100 TØ 160 PRINT THE ARRAY
100   FØR R=1 TØ 3
110   FØR C=1 TØ 4
120   PRINT A[R,C]S
130   NEXT C
140   PRINT
150   PRINT
160   NEXT R
200   END
RUN
MAT-1


-1      -1      -1      -1

-1      -1      -1      -1

-1      -1      -1      -1


DØNE
```

```
MAT-2

10   DIM A[3,4]
20   MAT  READ A
30   MAT  PRINT A;
40   DATA -1,-1,-1,-1,-1,-1,-1,-1,-1,-1,-1,-1
50   END
RUN
MAT-2

-1      -1      -1      -1

-1      -1      -1      -1

-1      -1      -1      -1


DØNE
```

would proceed as in MAT-1, using programming statements and techniques with which we are familiar. MAT-1 certainly does what we said we would do.

But consider MAT-2, which is a five-line program that does what required 13 lines to do in MAT-1. In MAT-2, line 10 instructs the computer to set up a 3 by 4 array. Then line 20 reads the data into the array named and dimensioned in line 10. (Some of you who had 0 subscripts will find that as soon as you specify a MAT instruction for a particular variable you also lose 0 subscripts for that variable. Others will find the situation unchanged. This depends on the system.) Note in line 20 a semicolon appears after the array A. Used in this way we are specifying semicolon spacing. To get comma spacing, we may place a comma there or leave it blank. If we wish to specify printing for several arrays in one print instruction, we may do so as follows:

XXX   MAT PRINT A, B; C

In this case A and C will be printed with comma spacing, and B will be printed with semicolon spacing.

In MAT-2 it may not be clear just how the computer takes the numbers in the data line and enters them in the array locations. MAT-3 is intended to show what numbers are entered where in the array.

```
MAT-3

10   DIM A[3,5]
20   MAT  READ A
30   MAT  PRINT A;
40   DATA 1,2,3,4,5,6,7,8,9,10,11,12,13,14,15
50   END
RUN
MAT-3

1       2       3       4       5

6       7       8       9       10

11      12      13      14      15


DØNE
```

It should be clear now that MAT READ enters numbers just as we read across the printed page. It reads and enters across until it runs out of space in the row and then reads the next data item into the first location of the next row. This is the method we have been using in all array programs throughout this text.

It was stated earlier that a list is just a special array consisting of a single column or a single row, depending on the computer. Now we will look at arrays of just one column or just one row. See MAT-4 and MAT-5.

```
MAT-4

10   DIM A[5,1]
20   MAT   READ A
30   MAT   PRINT A
40   DATA 1,2,3,4,5
50   END
RUN
MAT-4

1

2

3

4

5

DONE
```

```
MAT-5

10   DIM A[1,5]
20   MAT   READ A
30   MAT   PRINT A;
40   DATA 1,2,3,4,5
50   END
RUN
MAT-5

1     2     3     4     5

DONE
```

Some systems may permit you to dimension a list as DIM A[5] and then MAT READ A. If this works, then you can determine whether your system thinks of a list as a row vector or a column vector, by having it MAT PRINT A when A is a list.

The MAT READ statement has an optional redimensioning capability. MAT READ A[R, C] redimensions A to have rows numbered up to R and columns numbered up to C and then reads data into that redimensioned array. See MAT-6.

```
MAT-6

10   DIM A[8,8]
20   MAT   READ A[2,5]
30   MAT   PRINT A;
40   DATA 6,3,4,8,-1,0,17,31,899,10
50   END
RUN
MAT-6

6     3     4     8     -1

0     17    31    899   10

DONE
```

Some systems permit the use of MAT READ A[R, C] to perform the initial dimensioning within certain limits (usually up to [10, 10]).

An array of just one column is called a *column vector* by mathematicians. An array of one row is called a *row vector*. Mathematicians use the term *matrix* to describe all arrays. Thus the term MAT is used in BASIC.

MAT READ X
  Reads data into the array named X according to previously determined dimensions.

MAT READ Y[R, C]
  Dimensions or redimensions an array named Y with R rows and C columns and reads data into the array Y. R and C may be explicit integers or variables.

MAT PRINT P; Q, R;
  Prints array P with semicolon spacing, then prints array Q with comma spacing, and then prints array R with semicolon spacing.

Even though you use MAT READ in a program, you are not required to use MAT PRINT. You may often want to use nested loops to print an array as we have been doing up to this section. You will do this if you do not want the blank line between printed rows and if you want to print headings in front of each row or if you only want to print a portion of the array. Note too, that you may use MAT PRINT even if you have not used MAT READ. This will be the case if we analyze data and enter results into an array as we did in Chap. 5.

PROBLEMS FOR SEC. 12-1

1) Fill an array with the numbers 1, 2, 3, 4, 5, 6, 7, 23, 51, 47, 56, and 234 and fill another array of the same dimensions with the numbers 2, −3, 43, 90, 45, 32, −89, 65, 43, −96, 0, and 1. Fill a third array of the same dimensions with the sums of the numbers in order. The sum array should contain the numbers 3, −1, 46, 94, etc.

2) Use the data of problem 1). Dimension a 3 by 12 array. MAT READ the above data into the first two rows and 0's into the third row and then replace the 0's with the sums of the entries in the first two rows column by column.

3) Fill an array with the multiplication table up to 12 × 12. MAT PRINT the result.

4) Fill a 4 by 3 array with the following numbers: 2, 56, 78, 3, 20, 45, 3, 9, 673, 564, 90, and 234. Have the computer multiply each number in the array by 3 and enter the product to replace the old number. Print the result.

5) Use the data of problem 4), but this time multiply each entry by the product of the row and column number. MAT PRINT the result.

6) Fill a 2 by 5 array with the following numbers: 3, 67, 32, 45, 90, 2, 9, 57, —3, and 1. Multiply each entry by —3 if the sum of the row and column numbers is odd and by —1 if the sum of the row and column numbers is even. Print the result.

7) Fill a square array so that the locations along the top left to bottom right diagonal are filled with 1's and all other entries are 0's. MAT PRINT the array.

8) Fill an array with all 1's and print it.

9) Have the computer read the following array:

```
1    6    11

2    7    12

3    8    13

4    9    14

5    10   15
```

and have it create the new array:

```
1    2    3    4    5

6    7    8    9    10

11   12   13   14   15
```

10) Fill a 2 by 8 array with all 0's and print it.

11) A company has salesmen on the road four days a week. At the end of each week each salesman turns in an expense sheet. Here is a sample expense sheet:

	Mon.	Tue.	Wed.	Thur.
Lodging	$12.00	$11.00	$10.50	$14.00
Meals	$ 4.00	$ 7.50	$ 6.90	$ 7.40
Transportation	$ 2.00	0	0	$ 3.50
Customer entertainment	0	$18.00	$ 4.50	$ 4.50
Miscellaneous	$ 2.31	$ 1.84	$ 3.15	$ 1.83

Write a program that will find total expenses for the week, total expenses for each day of the week, and total expenses in each of the five categories listed on the expense sheet.

12-2   SOLVING A PROBLEM

To get from a certain town to another town one must travel over a toll road, through a toll tunnel, and over a toll bridge. At the beginning of the trip there is a sign posted, listing the rates as in Table 12-1.

TABLE 12-1.

	Tolls per Vehicle		
	Road	Tunnel	Bridge
Trucks	$6.00	$3.00	$2.00
Buses	$5.00	$3.00	$2.00
Passenger Cars	$4.00	$3.00	$2.00
Motorcycles	$3.00	$2.00	$1.00

On a particular day there were five caravans which traveled this route. The caravans consisted of different types of vehicles as shown in Table 12-2.

TABLE 12-2.

	Vehicles per Caravan			
	Trucks	Buses	Cars	Cycles
Caravan 1	1	3	4	2
Caravan 2	1	5	3	6
Caravan 3	2	4	2	5
Caravan 4	1	6	3	2
Caravan 5	3	1	0	2

The Road Commission would like to have a report which would include the amount each caravan paid in tolls at each toll booth. The problem will be solved, when we are able to fill in Table 12-3.

TABLE 12-3.

	Tolls Paid		
	Road	Tunnel	Bridge
Caravan 1	A	B	C
Caravan 2	D	E	F
Caravan 3	G	H	I
Caravan 4	J	K	L
Caravan 5	M	N	Ø

Before we actually attempt the problem solution, let us write just the portion of our program that we will use later, which will read the data into two arrays. One array, which we call A, stores the values of Table 12-1, the other array, which we call B, stores the values of Table 12-2. Then let us print the two arrays with headings so that we may later concentrate on the actual problem solution, having taken care of the mechanics of getting the data into the proper arrays. Taken by itself, the task of getting the data into the two arrays is reasonably straightforward. See program TØLL-1.

```
TØLL-1

20   DIM A[4,3],B[5,4]
40 , MAT   READ A
60 ' DATA  6,3,2,5,3,2,4,3,2,3,2,1
80   PRINT "TØLLS PER VEHICLE"
100   PRINT "RØAD  TUNL  BRIDGE"
120   MAT  PRINT A;
140   MAT  READ B
160   DATA  1,3,4,2,1,5,3,6,2,4,2,5,1,6,3,2,3,1,0,2
180   PRINT "VEHICLES PER CARAVAN"
200   PRINT "TRUCK BUS   CARS  MØTØRCYCLES"
220   MAT  PRINT B;
240   END
RUN
TØLL-1


TØLLS PER VEHICLE
RØAD   TUNL   BRIDGE
  6      3      2

  5      3      2

  4      3      2

  3      2      1

VEHICLES PER CARAVAN
TRUCK BUS    CARS  MØTØRCYCLES
  1      3      4      2

  1      5      3      6

  2      4      2      5

  1      6      3      2

  3      1      0      2


DØNE
```

Writing the program in parts like this will help us isolate any errors that we might encounter while writing the program. We may now strike out lines 80, 100, 120, 180, 200, and 220 as we will not need these values printed again.

Now to tackle the problem itself. We can find out how much Caravan 1 paid at the road toll booth. It had one truck which paid $6, three buses at $5 each for $15, four cars at $4 each for $16, and two motorcycles at $3 each for $6. Totaling 1 ° 6, 3 ° 5, 4 ° 4, and 2 ° 3 we get $43. So, $43 is the value of A in Table 12-3. How much did Caravan 1 pay at the tunnel? It paid 1 ° 3 for the truck, 3 ° 3 for the buses, 4 ° 3 for the cars, and 2 ° 2 for the motorcycles for a total of $28, which is the value of B in Table 12-3. We repeat this process at the bridge substituting 2, 2, 2, and 1 for 3, 3, 3, and 2 and sum up 1 ° 2, 3 ° 2, 4 ° 2, and 2 ° 1 getting a total of $18 for the value of C in Table 12-3. Then we would go to Caravan 2 and step through the road tolls, then the tunnel tolls, and finally the bridge tolls. Then on to the next caravan until we have gotten results for all the five caravans. This is just the kind of repetitive process that we use the computer for.

We will find it helpful to think of Table 12-3 as an array with C[I, J] as the values of the entries rather than A, B, . . . , M, N, Ø. Calling that array C we get C[1, 1] = A, C[1, 2] = B, etc. down to C[5, 3] = Ø.

Note that after we step across row 1 in MAT B and down column 1 in MAT A, the final sum is entered in row 1 and column 1 of MAT C. When we step across row 1 of MAT B and down column 2 of MAT A, the sum is entered in row 1 column 2 of MAT C. You should see that stepping across row R of MAT B and down column C of MAT A results in a sum that is entered in row R, column C of MAT C. Note too, that the row headings of MAT B correspond to the row headings of MAT C and the column headings of MAT A correspond to the column headings of MAT C, and that the row headings of MAT A and the column headings of MAT B coincide. With some experimentation, you should be able to convince yourself that this is a natural consequence of the problem and not mere coincidence for this particular set of data. If you change the number of toll booths, all of the above statements still hold.

Summarizing, we have just tried to establish that we sum up the following products:

$$B[R, X] \text{ ° } A[X, C] \tag{12-1}$$

where R is the row number in MAT B, C is the column number in MAT A, and X goes from 1 to the number of columns in MAT B which is the same as the number of rows in MAT A. Having found the sum of all products in Eq. (12-1) for a fixed [R, C] pair, we enter that sum in C[R, C]. We do this for all rows of MAT B and all columns of MAT A.

You should run through the calculations by hand with pencil and paper to verify the procedure and to become more familiar with it. We draw a flowchart in Fig. 12-1 and call the program TØLL-2.

PROBLEMS FOR SEC. 12-2

1) Suppose on a particular day there were four caravans. Caravan 1 had one truck, Caravan 2 had one bus, Caravan 3 had one car, and Caravan 4 had one motorcycle. Have the computer print the amounts that each caravan paid at each toll booth.

2) Suppose there were no vehicles on a particular day. What would the Road Commission report look like?

3) Suppose there were three caravans, each having one vehicle of each type. Print the schedule of payments for this situation.

4) On a given day there were four caravans. Caravan 1 had one motorcycle, Caravan 2 had one car, Caravan 3 had one bus, and Caravan 4 had one truck. Have the computer print the schedule of payments.

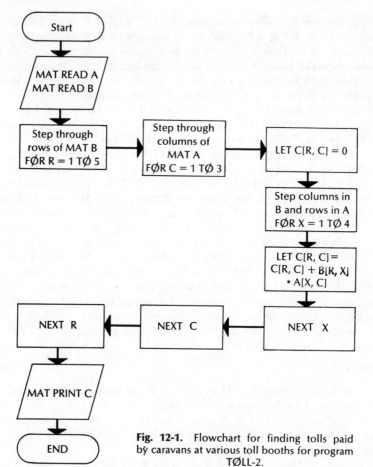

Fig. 12-1. Flowchart for finding tolls paid by caravans at various toll booths for program TØLL-2.

TØLL-2

```
20    DIM A[4,3],B[5,4]
25    DIM C[5,3]
40    MAT   READ A
60    DATA 6,3,2,5,3,2,4,3,2,3,2,1
140   MAT   READ B
160   DATA 1,3,4,2,1,5,3,6,2,4,2,5,1,6,3,2,3,1,0,2
235   REM   WE STEP THRØUGH RØWS ØF B   THE CARAVANS
240   FØR R=1 TØ 5
255   REM WE STEP THRØUGH CØLUMNS ØF   MAT A
256   REM    THE TØLL BØØTH IDENTIFICATIØN
260   FØR C=1 TØ 3
275   REM   INITIALIZE  C[R,C]  HERE
280   LET C[R,C]=0
295   REM  X  STEPS THRØUGH THE RØWS ØF A AND THE CØLUMNS ØF B
296   REM    THERE WE FIND 'TRUCKS BUSES CARS MØTØRCYCLES'
297   REM   IN EACH ARRAY
300   FØR X=1 TØ 4
320   LET C[R,C]=C[R,C]+B[R,X]*A[X,C]
335   REM  GØ TØ THE NEXT CØLUMN ØF B AND THE NEXT RØW ØF A
340   NEXT X
```

```
355   REM  GØ  TØ  THE  NEXT  CØLUMN  ØF   MAT  A
360   NEXT  C
375   REM   GØ  TØ  THE  NEXT  RØW  ØF  MAT  B
380   NEXT  R
500   PRINT  "RØAD", "TUNNEL", "BRIDGE"
520   MAT   PRINT  C
999   END
RUN
TØLL-2
```

RØAD	TUNNEL	BRIDGE
43	28	18
61	39	24
55	34	21
54	34	22
29	16	10

DØNE

5) Let

$$A = \begin{bmatrix} 1 & 2 & 3 \\ 4 & 5 & 6 \\ 7 & 8 & 9 \\ 10 & 11 & 12 \end{bmatrix} \quad \text{and} \quad B = \begin{bmatrix} 1 & 2 & 3 & 4 \\ 5 & 6 & 7 & 8 \end{bmatrix}$$

Perform the operations of this section to get MAT C.

6) Suppose we let

$$A = \begin{bmatrix} 1 & 2 & 3 & 4 \\ 5 & 6 & 7 & 8 \end{bmatrix} \quad \text{and} \quad B = \begin{bmatrix} 10 & 11 & 12 & 13 \\ 14 & 15 & 16 & 17 \end{bmatrix}$$

Why could not we perform the set of operations of program TØLL-2?

12-3 OPERATIONS AND SPECIAL MATRICES

While the MAT operations have specialized and rigid definitions in matrix algebra, we will find at times that some of the MAT capabilities will help us in writing programs not deeply involved in a matrix algebra setting. It is the purpose of this section to list the MAT capabilities, but not to develop the matrix algebra to any great extent. For such a treatment, you should see any text in advanced algebra.

Multiplication

The requirements of the Road Commission report in Sec. 12-2 led us to evolve a set of steps that occurs often in both applied and theoretical mathematics. The set of steps carried out there exactly fits the definition of matrix multiplication. Using the array names of Sec. 12-2, we define the product of B and A as the array C, which is written as $C = B \ ^\circ \ A$.

From the discussion in Sec. 12-2, we should see that the dimensioning must conform as

B[R, M] ° A[M, C] = C[R, C]

Calling for a product of two nonconforming matrices will generate an error message from the computer. The program statement for multiplication is

XXX   MAT C = B ° A

We may now have the computer do everything from lines 240 through 380 with a single statement. Having worked through the operation in considerable detail in Sec. 12-2, you should have little difficulty in having the dimensions correctly provided for. See TØLL-3.

```
TØLL-3

20   DIM A[4,3],B[5,4]
25   DIM C[5,3]
40   MAT   READ A
60   DATA  6,3,2,5,3,2,4,3,2,3,2,1
140  MAT   READ B
160  DATA  1,3,4,2,1,5,3,6,2,4,2,5,1,6,3,2,3,1,0,2
200  MAT C=B*A
210  PRINT "RØAD","TUNNEL","BRIDGE"
230  MAT   PRINT C
999  END
RUN
TØLL-3
```

RØAD	TUNNEL	BRIDGE
43	28	18
61	39	24
55	34	21
54	34	22
29	16	10

```
DØNE
```

Addition and Subtraction

Some past problems have asked you to add two arrays. For two arrays of the same dimensions, the sum is defined as an array containing the sums of corresponding entries of the given arrays. In other words, for all I, J pairs, $S[I, J] = A[I, J] + B[I, J]$, where the sum array is S. Matrix addition is accomplished with the program statement

XXX   MAT S = A + B

or   XXX   MAT A = A + B

may be used if you no longer need MAT A.

Subtraction is defined just as you would expect. For A − B, the difference must be an array so that for all I, J pairs, $D[I, J] = A[I, J] − B[I, J]$. The program statement is

XXX   MAT D = A − B

or   XXX   MAT A = A − B

Neither addition nor subtraction is defined for arrays of different dimensions.

Scalar Multiplication

You may multiply each element of an array by some constant or algebraic expression using

XXX   MAT Z = (SIN(G)) ° X

which multiplies every entry in MAT X by SIN(G) and enters the product in MAT Z.

Equality

A matrix may be created to be identical to an already existing matrix by

XXX   MAT P = Q   (12-2)

or, in systems which do not permit Eq. (12-2), you should be able to achieve the same result by

XXX   MAT P = (1) ° Q

Special MAT's

There are three special matrices available with a single assignment statement in BASIC. They are

XXX MAT A = ZER		(12-3A)
XXX MAT B = ZER[R, C]		(12-3B)
YYY MAT C = CØN		(12-4A)
YYY MAT D = CØN[R, C]		(12-4B)
ZZZ MAT E = IDN		(12-5A)
ZZZ MAT F = IDN[N, N]		(12-5B)

Equation (12-3A) sets all entries in MAT A equal to 0 according to previously determined dimensions, while Eq. (12-3B) sets the dimensions of B at [R, C] and fills MAT B with 0's. Equation (12-3B) is often used to change the dimensions of a matrix during the RUN of a program.

Equation (12-4A) sets all entries in MAT C equal to 1 according to previously determined dimensions, while Eq. (12-4B) sets the dimensions of MAT D at [R, C] and fills it with 1's.

Equation (12-5A) requires that MAT E be a square array, and fills the upper left to lower right diagonal with 1's and all other locations with 0's. Equation (12-5B) has the same effect as Eq. (12-5A), but the dimensions are set at [N, N]. The matrix created in this form is called an *identity matrix*. Program MATSP1 is intended to show how these special arrays are established.

```
MATSP1

10   DIM A[2,4],B[2,12],C[10,11]
20   PRINT "MAT A=ZER ** PREVIØUSLY DIMENSIØNED AT 2BY4"
30   MAT A=ZER
40   MAT   PRINT A
50   PRINT "MAT B=CØN[3,7]"
60   MAT B=CØN[3,7]
70   MAT   PRINT B;
80   PRINT "MAT C=IDN[4,4]"
90   MAT C=IDN[4,4]
100  MAT   PRINT C;
110  PRINT "MAT A=CØN[1,6]"
120  MAT A=CØN[1,6]
130  MAT   PRINT A;
140  END
RUN
MATSP1

MAT A=ZER ** PREVIØUSLY DIMENSIØNED AT 2BY4
 0          0          0          0

 0          0          0          0

MAT B=CØN[3,7]
 1     1     1     1     1     1     1

 1     1     1     1     1     1     1

 1     1     1     1     1     1     1

MAT C=IDN[4,4]
 1     0     0     0

 0     1     0     0

 0     0     1     0

 0     0     0     1

MAT A=CØN[1,6]
 1     1     1     1     1     1

 DØNE
```

SUMMARY

We have introduced the matrix operations—multiplication, addition, subtraction, and scalar multiplication. The special matrices ZER, CØN, and IDN have been specified.

PROBLEMS FOR SEC. 12-3

1) Redo program TØTAL using a row vector for the numbers of items and a column vector for the prices. Obtain the total cost with a single MAT statement.

2) Have the computer find the product of

$$\begin{bmatrix} 1 & 3 & -2 & -1 \\ 2 & -3 & 1 & -3 \\ -7 & 5 & -1 & 11 \\ 3 & -1 & 1 & -1 \end{bmatrix} \text{ and } \begin{bmatrix} -1 \\ 2 \\ -3 \\ 4 \end{bmatrix}$$

If we think of the above as

$$\begin{bmatrix} 1 & 3 & -2 & -1 \\ 2 & -3 & 1 & -3 \\ -7 & 5 & -1 & 11 \\ 3 & -1 & 1 & -1 \end{bmatrix} \quad \text{and} \quad \begin{bmatrix} W \\ X \\ Y \\ Z \end{bmatrix}$$

then we are really finding the values of $W + 3X - 2Y - Z$, $2W - 3X + Y - 3Z$, $-7W + 5X - Y + 11Z$, and $3W - X + Y - Z$.

3) Multiply

$$\begin{bmatrix} 0 & 0 & 1 \\ 0 & 0 & 2 \\ 0 & 0 & 3 \end{bmatrix} \quad \text{by} \quad \begin{bmatrix} 5 & 7 & -5 \\ 4 & 5 & 3 \\ 0 & 0 & 0 \end{bmatrix}$$

and multiply

$$\begin{bmatrix} 0 & 0 & 1 \\ 0 & 0 & 2 \\ 0 & 0 & 3 \end{bmatrix} \quad \text{by} \quad \begin{bmatrix} 5 & 6 & 2 \\ 4 & 1 & 3 \\ 0 & 0 & 0 \end{bmatrix}$$

Any conclusions about the matrix of 0's?

4) Let

$$A = \begin{bmatrix} 3 & 12 \\ 1 & 4 \end{bmatrix} \quad \text{and} \quad B = \begin{bmatrix} -12 & 28 \\ 3 & -7 \end{bmatrix}$$

Find the product A ° B and the product B ° A. What do you conclude?

5) Let

$$A = \begin{bmatrix} 1 & 2 \\ 3 & 4 \end{bmatrix} \quad B = \begin{bmatrix} -1 & -2 \\ 5 & 3 \end{bmatrix} \quad C = \begin{bmatrix} 2 & -11 \\ 25 & 31 \end{bmatrix}$$

Find [A ° B] ° C and A ° [B ° C].

6) Using A, B, and C from problem 5), find A ° [B + C] and A ° B + A ° C.

7) Multiply

$$\begin{bmatrix} 1 & 2 & -1 \\ 2 & -1 & 3 \\ 7 & -2 & 4 \end{bmatrix} \quad \text{by} \quad \begin{bmatrix} .08 & -.24 & .2 \\ .52 & .44 & -.2 \\ .12 & .64 & -.2 \end{bmatrix}$$

8) Let

$$A = \begin{bmatrix} -2 & 1 \\ 1.5 & -.5 \end{bmatrix} \quad \text{and} \quad B = \begin{bmatrix} 1 & 2 \\ 3 & 4 \end{bmatrix}$$

Find A ° B and B ° A.

√ 9) Write a program to raise a matrix to a power. Let the power be determined by an item of data.

10) Enter the integers 1 through 12 into a row vector and into a column vector, using MAT READ. (You can avoid typing the data twice by using RESTØRE.) Find the 12 by 12 product matrix and print it.

12-4 SOLVING SIMULTANEOUS LINEAR EQUATIONS

You should see that the matrix equation

$$\begin{bmatrix} A_1 & B_1 & C_1 \\ A_2 & B_2 & C_2 \\ A_3 & B_3 & C_3 \end{bmatrix} \bullet \begin{bmatrix} X \\ Y \\ Z \end{bmatrix} = \begin{bmatrix} D_1 \\ D_2 \\ D_3 \end{bmatrix} \tag{12-6}$$

can be multiplied out on the left-hand side to obtain

$$\begin{bmatrix} A_1X + B_1Y + C_1Z \\ A_2X + B_2Y + C_2Z \\ A_3X + B_3Y + C_3Z \end{bmatrix} = \begin{bmatrix} D_1 \\ D_2 \\ D_3 \end{bmatrix} \tag{12-7}$$

Defining equality for two matrices as existing if and only if for all I, J pairs the entry of one matrix equals the corresponding entry of the other, or for MAT A and MAT B, $A[I, J] = B[I, J]$, we may say that

$$A_1X + B_1Y + C_1Z = D_1$$
$$A_2X + B_2Y + C_2Z = D_2 \tag{12-8}$$
$$A_3X + B_3Y + C_3Z = D_3$$

which constitutes a system of three linear equations.

Equations (12-6), (12-7), and (12-8) are simply three different ways of writing the same set of equations. If we can find the values of X, Y, and Z in Eq. (12-6), we will have solved the set of linear equations in Eq. (12-8).

Let us rewrite Eq. (12-6) as

$$C \bullet S = K$$

where

$$C = \begin{bmatrix} A_1 & B_1 & C_1 \\ A_2 & B_2 & C_2 \\ A_3 & B_3 & C_3 \end{bmatrix} \qquad S = \begin{bmatrix} X \\ Y \\ Z \end{bmatrix} \qquad K = \begin{bmatrix} D_1 \\ D_2 \\ D_3 \end{bmatrix}$$

It would be very convenient if we could just divide both sides by C. But it turns out that the division of one matrix by another is not an easily describable process. However, we may instead multiply each side by the multiplicative inverse of C. We write that as C^{-1}. Doing that we get

$$S = C^{-1} \bullet K$$

We note here without elaboration, the following facts:

1) In order to have an inverse, a matrix must be square.
2) Not all matrices have inverses.
3) The product of a square matrix and its inverse is the identity matrix.

To see more clearly what the inverse of a matrix is, let us find the inverse of

$$\begin{bmatrix} 5 & 6 \\ 7 & 8 \end{bmatrix}$$

We may call its inverse the matrix with entries A, B, C, and D such that

$$\begin{bmatrix} A & B \\ C & D \end{bmatrix} \cdot \begin{bmatrix} 5 & 6 \\ 7 & 8 \end{bmatrix} = \begin{bmatrix} 1 & 0 \\ 0 & 1 \end{bmatrix}$$

Finding the product on the left, we get

$$\begin{bmatrix} 5A + 7B & 6A + 8B \\ 5C + 7D & 6C + 8D \end{bmatrix} = \begin{bmatrix} 1 & 0 \\ 0 & 1 \end{bmatrix}$$

Two matrices are equal if their corresponding entries are equal. So we get the following four equations:

$$5A + 7B = 1 \qquad 6A + 8B = 0$$
$$5C + 7D = 0 \qquad 6C + 8D = 1$$

Solving these for A, B, C, and D we get A $= -4$, B $= 3$, C $= 3.5$, and D $= -2.5$. So

$$\begin{bmatrix} 5 & 6 \\ 7 & 8 \end{bmatrix}^{-1} = \begin{bmatrix} -4 & 3 \\ 3.5 & -2.5 \end{bmatrix}$$

BASIC provides a statement to find the inverse of a square matrix, if it exists. After we have arranged for proper dimensioning, we may use

XXX   MAT X = INV(A)

```
MATINV

10   DIM X[2,2],A[2,2],P[2,2]
20   MAT  READ A
30   MAT X=INV(A)
40   PRINT "ORIGINAL MATRIX"
50   MAT  PRINT A;
60   PRINT "INVERSE MATRIX"
70   MAT  PRINT X;
80   PRINT "THE PRODUCT IS"
90   MAT P=X*A
100  MAT  PRINT P;
110  DATA 5,6,7,8
120  END
RUN
MATINV

ORIGINAL MATRIX
 5     6

 7     8

INVERSE MATRIX
-4.          3.

 3.5         -2.5

THE PRODUCT IS
 1     0

 0     1

DONE
```

and matrix X will be the inverse of matrix A. We may easily verify our calculations for finding the inverse above. See MATINV.

(You are cautioned that the computer may be susceptible to slight errors when using the INV( ) statement.)

So with the MAT INV( ), we should be able to solve sets of simultaneous linear equations such as the following:

$$4W - X + 2Y + 3Z = -3 \tag{12-9A}$$
$$-W + 4X + 2Y = -15 \tag{12-9B}$$
$$W + 2X - Y + 3Z = -3 \tag{12-9C}$$
$$-4W + 3X + 2Y + Z = -17 \tag{12-9D}$$

We let

$$C = \begin{bmatrix} 4 & -1 & 2 & 3 \\ -1 & 4 & 2 & 0 \\ 1 & 2 & -1 & 3 \\ -4 & 3 & 2 & 1 \end{bmatrix}$$

where C is usually referred to as the *coefficient matrix*, and we let

$$K = \begin{bmatrix} -3 \\ -15 \\ -3 \\ -17 \end{bmatrix}$$

Now we can read the data into two matrices C and K, have the computer find the inverse of C, and multiply it by K to get matrix S consisting of the values for W, X, Y, and Z, which satisfy Eq. (12-9). See program SØLVE.

```
SØLVE

10   DIM C[4,4],K[4,1],S[4,1],I[4,4]
20   MAT   READ C,K
30   MAT I=INV(C)
40   MAT S=I*K
50   PRINT "SØLUTIØNS:"
60   MAT   PRINT S
70   DATA 4,-1,2,3,-1,4,2,0,1,2,-1,3,-4,3,2,1,-3,-15,-3,-17
80   END
RUN
SØLVE

SØLUTIØNS:
 1.

-2

-3.

-1


DØNE
```

The column vector

is to be interpreted as, $W = 1$, $X = -2$, $Y = -3$, and $Z = -1$. We may now substitute these values in Eq. (12-9) to verify that they do in fact constitute the unique solution.

SUMMARY

We have seen that sets of simultaneous linear equations may be solved by considering an equivalent matrix equation $C \circ X = K$, where C is the coefficient matrix, X is a column vector which contains the values of the variables in the original set of linear equations, and K is a column vector containing the constant terms in the original set of linear equations. We may solve for X by finding the inverse of matrix C, so that $X = C^{-1} \circ K$. The inverse may be found with the BASIC statement MAT $I = INV(C)$. For systems of simultaneous linear equations having a unique solution, MAT C will always be square, which is one of the requirements for having an inverse.

PROBLEMS FOR SEC. 12-4

1) Let
$$A = \begin{bmatrix} 4 & -4 & 4 \\ 1 & 1 & 7 \\ -3 & 9 & -8 \end{bmatrix}$$
Find and print A^{-1}, $A \circ A^{-1}$, and $A^{-1} \circ A$.

2) Let
$$B = \begin{bmatrix} -8 & -3 \\ 0 & -1 \end{bmatrix}$$
Find B^{-1} and print it. Verify by hand-computing the inverse of B. Find and print $B \circ B^{-1}$ and $B^{-1} \circ B$.

3) Solve for X and Y:
$$-2X - 5Y = -16$$
$$- X + 4Y = 31$$

4) Solve for X, Y, and Z:
$$2X - 9Y - 5Z = 2$$
$$7X - 6Y + 5Z = -35$$
$$9X - 6Y + 5Z = -39$$

5) Solve for X, Y, and Z:

$$3X + 4Y + Z = 7$$
$$5X - 6Y + 3Z = 8$$
$$3X + 4Y + Z = -3$$

6) Solve for W, X, Y, and Z:

$$6W + 3X + 6Y + 5Z = -12$$
$$-7W + 5X - 7Y - Z = 77$$
$$-3W + X + 3Y + 6Z = 31$$
$$-2W - 4X + 4Y - 7Z = -76$$

7) Solve for W, X, Y, and Z:

$$-3W + 6X - 5Y - Z = -32$$
$$W + 9X - 5Y - 2Z = 9$$
$$W + 6Y + 5Z = 2$$
$$-7W + 4X - Y + 5Z = -86$$

8) Solve for X, Y, and Z:

$$2X + 4Y - 3Z = -11.9$$
$$-9X - 3Y = 58.5$$
$$-9X + 8Y + 5Z = 66.6$$

9) Solve for V, W, X, Y, and Z:

$$7V + 6W - 3X - Y + 9Z = 26.3$$
$$-9V + 2W + 9X + 5Y + Z = 91.1$$
$$-3V + 4W + 5X + 5Z = 62.9$$
$$6V - 8X - 2Y - 6Z = -55.6$$
$$-3V - 9W + 5X + 7Y + 3Z = -25.9$$

10) Let

$$A = \begin{bmatrix} 1 & -2 & 3 \\ 5 & -1 & -2 \\ 0 & 3 & 4 \end{bmatrix} \quad \text{and} \quad B = \begin{bmatrix} 2 & -4 & 0 \\ -3 & 1 & 2 \\ 5 & 2 & -5 \end{bmatrix}$$

Find and print $(A \circ B)^{-1}$ and $B^{-1} \circ A^{-1}$.

√ 11) Write a program that can solve sets of simultaneous linear equations having different numbers of equations. Have an item of data that is the number of equations and redimension all matrices accordingly.

12-5 TRANSPOSE OF A MATRIX

Suppose you have just solved a set of 10 simultaneous linear equations. The 10 values of the 10 unknowns are entered into a column vector that is called X in Sec. 12-4. Calling for MAT PRINT X prints the 10 values down the page with a blank line between every two. This takes up a lot of space. It might be convenient to enter these same values in a row vector and MAT PRINT that on one line. What we want is to create a new matrix whose row corresponds to the column of the matrix X and whose columns correspond to the rows of matrix X, i.e., an exchange of rows and columns. Of course we could make the exchange element by element or we could do the printing entry by entry, but both are unnecessary. BASIC provides a program statement to perform this set of exchanges. XXX MAT A = TRN(B) fills matrix A so that its rows correspond to the columns of B and its columns correspond to the rows of B. This set of exchanges creates a matrix called the *transpose* of B. We write the transpose of B as B^t.

As noted earlier, the transpose will enable us to have more compact printing in some programs. The transpose also introduces some matrix properties of theoretical interest. Some of these properties may be suggested by the exercises.

TRPØS1 is simply a demonstration program that finds and prints the transpose of a 10-element column vector.

```
TRPØS1

8   REM    A IS A CØLUMN VECTØR AND B IS A RØW VECTØR
10  DIM A[10,1],B[1,10]
20  MAT    READ A
30  DATA 1,2,3,4,5,6,7,8,9,10
40  MAT B=TRN(A)
45  PRINT "TRANSPØSE ØF CØLUMN VECTØR A"
50  MAT   PRINT B;
60  END
RUN
TRPØS1

TRANSPØSE ØF CØLUMN VECTØR A
 1      2      3      4      5      6      7      8      9      10


DØNE
```

The transpose differs from the inverse in that every matrix has a transpose. If MAT A has M rows and N columns, then A^t has N rows and M columns. Let us write a second demonstration program to print a 2 by 4 matrix and its transpose. See TRPØS2.

```
TRPØS2

10  DIM A[2,4],B[4,2]
20  PRINT "2 BY 4 MATRIX"
30  MAT    READ A
40  MAT    PRINT A;
50  MAT B=TRN(A)
60  PRINT "TRANSPØSE ØF THE ABØVE MATRIX"
70  MAT    PRINT B;
80  DATA 3,6,1,-5,0,18,999,11
90  END
```

```
RUN
TRPOS2

2 BY 4 MATRIX
 3     6     1    -5

 0    18   999    11

TRANSPOSE OF THE ABOVE MATRIX
 3     0

 6    18

 1   999

-5    11

DONE
```

MAT X = TRN(Y)
    Creates a matrix X so that for all I, J pairs, X[I, J] = Y[J, I]. Dimensions must be correctly provided for. X is called the transpose of Y.

PROBLEMS FOR SEC. 12-5

1) Let

$$A = \begin{bmatrix} 1 & -2 & 3 \\ 2 & 1 & -4 \\ -3 & 4 & 1 \end{bmatrix}$$

Find and print A^t, $A^t + A$, and $A^t - A$.

2) Let

$$A = \begin{bmatrix} 5 & 3 & 1 \\ 6 & -2 & 9 \\ 3 & 9 & 1 \end{bmatrix}$$

Print A^t, $A + A^t$, $A - A^t$, and $A^t - A$.

3) Let

$$A = \begin{bmatrix} 1 & 2 \\ 3 & 4 \end{bmatrix}$$

Let $B = A^t$ and let $C = A^{-1}$. Print B^{-1} and C^t.

4) Let

$$A = \begin{bmatrix} 2 & -1 & 3 \\ 5 & 0 & 8 \\ -3 & 4 & 2 \end{bmatrix} \quad \text{and} \quad B = \begin{bmatrix} 6 & 3 & 8 \\ 9 & 5 & 4 \\ 11 & -2 & 0 \end{bmatrix}$$

Print $[A * B]^t$, $B^t * A^t$, and $A^t * B^t$.

CHAPTER 13

Elementary Probability

13-1 INTRODUCTION

It is the purpose of this chapter to introduce some fundamental concepts of probability and to develop program routines for some of these applications.

Taking an intuitive approach to probability, we may think of rolling a die. The term *experiment* is used to describe a particular trial, or in the case of rolling a die, an experiment is the actual rolling of the die. The *outcome* is the number that comes up. There are six possible outcomes for rolling a die. We may say that the probability of the die coming up 2 is one in six or ⅙, because there is only one 2 and there are six different numbers, each of which is equally likely to come up. We refer to the outcome we are looking for as a success and all others as failure. We define probability so that the probability of success P added to the probability of failure Q is 1, or $P + Q = 1$.

Often our requirements for success permit more than one single outcome, all of which are equally likely to occur. We define probability as the quotient of the number of outcomes that constitute success and the total possible number of outcomes:

$P = S/T$

where P is the probability of success, S is the number of outcomes that constitute success, and T is the total number of possible outcomes. All outcomes are equally likely to occur.

So, before we work with probability, we will have to develop ways of counting the numbers of outcomes of various kinds of experiments.

13-2 ENUMERATION

Fundamental Principle of Enumeration

The Fundamental Principle of Enumeration states that, if one choice can occur in A ways and then a second choice can occur in B ways, the total number of ways that the two choices may occur is the product of A and B, or A * B.

197

So, if you are going to buy a car that comes in five models and seven colors, the number of cars you have to choose from is 5 * 7, or 35. The Fundamental Principle of Enumeration may be extended to cover any number of choices so that, if in buying the car you also may choose airconditioning and whitewalls and you have four engines from which to choose, the number of cars available is 5 * 7 * 2 * 2 * 4, or 560.

Permutations

How many four-letter combinations may be formed using the letters of the word FLAG each used once?

We could approach this problem in one of several ways. We could sit down with pencil and paper and try to write them all, or we might write a program to write them all.

The techniques required for this vary so greatly from system to system that we will not present the program, but only the RUN.

```
RUN
FLAG

FLAG  FLGA  FALG  FAGL  FGLA  FGAL
LFAG  LFGA  LAFG  LAGF  LGFA  LGAF
AFLG  AFGL  ALFG  ALGF  AGFL  AGLF
GFLA  GFAL  GLFA  GLAF  GAFL  GALF

DONE
```

We can easily see that the number of different combinations is 24. Each of the combinations listed is a permutation of the four letters F, L, A, and G, and each is different from the others because the letters are in a different order. In other words, when we talk about permutations, order matters.

One other approach to solving the original problem will lead us to a more general enumeration technique. We observe that to form a four-letter word using four different letters once, we may use any one of the four letters for the first letter. Now there are only three letters left from which to choose the second letter, two left from which to pick the third letter, and finally we have exactly one letter for the fourth letter of the new word. Using the Fundamental Principle of Enumeration, there are four choices. The first can occur in four ways, the second can occur in three ways, the third in two ways, and the fourth in one way. This makes 4 * 3 * 2 * 1 or 24, ways that the four choices can occur.

This kind of calculation occurs often in mathematics and so is given a special name. 4 * 3 * 2 * 1 is called *4 factorial* written as 4! . In general,

$$N(N - 1)(N - 2) \cdots (2)(1) = N!$$

where N is a positive integer. Let us write a routine to compute factorials (see program N!).

```
N !

10    PRINT "FIND THE FACTORIAL OF";
20    INPUT N
30    LET F=1
40    FOR X=N TO 1 STEP -1
50    LET F=F*X
60    NEXT X
70    PRINT N;"FACTORIAL =";F
80    END
RUN
N !

FIND THE FACTORIAL OF?4
   4    FACTORIAL = 24

DONE
```

Of course for larger integers, N! becomes very large.

```
RUN
N !

FIND THE FACTORIAL OF?20
  20    FACTORIAL = 2.43290E+18

DONE
```

Suppose we want to find the number of three-letter words that can be formed from the letters of the word COMPUTER without duplication. For the first letter we may pick from among eight, for the second we may pick from among seven, and for the third we may pick from among the remaining six letters. This makes 8 ° 7 ° 6, or 336, different words. Since the order is different, these are 336 different permutations. Notice that

$$8 \cdot 7 \cdot 6 = \frac{8 \cdot 7 \cdot 6 \cdot 5 \cdot 4 \cdot 3 \cdot 2 \cdot 1}{5 \cdot 4 \cdot 3 \cdot 2 \cdot 1} = \frac{8!}{5!} = \frac{8!}{(8-3)!}$$

We should see that for the number of arrangements of R letters taken from among N different letters with no duplications we get $N!/(N-R)!$. This defines the number of permutations of N things taken R at a time written as

$$_N P_R = \frac{N!}{(N-R)!} \tag{13-1}$$

Writing the right side of Eq. (13-1) as the quotient of products, we get

$$_N P_R = \frac{N(N-1)(N-2) \cdots (N-R+1)(N-R)(N-R-1) \cdots (2)(1)}{(N-R)(N-R-1) \cdots (2)(1)}$$

Dividing we get

$$_N P_R = N(N-1) \cdots (N-R+1)$$

which is ideal for computing with a loop that goes from N to $N-R+1$ STEP -1. See line 40 of program NPR.

```
NPR

10   READ N,R
20   IF N=0 THEN 100
30   LET P=1
40   FØR X=N TØ N-R+1 STEP -1
50   LET P=P*X
60   NEXT X
70   PRINT N;"THINGS";R;"AT A TIME HAVE";P;"PERMUTATIØNS"
80   GØTØ 10
90   DATA 8,3,4,4,0,0
100  END
RUN
NPR

8    THINGS 3    AT A TIME HAVE 336  PERMUTATIØNS
4    THINGS 4    AT A TIME HAVE 24   PERMUTATIØNS

DØNE
```

Combinations

The distinction between combinations and permutations is order. For combinations, order does not matter. We may think of combinations as selections of items while permutations are arrangements. The number of combinations of four letters selected from among four letters is one. The number of combinations of N different things taken R at a time is written $_NC_R$. We may find the number of combinations of N things taken R at a time by looking at the number of permutations. Each combination of R things could be arranged in R! ways and that gives us the number of permutations. So

$$(_NC_R)(R!) = _NP_R$$

and solving for $_NC_R$ we get

$$_NC_R = \frac{_NP_R}{R!} = \frac{N!}{(R!)(N-R)!}$$

Thus, the number of combinations of three letters selected from eight different letters with no duplications is

$$_8C_3 = \frac{8!}{3!5!} = 56$$

while the number of permutations is

$$_8P_3 = 336$$

Combinations pertain to such things as committees and dealing cards where order does not matter.

If we want to know the number of five-member committees that can be selected from among 20 people, we get $_{20}C_5$. For the purpose of writing a computer program, we might think of $_{20}C_5$ as $_{20}P_5/R!$. One approach is to compute $_{20}P_5$ and then successively divide by the integers from 5 down to 1. Let us draw a flowchart (Fig. 13-1) and call the program NCR.

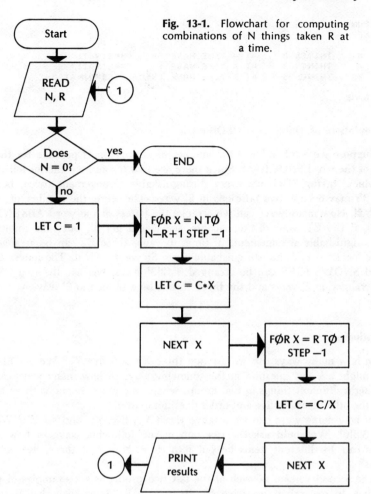

Fig. 13-1. Flowchart for computing combinations of N things taken R at a time.

```
NCR

10    READ N, R
20    IF N=0 THEN 150
30    LET C=1
40    REM 30 TO 50 FIND NPR
50    FOR X=N TO N-R+1 STEP -1
60    LET C=C*X
70    NEXT X
80    REM 60 TO 80 DIVIDE BY R!
90    FOR X=R TO 1 STEP -1
100   LET C=C/X
110   NEXT X
120   PRINT N;"THINGS";R;"AT A TIME HAVE";C;"COMBINATIONS"
130   GOTO 10
140   DATA 8,3,4,4,20,5,0,0
150   END
```

```
RUN
NCR

 8     THINGS 3    AT A TIME HAVE 56     COMBINATIONS
 4     THINGS 4    AT A TIME HAVE 1      COMBINATIONS
20     THINGS 5    AT A TIME HAVE 15504  COMBINATIONS

DONE
```

Permutations of Things Not All Different

Suppose we want to know the number of arrangements possible for the letters of the word PROGRAM. Since there are two R's and we cannot tell which is which, taking 7! counts every distinguishable arrangement twice, because the R's may occupy two positions in 2! ways. Therefore, the number of words is 7!/2!. How many ways can we arrange the letters of the word ABSENTEE? Well, if the E's were distinguishable, we would get 8!; but that counts the indistinguishable arrangements 3! times, because three E's can be arranged in three locations in 3! indistinguishable ways. So we get 8!/3!. The letters of the word SNOWSHOES can be arranged 9!/2!3! ways, because the two O's can be arranged in 2! ways and the three S's can be arranged in 3! ways.

Partitioning

In how many ways can we arrange three X's and five Y's? We get 8!/3!5!. We might ask this question in the following way: In how many ways can we put eight different things in two groups where one group contains three things and the other contains five and order does not matter?

In how many ways can we arrange three X's, five Y's, and six Z's? We get 14!/3!5!6!. We could ask the question in the following way: In how many ways can 14 different items be put into three groups of three, five, and six items?

The second version of each of the last two problems are examples of partitioning. In general, if we have $R_1, R_2, \ldots , R_n$ items such that $R_1 + R_2 + \cdots + R_n = T$, then the number of ways that we can put the T items in n groups of $R_1, R_2, \ldots , R_n$ is

$$N = \frac{T!}{R_1!R_2! \cdots R_n!}$$

Note that all the problems treated under permutations and combinations were really special cases of partitioning. The combinations of N things taken R at a time may be thought of as partitioning into two groups of R and N − R items. The problem of arranging SNOWSHOES may be thought of as partitioning into six groups of three items for the S's, two items for the O's, and one item each for the four remaining letters N, W, H, and E. Finally, the permutations of N different items taken R at a time may be thought of as R + 1 groups of N − R in the first group and one item each for the other R groups.

SUMMARY

This section has been devoted to introducing the Fundamental Principle of Enumeration and the enumeration of permutations, combinations, and partitionings of objects. In counting permutations order matters. Permutations count such things as arrangements of letters in a word and books lined up on a bookshelf. When counting combinations order does not matter. We use combinations for such things as the number of different committees formed from a group of people and hands dealt in a game of cards.

PROBLEMS FOR SEC. 13-2

1) In how many orders can 15 people enter a classroom?

2) In how many different ways can 15 keys be put on a circular key ring?

3) Cars come in 18 colors, seven models, four engines, and there are 15 options such as whitewalls, outside mirror, radio, etc. How many different cars are available?

4) You have 25 different books and two bookshelves, one of which holds exactly 12 books and the other holds exactly 13 books. In how many ways can the books be arranged on the shelves?

5) In a class of 30, a six-member committee is to be selected. How many different committees are possible? If there are 15 girls in the class, how many of the committees consist of six girls?

6) How many different five-card hands may be dealt from a deck of 52 cards?

7) How many different 13-card hands may be dealt from a deck of 52 cards?

8) There are five people in a room. In how many ways can they all have different birthdays? Use a 365-day year and ignore Feb. 29.

9) In how many ways can 10 people have all different birthdays? Ignore Feb. 29.

10) If a state uses three letters followed by three digits for its license plates, how many different license plates can it produce?

11) You have five different flags with which to form signals by arranging them all on a flagpole. How many signals can you form?

12) You have five different flags with which to form signals by arranging up to five of them on a flagpole. How many signals can you form? Let zero flags constitute a signal.

13) You have 10 different flags with which to form signals by arranging up to five of them on a flagpole. How many signals can you form?

14) You have 50 friends. You are going to have a party and can only invite 25 people. How many different guest lists could you have?

15) In how many ways can 15 people sit in a row of 15 chairs?

16) Do problem 15) if two of the people must sit next to each other.

17) How many different words can be formed from the letters of the word COMPUTERS if 1) you must use all of the letters and 2) you must leave out one letter?

18) A class consists of 30 students of which 17 are girls. In how many ways can we select a committee of four? How many will have two boys and two girls? How many will have one boy and three girls? How many will have four girls? How many will have four boys?

19) How many outcomes are possible for rolling two dice followed by drawing three cards from a 52-card deck?

20) How many different sets of two five-card hands can be dealt from a 52-card deck?

21) How many words can be formed using all the letters in MISSISSIPPI?

13-3   SIMPLE PROBABILITY

We defined probability in Sec. 13-1 as S/T, where S is the number of ways in which an outcome may constitute a success and T is the number of possible outcomes, and all outcomes are equally likely. For flipping a coin, we see that the probability of coming up heads is 1/2 or .5. For drawing a card from a 52-card deck, the probability of getting the ace of spades is 1/52 or about .0192.

Suppose you are in a class of 29 students and a committee of four members is to be selected at random. What is the probability that you get on the committee? Well, the total number of committees possible is $_{29}C_4$. Now all we have to find is how many of those committees count yourself as a member. We can find out by saying in effect, "Let us put you on the committee and pick the other three members from the remaining 28 class members." This means that you will be on $_{28}C_3$ of the committees, and the probability that you get on the committee is $_{28}C_3/_{29}C_4$. Let us write a program to compute this probability. We can use lines 30 through 110 of program NCR as a subroutine to first find $_{28}C_3$ and then find $_{29}C_4$. See program CLASS. You can see that your chances are about 14%. You should also see that the probability that you do not get on the committee is about $1 - .14$ or .86.

```
CLASS

10    READ N,R
20    GØSUB 500
30    LET C1=C
32    REM   C1 STØRES THE NUMBER ØF CØMMITTEES ØF WHICH
33    REM YØU ARE A MEMBER
40    READ N,R
50    GØSUB 500
60    LET P=C1/C
70    PRINT "THE PRØBABILITY THAT YØU GET ØN A 4 MEMBER"
75    PRINT "CØMMITTEE FRØM A CLASS ØF 29 IS";P
80    STØP
490   REM   FIND CØMBINATIØNS ØF N THINGS TAKEN R AT A TIME
500   LET C=1
510   FØR X=N TØ N-R+1 STEP -1
520   LET C=C*X
530   NEXT X
540   FØR Y=R TØ 1 STEP -1
550   LET C=C/Y
560   NEXT Y
570   RETURN
600   DATA 28,3
610   DATA 29,4
999   END
RUN
CLASS

THE PRØBABILITY THAT YØU GET ØN A 4 MEMBER
CØMMITTEE FRØM A CLASS ØF 29 IS .137931

DØNE
```

Suppose we roll a die. The probability that a 3 comes up is one in six or 1/6. Now roll the die again. Again, the probability of a 3 is 1/6. We can see that if we roll the die twice, the probability of both rolls coming up 3 is (1/6) ° (1/6), or 1/36. We define an *event* as a set of outcomes for a particular experiment. If we have two events A and B such that the probability of success for A is P and the probability of success for B is Q, the events A and B are said to be independent if the probability of success for A and B both is P ° Q. This is exactly the case for rolling a 3 on each of two dice, which enables us to arrive at probabilities without actually enumerating outcomes. Thus we have extended our definition of probability.

For rolling two dice, the events associated with the first die are independent of the events associated with the second die. The same may be said of rolling the same die twice. Flipping two coins are independent. Drawing a card from a deck is independent of rolling a die. So, the probability of getting a 1 and an ace upon rolling a die and drawing a card is (1/6) ° (4/52), or (1/78).

Let us look at a problem often referred to as the "birthday problem." Suppose you are in a room with 29 other people. What is the probability that at least two people have the same birthdate? We can say that if the probability of no two people having the same birthdate is P, then the probability that at least two do have the same birthdate is 1 − P. The birthdates for two people are independent events, so we may multiply individual probabilities. Picking any person first, we say that his probability of having a different birthdate from those already picked is 365/365. Picking a second person, the probability that his birthdate is different from the first person's is 364/365. For the third person we get 363/365 as the probability that his birthdate is different from the first two, and for the 30th person we get 336/365 as the probability that his birthdate is different from each of the first 29 birthdates. So, the probability that all are different is

$$P = \frac{365}{365} \text{ ° } \frac{364}{365} \text{ ° } \ldots \text{ ° } \frac{336}{365}$$

and the probability that at least two people have the same birthdate is 1 − P. We can write a short program to compute 1 − P. See BIRTH.

The chances are about 71%, which is much higher than many people would

```
BIRTH

10   LET P=1
20   FOR D=365 TO 336 STEP -1
30   LET P=P*D/365
40   NEXT D
50   LET Q=1-P
60   PRINT "THE PROBABILITY OF TWO OR MORE"
70   PRINT "IDENTICAL BIRTHDATES AMONG 30 PEOPLE IS";Q
80   END
RUN
BIRTH

THE PROBABILITY OF TWO OR MORE
IDENTICAL BIRTHDATES AMONG 30 PEOPLE IS .706316

DONE
```

guess before doing the problem. Note that this is not the probability that someone else in the room has the same birthday that you have. That problem is left as an exercise.

SUMMARY

We have initially defined probability as the quotient of the number of ways to constitute success and the total number of possible outcomes for equally likely outcomes. We see that this can easily be applied to situations of enumeration. Independent events which have individual probabilities P and Q occur together with a probability of P ° Q. This produces an extended definition of probability which does not always require enumeration, but requires only that we know individual probabilities for successive events.

PROBLEMS FOR SEC. 13-3

1) A class of 29 has 16 girls. A committee of five is selected at random. What is the probability that all five committee members are girls?

2) Ten people are to sit in a row of 10 chairs. What is the probability that two particular persons sit next to each other?

3) What is the probability of being dealt the ace of spades, the three of clubs, the eight of hearts, the seven of diamonds, and the 10 of clubs?

4) What is the probability of being dealt the ace, king, queen, jack, and 10 of spades from a 52-card deck?

5) What is the probability of the first six flips coming up heads and the last four tails when flipping a coin 10 times?

6) What is the probability of getting all heads when flipping a coin 10 times?

7) You have a list of 20 true–false questions from which 10 will be selected at random for a test. Of the 20, there are 15 you are guaranteed to get right and five that you are guaranteed to get wrong. What is the probability that you will get exactly eight right?

8) An experiment consists of drawing a card from a 52-card deck until the first ace appears. Find the probability of the first ace appearing on the fourth draw.

9) For the experiment of problem 8), find the probability of the first ace appearing on draws one through ten.

10) An experiment consists of rolling a die until it comes up 2. Find the probability of the first 2 coming up on the fourth roll, on the tenth roll.

√ 11) Refer to the birthday problem. How many people must be in a room to have the probability of at least two identical birthdates be .5?

12) You are in a room with 29 other people. What is the probability that one of them has your birthdate?

√ 13) How many people must be in a room for the probability of another person to have your birthdate be .5?

13-4   RANDOM SIMULATION

We may use the random number generator to simulate experiments that occur at random. We can have the computer flip a coin by generating two random digits. We can roll a die by generating six random digits, etc.

```
FLIP

5   LET C=0
10  FOR X=1 TO 50
20  LET F=INT(2*RND(1))
30  IF F=1 THEN 60
40  PRINT "T";
50  GOTO 100
58  REM  C COUNTS THE NUMBER OF HEADS
60  LET C=C+1
70  PRINT "H";
100  NEXT X
110  PRINT
120  PRINT "HEADS  ";C;"OUT OF 50 FLIPS"
130  END
RUN
FLIP

HTTHTTTHTTHHHTTTHHHTHTTHHHTTTTHHHHHTTTHTHTHTHTTTTTHTH
HEADS   23   OUT OF 50 FLIPS

DONE
```

Let us begin by having the computer flip a coin 50 times. See program FLIP. We get 23 heads out of 50 flips. One of the intriguing things about flipping a coin many times is that we do not get heads for half of the flips for each experiment. In fact, it is possible to flip a coin 50 times and get no heads or to get all heads. Of course the probability of all heads or no heads is very small compared to the probability of half heads. We will be able to compute those probabilities in the next section. For now we are concentrating on simulation.

In many ways, flipping a coin 50 times is the same as flipping 50 coins once. Let us put program FLIP in a loop to perform the experiment 10 times to see a range of results. See FLIP-1.

We get a range of 17 to 34 heads for this RUN of the program, and it turned out this time that none of the trials came out 25 heads.

One of the nice features of simulation by computer is that we can have the computer perform hundreds or thousands of trials of an experiment that might take days to do with physical apparatus.

```
FLIP-1

2   FOR Y=1 TO 10
5   LET C=0
10  FOR X=1 TO 50
20  LET F=INT(2*RND(1))
30  IF F=1 THEN 60
40  PRINT "T";
50  GOTO 100
58  REM  C COUNTS THE NUMBER OF HEADS
60  LET C=C+1
70  PRINT "H";
100  NEXT X
110  PRINT
120  PRINT "HEADS  ";C;"OUT OF 50 FLIPS"
125  NEXT Y
130  END
```

```
RUN
FLIP-1

HTTTTTHTTHHTTHTTTTTTTTHTHTHHHHHHTTTTTHTHHHTHHHTTHHTT
HEADS   21   OUT OF 50 FLIPS
HTTHTHHTTHTTHTHHHTTTHHHTTTTTTHHHHTTHTHTHHHHTHHTTHHH
HEADS   26   OUT OF 50 FLIPS
HTHTTTHTTHTTHTTTTTTTTHTTHTTTHTHTHTHTTTHTTTTTHHHHTHHHT
HEADS   17   OUT OF 50 FLIPS
THTTTTTTHTHTHTHHHTHHHHHHTHTTTHHTTHTTTTTTTTHHTHTTHHTT
HEADS   21   OUT OF 50 FLIPS
TTHHTTTTHTHHHTTHTHTHHHHTTHHHTHHHTTTTTTHTHHHHTTHTHHTT
HEADS   24   OUT OF 50 FLIPS
HTHTHHHHHHHHTHTTTTTTTTHTTHHHHHHHTTTHTTTTHTHTTHHTHHHTHH
HEADS   26   OUT OF 50 FLIPS
HTTTTTHTTTTHHTTHTTHTHHHHTHTHHTTHHHHHTHTTHTHTHTHTTTTHT
HEADS   22   OUT OF 50 FLIPS
THTHHHHHHHTHTHHHHHTTTHHTHTHHHHHHTHHHTHHTHHHHHHHHTTTHTH
HEADS   34   OUT OF 50 FLIPS
HTTHHTHHTTHTTTTTTTHHHTTTHTTTHHTTHTHTHTHHHHHTTHHHTHHHTHT
HEADS   24   OUT OF 50 FLIPS
TTHHTHHTHHHTHTTHTHHHTHHHTTTTHHHTTTTHTTHTHHTHHTHTHT
HEADS   26   OUT OF 50 FLIPS

DONE
```

Let us set up an experiment to roll six dice 1000 times, counting the number of times 1 comes up for each roll of six dice. The possibilities are from zero to six. Then let us count the number of times each of those seven numbers occurs. We can keep track of all seven totals in a 1 by 7 row vector. We will count the number of times no 1's come up in column 1 and the number of times one 1 comes up in column 2, etc. See the flowchart in Fig. 13-2 and program RØLL.

```
RØLL

5   REM   THE MAT INSTRUCTIONS ARE CONVENIENT HERE
10  DIM L[1,7]
20  MAT L=ZER
38  REM   THE COMPUTER DOES 50 THROUGH 110 1000 TIMES
40  FOR X=1 TO 1000
50  LET C=0
55  REM   C IS GOING TO COUNT 1'S
58  REM   LINES 60 THROUGH 100 ROLL 6 DICE AND COUNT 1'S
60  FOR R=1 TO 6
70  LET U=INT(6*RND(1)+1)
80  IF U>1 THEN 100
90  LET C=C+1
100 NEXT R
110 LET L[1,C+1]=L[1,C+1]+1
120 NEXT X
130 PRINT "NØNE  ØNE   TWØ   THREE FOUR  FIVE   SIX"
140 MAT PRINT L;
150 END
RUN
RØLL

NØNE  ØNE   TWØ   THREE FØUR  FIVE  SIX
 343   410   193    44     9     1    0


DONE
```

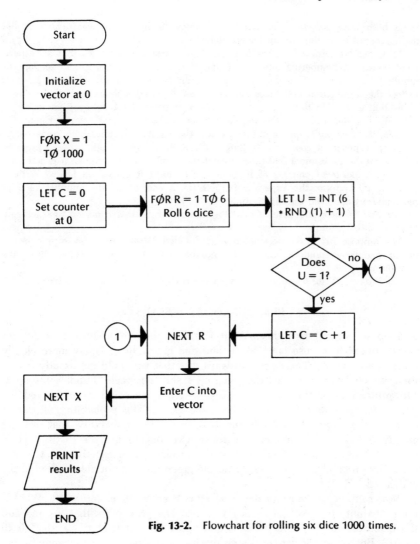

Fig. 13-2. Flowchart for rolling six dice 1000 times.

PROBLEMS FOR SEC. 13-4

1) Have the computer flip six coins 1000 times and print the distribution of outcomes.

2) Sketch a graph of the distribution for problem 1) and the distribution for program RØLL.

3) Write a program to deal five-card hands from a 52-card deck. Be sure not to deal the same card twice.

4) A company manufactures light bulbs and can openers. For light bulbs it is known that 1 in 20 is defective and for can openers 1 in 25 is defective. Write a program to select at random one light bulb and one can opener 1000 times. Total each of the following: the number of times neither was defective, the number of

times both were defective, the number of times the light bulb was defective, and the number of times the can opener was defective.

5) A regular tetrahedron has four equilateral triangles as faces. Let an experiment consist of numbering one face 1 and the remaining faces 2, and tossing the tetrahedron into the air to determine which number faces down. Write a program to toss the tetrahedron 500 times and count the number of times the 1 faces down.

6) Roll a die 500 times. Count the number of times the 1 or the 5 comes up.

7) Roll a die and toss the tetrahedron of problem 5) 1000 times. Count the number of times both come out 1 and count the number of times both come out 2.

8) An experiment consists of rolling a die until a 1 comes up. Write a program to perform the experiment 500 times. Count the number of rolls for each experiment.

9) An experiment consists of flipping a coin until it comes up heads. Write a program to perform the experiment 1500 times and count the number of flips required for each. Print the distribution.

10) Roll 10 dice 500 times. Count the number of 1's that come up for each roll. Print the distribution.

11) Suppose 10% of the population is left handed. Write a program to pick groups of 10 people at random. Count the number of left-handed people. Print the distribution.

12) *Project:* Write a program to make the computer the dealer in a game of 21.

13-5 BINOMIAL TRIALS

Suppose we roll two dice. What is the probability that a 1 comes up exactly once? If we use one red die and one green die, we may more clearly describe the results. There are two ways that that we could get exactly one 1. First, we could have the red die come up 1 and the green die not come up 1. The probability of this is $(1/6) \cdot (5/6)$. Second, we could have the red die not come up 1 and the green die come up 1. The probability of this is $(5/6) \cdot (1/6)$. Now, if we roll the two dice, the probability that we get exactly one 1 is the sum of the above two possibilities, or $(5/6) \cdot (1/6) + (1/6) \cdot (5/6)$. Or we can say that the probability of exactly one 1 is two times the probability of getting a 1 on the green die and not a 1 on the red die which is $2 \cdot (5/6) \cdot (1/6)$.

Now suppose we roll four dice colored red, green, blue, and white. What is the probability that we get exactly two 1's? The probability that the red and the green dice are 1's and the blue and white are not is $(1/6) \cdot (1/6) \cdot (5/6) \cdot (5/6)$. But we might get the 1's on the green and blue with the same probability, or we might get 1's on the red and white dice with the same probability. In fact, there are $_4C_2$ ways that we could select two dice from the four to come up with 1's. Each selection has probability of $(1/6) \cdot (1/6) \cdot (5/6) \cdot (5/6)$. So the probability of exactly two 1's up for a roll of four dice is

$$P = {_4C_2} \cdot (1/6)^2 \cdot (5/6)^2$$

which simplifies to 25/216.

Suppose we have 10 dice. What is the probability that exactly two dice come up 1 when all 10 are rolled? For a particular selection of two dice, we get $(1/6)^2 \cdot (5/6)^8$ and we can select the two dice in $_{10}C_2$ ways. So,

$$P = {_{10}C_2} \cdot (1/6)^2 \cdot (5/6)^8$$

We can write a short program to find the value of P. Note that in program DICE lines 15 through 40 compute the value of $_{10}C_2$.

```
DICE

10   READ R
15   LET C=1
20   FØR X=10 TØ 10-R+1 STEP -1
30   LET C=C*X/(10-X+1)
40   NEXT X
50   LET P=C*(1/6)↑R*(5/6)↑(10-R)
60   PRINT P
65   DATA 2
70   END
RUN
DICE

 .29071

DØNE
```

Program DICE is for exactly two 1's. What about the other possible numbers of 1's? With just a few changes in program DICE, we can answer that question. Instead of computing for R = 2 only, we can let R go from 0 to 10 in a FØR–NEXT loop. This can be done by changing only lines 10 and 65 in DICE. See DICE-1.

In DICE-1 we have defined 11 events that cover all possible outcomes in this experiment. There can be no outcomes that do not give from 0 to 10 1's. It is also true that no two of the events have any outcomes in common. Events which do not have any outcomes in common are called *mutually exclusive*

```
DICE-1

5    PRINT "ØNES  PRØBABILITY"
10   FØR R=0 TØ 10
15   LET C=1
20   FØR X=10 TØ 10-R+1 STEP -1
30   LET C=C*X/(10-X+1)
40   NEXT X
50   LET P=C*(1/6)↑R*(5/6)↑(10-R)
60   PRINT R;P
65   NEXT R
70   END
RUN
DICE-1

ØNES   PRØBABILITY
 0      .161506
 1      .323011
 2      .29071
 3      .155045
 4      5.42659E-02
 5      1.30238E-02
 6      2.17063E-03
 7      2.48072E-04
 8      1.86054E-05
 9      8.26908E-07
10      1.65382E-08

DØNE
```

events. If we have a set of mutually exclusive events that also cover all possible outcomes, then the sum of the individual probabilities must total 1. We can verify that the sum of the probabilities in DICE-1 is in fact 1. Of course one way to do that would be to rewrite the program to total the probabilities in DICE-1.

Suppose we know that 10% of a certain population is left handed. If we select 100 people at random, what is the probability that exactly 10 of them will be left handed? The probability that a particular set of 10 people will be left handed will be $(1/10)^{10} * (9/10)^{90}$ and from 100 people there are $_{100}C_{10}$ ways that 10 of them can be left handed. So the probability is

$$P = {}_{100}C_{10} * (1/10)^{10} * (9/10)^{90}$$

This too, can be done with a short program. See LEFT.

```
LEFT

10    LET C=1
20    FOR X=100 TO 100-10+1 STEP -1
30    LET C=C*X/(100-X+1)
40    NEXT X
50    LET P=C*(.1)↑10*(.9)↑90
60    PRINT P
70    END
RUN
LEFT

 .131865

DONE
```

In general, we should see that if an outcome has probability P of success and Q of failure and we perform an experiment consisting of N trials, the probability of exactly R successes is

$$P = {}_{N}C_{R} * P^{R} * Q^{N-R}$$

Experiments that behave in this way are called *binomial experiments* because the values of $_{N}C_{R} * P^{R} * Q^{N-R}$ are the terms of the expansion of the binomial $(P + Q)$ raised to the Nth power.

Binomial Theorem

Looking at $(P + Q)^{N}$, we should be able to see the general term in the product. $(P + Q)^{N}$ means, write $(P + Q)$ as a factor N times. So

$$(P + Q)^{N} = (P + Q)(P + Q)(P + Q) \cdots (P + Q)$$

When we multiply this out, we are actually taking one term from each factor in such a way that we can sum up all possible products of combinations of N factors one from each $(P + Q)$ factor. How many factors are there in the product? There is one term that takes P as a factor N times. There is one term that takes P as a factor $N - 1$ times and Q as a factor once. There is also a term that takes P as a factor $N - 2$ times and Q as a factor twice, etc., down to the term that takes Q as a factor N times. That makes $N + 1$ terms. Now, for a particular term, say P^3Q^{N-3}, we want three P's and N minus three Q's. We can select three P's from among N terms in $_NC_3$ ways and so the value of this term is $_NC_3 \cdot P^3Q^{N-3}$. For the Rth term we get $_NC_R \cdot P^RQ^{N-R}$, which is exactly what we get for a probability of R successes in N trials where the probability of success on a single trial is P and the probability of failure on a single trial is Q. So to find $(P + Q)^N$ we simply evaluate $_NC_R \cdot P^RQ^{N-R}$ for all values of R from 0 to N.

Taking a look at the probability of any binomial experiment, we see that since $P + Q = 1$ and the sum of all $_NC_R \cdot P^RQ^{N-R}$ terms is $(P + Q)^N$, we get

if $\quad$ $P + Q = 1$ $\quad$ then $\quad$ $(P + Q)^N = 1$

which can be verified by summing up the probabilities in program DICE-1.

Finally, if we look at $(X + Y)^N$ for X and Y both equal to 1, we get the general term in the expansion to be $_NC_R1^R1^{N-R}$, which is the same as $_NC_R$, so that the numerical coefficients of any binomial expansion are simply the corresponding values of $_NC_R$. Since the values of X and Y are both 1, we are really finding the value of 2^N if we sum up all of the coefficients. Let us write a program to print the coefficients for values of N from 0 to 11. See program PASCAL.

You may recognize these numbers as Pascal's Triangle which has many interesting properties. Problem 9) in Sec. 11-1 and problem 7) in Sec. 5-3 should also have given the results of program PASCAL.

PASCAL

```
10   FØR N=0 TØ 11
20   FØR R=0 TØ N
30   LET C=1
40   FØR X=N TØ N-R+1 STEP -1
50   LET C=C*X/(N-X+1)
60   NEXT X
70   PRINT C;
80   NEXT R
90   PRINT
100  NEXT N
110  END
RUN
PASCAL
```

1											
1	1										
1	2	1									
1	3	3	1								
1	4	6	4	1							
1	5	10	10	5	1						
1	6	15	20	15	6	1					
1	7	21	35	35	21	7	1				
1	8	28	56	70	56	28	8	1			
1	9	36	84	126	126	84	36	9	1		
1	10	45	120	210	252	210	120	45	10	1	
1	11	55	165	330	462	462	330	165	55	11	1

DØNE

PROBLEMS FOR SEC. 13-5

1) Modify PASCAL to sum up the coefficients. Print the values of R and the sum of the coefficients. Do not print the coefficients.

2) Modify DICE-1 to sum up the individual probabilities. Have the loop go from 10 to 0.

3) It is known that 1% of the population has a certain type of blood. In a class of 25 persons, what is the probability that exactly two people have this blood type?

4) A company makes bolts. It is known that 1 in 1000 is defective. You buy a box of 100 bolts. What is the probability of getting exactly one defective bolt?

5) For the company in problem 4), what is the probability of getting 10 defective bolts.

6) For the company in problem 4), what is the probability of getting at least one defective bolt.

7) For the company in problem 4), what is the probability of getting less than five defective bolts.

8) Find the probabilities of getting zero through six 1's when rolling six dice. Compare your results with the random simulation in program RØLL.

9) What is the probability of getting zero through 10 heads when flipping 10 coins.

10) What is the probability of getting more heads than tails when flipping 10 coins.

11) A test consists of 25 true–false questions. You know that your probability of guessing right on any given question is 75%. Find the probability of getting 76% on the test, if you guess on all questions. Find your probability of getting 76% or better.

√ 12) An experiment consists of flipping a coin until it comes up heads. Find the probability of success for 1 to 10 flips.

√ 13) An experiment consists of rolling a die until it comes up 1. Find the probability of success for 1 to 10 flips. Find the probability that success will require more than 10 rolls. Find the probability that success will require more than 20 rolls.

APPENDIX A

Storing Programs on Paper Tape

A-1 INTRODUCTION

Once you have written your program, you would like to have the computer execute it. In order to execute a program it must be typed into the computer. Ideally, we should all be expert typists, but many of us are not. So, many time-share terminals provide for punching programs on paper tape when the terminal is not connected to the computer. Then the high-speed tape reader may be used for reading the program in on-line. Even so, the considerate student will do his utmost to improve his typing speed so as not to tie up the terminal when others would like to be typing. One suggestion is to type all programs in advance before sitting in front of the terminal to punch tape. You will benefit in two ways: by getting practice in typing and by being able to read the program easily.

A-2 PUNCHING PAPER TAPE OFF-LINE

Programs may be stored on a narrow strip of paper tape by punching rows of holes in a code. Each row represents a character, space, line feed, carriage return, or other nonprinting character.

There are so many variations from one time-share company to the next, that we cannot list them all here. But we can outline the general procedure. First the terminal must be switched to *local*. Then the tape punch apparatus must be turned on. Now you want some blank leading tape so that the tape reader will be able to read the first character of your program. Some terminals generate the blank leader by depressing the HERE IS key. On others, you may have to depress the REPT and RUBOUT keys simultaneously until sufficient tape shows, or try depressing CTRL, SHIFT, REPT, and P all at once.

Now you may type your program. As you type, holes will be punched, which the tape reader will interpret when you feed the finished tape back. Be sure to begin each line with a line number and touch the RETURN and

LINE FEED keys at the end of each line. (There may be a special key for RETURN.)

If you make a typing error, you may correct it in one of several ways. If it is the previous character or within a few characters, depress the backspace button on the tape punch apparatus once for each character you wish to erase. Then touch the RUBOUT key once for each backspace. The RUBOUT key punches out all holes in the row and will be ignored by the computer and will not print. Alternatively, you may depress the SHIFT key and the Ø key once for each character you wish to erase. A backwards arrow will be printed for each correction. Spaces do count as characters for this purpose. If the entire line is a lost cause, simply RETURN, LINE FEED, and begin typing from the beginning including the line number. After you have finished typing, touch RETURN and LINE FEED. Then generate blank tape as you did before typing your program. The idea is to get some paper that is not filled with holes so that you may write some kind of identification on the tape. As soon as you have your second tape, the need for this will become obvious. After tape preparation is completed, tear it off and roll it up. It is suggested that you not roll it less than about 2 in. in diameter, as the tape will take on a permanent curl and that may cause trouble in the reader later.

A-3 READING PAPER TAPE

With the terminal on-line and the previous program erased, you are ready to enter your program into the computer via the tape reader. Again computers vary, but most require a system command, and for some the command is TAPE followed by turning the tape reader on. After the tape is read in, remove your tape from the reader and roll it up again. If the computer requires a system command to enter tape mode, then a second command will be required to remove it from that mode. The command KEY removes the computer from tape mode and prepares it for instructions from the keyboard. The command RUN usually will serve the same purpose.

At this time the computer takes your entire program and compiles it. To compile a program means to put all instructions in order and convert it to a form that the computer uses to actually perform the instructions. In order to run, all statements must be legal BASIC statements and the entire program must fit certain requirements that vary depending on the computer.

At this point, you should read all of Appendix B and then return and finish this appendix.

A-4 GETTING THE COMPUTER TO PUNCH PAPER TAPE

Having read Appendix B, you can see that after you have read in a program on tape, you may make many changes or additions. After you have made all of the necessary changes or after it becomes clear that you cannot make all of the necessary corrections in a reasonable length of time at the keyboard, you may want a new tape of the program in its latest form. Here again, time-share systems will vary, but you will have a way of getting the computer to punch your program. Some will automatically provide blank leading and trailing tape, others will require you to use the method you used when you typed off-line. Two of the system commands in use are PUNCH and LIST-NØ-HEADER.

Now you have two tapes for the same program. Most likely you will want to throw the old one away. Be sure to write some identification on the new tape.

APPENDIX B

Error Diagnosis

B-1 INTRODUCTION

From the time you type the last line of your program to the completion of a successful RUN, there are three types of errors that may show up: 1) those errors that prevent a RUN; 2) those errors that allow a RUN to begin but cause it to terminate during execution; and 3) those that permit a complete RUN, but cause the computer to produce an unexpected or incorrect result. The whole process of taking a program that does not work and turning it into one that does is called *debugging*. Let us look at the errors by type.

B-2 ERRORS THAT PREVENT RUN

These are very often simply typing errors:

```
10 LT←ET X=5
20 PRØNT X
30 END
RUN
NØ STATEMENT TYPE FØUND  IN LINE 20
```

The exact wording will vary from computer to computer, but the message is clear. We retype line 20 as in the following:

```
20  PRINT X
RUN

5

DØNE
```

Even though BASIC does use English words, you may not get too conversational as in the following:

```
10   READ X AND Y
20   PRINT X,Y
30 DATA 4, 5, 7, -11
40 GØ TØ 10
50 END
RUN
CHARACTERS AFTER STATEMENT END IN LINE 10
```

As far as BASIC is concerned, line 10 says READ X. The AND Y is not part of the language and so is rejected. Since there is no way to know just what the characters after X mean, if the first one is not a comma or a single digit, the computer will not take a guess at what you meant. You must say exactly what you mean; the computer is not clairvoyant. So, change line 10 as follows:

```
10 READ X,Y
RUN
```

```
4               5
7              -11

ØUT ØF DATA   IN LINE 10
```

To multiply X times Y in algebra we write XY.

```
10 LET X=5
20 LET Y=10
30 LET Z=XY
40 PRINT Z
50 END
RUN
CHARACTERS AFTER STATEMENT END IN LINE 30
```

However, even though in algebra XY is understood to mean X times Y, you must be more explicit for the computer, and write X * Y.

```
30 LET Z=X*Y
RUN
```

```
50

DØNE
```

Let us put many errors in one program and see what happens.

```
10   LET X= 5
20   READ Y  , Z
30 LER W=Y* Z
40 PRINT X
50 LET A*B=X
60   READ W
70 GØTØ 9010
80 LET S=(AX+B)*(CX+D)
90   LET A1
100 GØ BACK TØ 10
110 LET X=3*4+5)
```

```
120  DATA  5, 11,   25, -5
130  PRINT  W*2
140  GØTØ  60
150  DATA  2, 67,-1,
RUN
NØ STATEMENT TYPE FØUND  IN LINE 30
MISSING ASSIGNMENT ØPERATØR  IN LINE 50
MISSING RIGHT PARENTHESIS   IN LINE 80
MISSING ASSIGNMENT ØPERATØR  IN LINE 90
NØ STATEMENT TYPE FØUND  IN LINE 100
CHARACTERS AFTER STATEMENT END IN LINE 110
MISSING ØR ILLEGAL DATA ITEM IN LINE 150
```

Now let us see what we can do to fix the program so it will run. First v
would like to see what is left of our program. The system command LIST w
do that for us.

```
LIST

10   LET X=5
20   READ Y,Z
40   PRINT X
60   READ W
70   GØTØ 9010
120   DATA 5,11,25,-5
130   PRINT W*2
140   GØTØ 60
```

The computer automatically wiped out all of the statements that did n
conform to BASIC requirements. So what remains ought to run, right? Wron;
The computer has only eliminated the errors that are self-contained in singl
statements. These are sometimes called *syntax errors* or *errors of form*. Th
computer has not yet looked to see if the statements fit together into a set (
executable statements. To achieve that we type RUN again:

```
RUN
UNDEFINED STATEMENT REFERENCE  IN LINE 70
```

We can easily see that the computer cannot GØTØ 9010 as there is 1
line 9010 in the program. We take line 70 out by typing 70 followed
RETURN and try again.

```
70

RUN
LAST STATEMENT NØT 'END' IN LINE 140
9999   END
RUN


5
625
25

ØUT ØF DATA  IN LINE 60
```

Now we have gotten something printed, but the program is all over the place. We can assemble it again with the LIST command or we may use a new command first. We can get nice numbering by the command RENUM-BER. Some computers use EDIT RESEQUENCE. We RENUMBER here and LIST the program in its present form.

```
RENUMBER
LIST


10    LET  X=5
20    READ  Y,Z
30    PRINT  X
40    READ  W
50    DATA  5,11,25,-5
60    PRINT  W↑2
70    GOTO  40
80    END
RUN


  5
 625
 25

OUT OF DATA   IN LINE 40
```

There is no substitute for experience.

B-3   ERRORS THAT TERMINATE A RUN

The possible errors in this category become more and more plentiful as you use more and more advanced capabilities. However, the error messages are rather explicit and so the most fundamental examples should serve to demonstrate how termination errors operate. Probably the most common error for beginning programmers is that the data is either missing or not matched correctly for the READ variables.

```
10    PRINT "THE RUN HAS BEGUN"
20    LET A=2
30    READ B,C,D
40    PRINT B*C↑A
50    PRINT "D ="; D
60    PRINT "WE GOT TO LINE 60 AT LEAST"
70    READ X
80    PRINT X
90    DATA 3,17,11
100   END
RUN


THE RUN HAS BEGUN
 867
D = 11
WE GOT TO LINE 60 AT LEAST

OUT OF DATA   IN LINE 70
```

Not all computers will print the out of data message, but they will terminate after the last item of data is read if the program sends it back to READ again.

You might instruct the computer to perform an illegal operation as follows:

```
10   PRINT "A","B","A-B","A↑B"
20   READ A,B
30   PRINT A,B,A-B,A↑B
40   GØTØ 20
50   DATA 1,2,5,3,3.41,2,1.23,4,0,0,4.03,5
60   END
RUN
```

A	B	A-B	A↑B
1	2	-1	1
5	3	2	125
3.41	2	1.41	11.6281
1.23	4	-2.77	2.28887
0	0	0	

ZERØ TØ ZERØ PØWER IN LINE 30

Zero to the zero power is not defined. So the computer notifies you that it has come to this undefined condition and halts execution awaiting your program change. There are many more errors that will halt execution, but these examples should demonstrate the principle involved.

B-4   ERRORS THAT CAUSE UNEXPECTED OR INCORRECT RESULTS

These are the most difficult errors to find. Suppose you write a program and the computer prints nothing, but notifies you that it has run the program in the usual manner.

```
15   LET X=5
25   LET Y=10
30   LET Z=X↑2
40   LET W=Y↑2
70   END
RUN


DØNE
```

We got three blank lines and that is not what we wrote the program to do. It is reasonably obvious that we forgot to put in any PRINT statements.

```
50 PRINT X,Y,Z,W
10 PRINT "X      Y      X↑2     Y↑2"
RUN


X      Y      X↑2     Y↑2
5      10     25      100

DØNE
```

If you think that you have the PRINT statements and do not get any printed results, look for a GØTØ that causes the computer to bypass the PRINT statements.

The ways in which programs can give incorrect results are unlimited. And to make matters worse, the computer has no way of determining that the result is correct. This is the responsibility of the programmer. Consider the following program to read pairs of numbers and print their sum and their product and the number of pairs:

```
10   PRINT "A      B      SUM    PROD   "
20   LET C=0
30   READ A, B
40   LET C=C+1
50   PRINT A; B; A+B; A*B; C; "PAIRS SØ FAR"
60   GØTØ 10
70   DATA 10, 20, 11, 9
80   DATA 1, 2, -45, 18
90   END
RUN
```

```
A      B      SUM    PROD
 10     20     30     200    1    PAIRS SØ FAR
A      B      SUM    PROD
 11      9     20      99    1    PAIRS SØ FAR
A      B      SUM    PROD
  1      2      3       2    1    PAIRS SØ FAR
A      B      SUM    PROD
-45     18    -27    -810    1    PAIRS SØ FAR
A      B      SUM    PROD

ØUT ØF DATA  IN LINE 30
```

We certainly do not need to have the headings printed more than once. So we want to change the GØTØ in line 60 as follows:

```
60  GØTØ20
RUN
```

```
A      B      SUM    PROD
 10     20     30     200    1    PAIRS SØ FAR
 11      9     20      99    1    PAIRS SØ FAR
  1      2      3       2    1    PAIRS SØ FAR
-45     18    -27    -810    1    PAIRS SØ FAR

ØUT ØF DATA   IN LINE 30
```

But now we still have to find out why the computer prints 1 for the number of pairs each time. Line 40 is LET $C = C + 1$. C must be 0 each time the computer comes to line 40. This is because the GØTØ sends the computer to line 20 which is LET $C = 0$. So we change line 60 again. This time we want the computer to go only to the READ statement in line 30.

```
60   GØTØ 30
RUN


A       B       SUM     PROD
 10     20      30      200     1   PAIRS SØ FAR
 11      9      20       99     2   PAIRS SØ FAR
  1      2       3        2     3   PAIRS SØ FAR
-45     18     -27     -810     4   PAIRS SØ FAR

ØUT ØF DATA  IN LINE 30
```

And now the program is as follows:

```
10   PRINT "A       B       SUM     PROD    "
20   LET C=0
30   READ A, B
40   LET C=C+1
50   PRINT A;B;A+B;A*B;C;"PAIRS SØ FAR"
60   GØTØ 30
70   DATA 10,20,11,9
80   DATA 1,2,-45,18
90   END
```

SUMMARY

We begin to see some of the types of errors and the way in which they affect the running of our program. There are errors of language or syntax errors. There are errors that prevent execution such as GØTØ 870 when there is no line 870 in the program. Some errors do not affect the computer until it tries to evaluate an expression that calls for an undefined condition. And finally we have seen some errors that give incorrect results. As we are making changes in programs we may find the LIST command helpful to see the program in its present form. As we change programs, the line numbers may become very scattered or very close together. The command RENUMBER or EDIT RESEQUENCE makes 10 the first line number and the intervals 10.

Special Formatting Functions

C-1   TAB(X)

The TAB(X) function is available on many BASIC systems. The TAB( ) function numbers the spaces across the terminal carriage and uses this number to designate where to print. XXX PRINT TAB (10); "HELLØ THERE" is an instruction to the computer to skip out to the space whose number is 10 and begin printing there. See program HELLØ.

```
HELLØ

5   PRINT "HELLØ THERE"
10  PRINT TAB(10);"HELLØ THERE"
20  END
RUN
HELLØ

HELLØ THERE
          HELLØ THERE

DØNE
```

Some systems call the leftmost space zero and others call it one. Some systems treat the argument of the TAB( ) function mod 72, so that TAB(100) and TAB(28) mean the same thing. Others use mod 75, in which case TAB(100) means the same as TAB(25).

There may be several TAB( )'s in the same PRINT instruction. The argument of TAB( ) may be a variable as in program TAB(1).

```
TAB(1)

10  LET X=10
20  PRINT TAB(X);X; TAB(X+10);X+10; TAB(X+25);X+25
30  END
RUN
TAB(1)

          10        20            35

DØNE
```

Notice that TAB( ) counts from the left margin every time it appears, not from the previous printed character.

We may use the TAB( ) function to make the formatting a little simpler in program BANK2 in Sec. 4-3. Turn back to that program and look at lines 132, 138, 156, 158, and 500 through 530. All of these lines were required to achieve flexible format. We may eliminate all of these as well as line 490 and replace line 140 with 140 PRINT TAB(X); "$";FNH(P) and replace line 160 with 160 PRINT TAB(X);"$";FNH(P1). Now all we need to take care of is a value for X. Let us try 35 the first time through. Anywhere before line 140 we may insert ZZZ LET X = 35 and call for a RUN.

```
530
520
510
500
490
158
156
138
132
140  PRINT TAB(X);"$";FNH(P)
160  PRINT TAB(X);"$";FNH(P1)
135 LET X=35
RUN
BANK2

FOR TEN YEARS
@4.5% COMPOUNDED MONTHLY...        $ 88.24
@4.75% COMPOUNDED QUARTERLY...     $ 90.29
```

The printed results are aligned nicely. Now let us list the new program in full with the value of X at 31 and call for a final RUN.

```
BANK2

2    DEF FNH(X)=INT(X*100+.5)/100
10   LET P=P1=56.31
20   FOR Y=1 TO 10
22   REM  FOR TEN YEARS
30   FOR M=1 TO 12
32   REM  COMPOUND MONTHLY AND COMPUTE INTEREST
40   LET I=P*4.5/100/12
50   LET P=P+I
60   NEXT M
62   REM THAT FIGURES THE INTEREST FOR THIS YEAR COMPOUNDED
     MONTHLY
70   FOR Q=1 TO 4
72   REM  COMPOUND QUARTERLY
80   LET I1=P1*4.75/100/4
90   LET P1=P1+I1
100  NEXT Q
102  REM  THAT TAKES CARE OF THE QUARTERLY INVESTMENT FOR THIS
     YEAR
108  REM  NOW TO COMPUTE THE NEXT YEAR
110  NEXT Y
120  PRINT "FOR TEN YEARS"
130  PRINT "@4.5% COMPOUNDED MONTHLY...";
135  LET X=31
```

```
140   PRINT TAB(X);"$";FNH(P)
150   PRINT "@4.75% COMPOUNDED QUARTERLY...";
160   PRINT TAB(X);"$";FNH(P1)
9999  END
RUN
BANK2

FOR TEN YEARS
@4.5% COMPOUNDED MONTHLY...      $ 88.24
@4.75% COMPOUNDED QUARTERLY...   $ 90.29

DONE
```

C-2 IMAGE STATEMENT

There may be an IMAGE statement available on your system. An IMAGE statement provides the printing pattern for a PRINT statement in yet another statement. For our BANK2 program, we would use the following set of statements:

130 PRINT USING 140, FNH(P)
140 :@4.5% COMPOUNDED MONTHLY ..... $ ## . ##
150 PRINT USING 160, FNH(P1)
160 :@4.75% COMPOUNDED QUARTERLY .. $ ## . ##

to achieve the results of the last RUN above. The IMAGE statement begins with a colon and the number signs specify the locations of the digits in the numerical results. In an IMAGE statement, you may specify the location of the decimal point and the number of digits on either side with the number of number signs. The IMAGE statement may specify printing for several numbers by having several sets of number signs. You may also specify E-format by following the number signs with four exclamation marks (... ##!!!!). In our problem above, if we decide to change the location of the printed results, we simply retype lines 140 and 160.

Summary of Flowchart Shapes

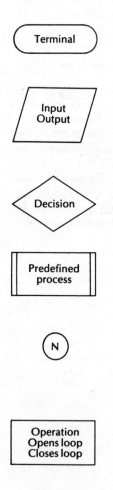

Used for beginning and ending of program.

Indicates data entered into the computer or results returned by the computer.

READ	MAT READ	READ#
PRINT	MAT PRINT	READ:
INPUT	MAT INPUT	WRITE#
		WRITE:

Indicates that a decision is being made.

IF   XXXXXX   THEN   YYY

Indicates a sequence of program statements not included in the flowchart. May be used for GØSUB statement.

Connector. Indicates transfer from one statement to another other than the next higher numbered statement in the program. N matches another N elsewhere in the same flowchart.

Used for anything not already specified.

NEXT X
LET
RETURN
STØP

Summary of Statements in BASIC

NOTE: Not all statements which appear in this appendix will run on all systems, and the list here does not cover every statement from some systems.

END	It is the highest numbered statement of every BASIC program. It is optional on some systems and required on others.
PRINT	Prints values of variables, calculated values, and literal expressions inside quotes. Spacing is controlled by semicolons or commas.
READ	Enters values stored in DATA statements into variables named in the READ statement. All legal BASIC variables (string and numeric) may be read in a single READ statement by separating them with commas.
DATA	Stores values for READ statements. Items of data must be separated by commas. Some systems require that strings be in quotes.
INPUT	Same as READ except that data is to be typed on the keyboard of the remote terminal.
LET	Assignment statement. The word LET is optional on many systems. Stores the value on the right of an equals sign in the variable named on the left. May be used to assign string variables. Multiple assignment is available on most systems.
GØTØ n	Names n as the next line number to be executed by the computer.
IF–THEN n	Tests the truth of an algebraic sentence placed between the IF and the THEN. Sends the computer to line n if the sentence is true. Control passes to the next line of the sentence is false.

REM — Permits the programmer to remark upon the program in the program itself without affecting the program operation. Some systems allow an apostrophe, ', to serve the same purpose.

FØR X = A TØ B STEP C — Opens a machine loop with first value for X at A, last number B, and increment C. If C is omitted, the step defaults to an increment of 1.

NEXT X — Closes machine loop. Sends the computer to the corresponding FØR statement to increment and test X.

GØSUB n — Sends the computer to a subroutine beginning at line n. Upon executing a RETURN statement, the computer returns to the line immediately following GØSUB n.

RETURN — Closes a subroutine.

DEF FNA(X) = — Program-defined function. The letter pair FN designates that a function is called for. The function name is A and the argument is X. Any letter of the alphabet may be placed where the A is. Some systems permit several variables as arguments.

DIM A( ),B$( ). . . . — Declares dimensions for one- or two-dimensional numeric arrays or string arrays or both. One number is required in the parentheses for a list, and two numbers separated by a comma are required for a two-dimensional array.

STØP — Execution of STØP statement causes termination of the RUN at that point.

RESTØRE — Restores all data in the program. The next item of data to be read will be the very first data item in the program (not discussed in text).

CHANGE A$ TØ A — Stores the ASCII code of the characters of the string A$ in the array A with the length of the string in characters stored in A(0).

CHANGE A TØ A$ — Stores a string in A$ with length specified in A(0) and characters determined by the ASCII code stored in the array elements of the A list.

MATRIX INSTRUCTIONS

MAT READ A — Enters data into the array named A. Several arrays can be read in the same MAT READ statement by separating the array names with commas.

MAT PRINT A — Prints the array named A with comma spacing. Several arrays may be printed with the same MAT PRINT statement by separating array names with a comma or a semicolon. The delimiter specifies the spacing for the preceding array.

MAT INPUT	Enters data into an array from the keyboard (not discussed in text).
MAT C = A ∘ B	Enters the product of A and B into array C.
MAT A = B + C	Enters the sum of B and C into array A.
MAT A = B − C	Enters the difference of B and C into array A.
MAT A = (K)∘B	Multiplies each entry of B by the scalar K and enters the result into A.
MAT A = ZER	Creates the zero matrix (fills each entry of A with zero). ZER may be followed by redimensioning specifications in parentheses.
MAT A = CØN	Fills each element of A with 1. CØN may be followed by redimensioning specifications in parentheses.
MAT E = IDN	Forms the identity matrix E. E must be square. All elements with equal row and column numbers are 1 and all other elements are 0. IDN may be followed by redimensioning specifications in parentheses.
MAT X = INV(A)	Finds the inverse of A (if it exists) and enters it in X.
MAT A = TRN(B)	Fills A with the transpose of B.

FUNCTIONS

SQR(X)	Computes the nonnegative square root of X. X must be nonnegative.
ABS(X)	Computes the absolute value of X.
SGN(X)	Returns the value 1 for X positive, 0 for X equals zero, and −1 for X negative.
INT(X)	Returns integer part of X. For some systems this is the mathematically greatest integer function. For others, the computer simply chops off the digits to the right of the decimal point. (The results are the same for nonnegative numbers.)
RND(X)	Generates a random number. In some systems the set of random numbers accessed is determined by the value of X. Some systems generate the same set of numbers each time the program is run, whereas others provide a different set and still others provide an option. See RND below.
RND	Returns a random number. The numbers will be the same on successive runs of the program if the RANDØMIZE statement is not present in the program and different on successive runs if the RANDØMIZE statement is present.
RANDØMIZE	Causes the random numbers generated in successive runs of the same program to vary.
SIN(X),CØS(X),TAN(X)	Computes the sin, cos, or tan of X, where X must be in radians.

ATN(X)   Computes the arctan of X. ATN(X) is in radians. The program must be written to determine the correct quadrant for the result.

LØG(X)   Computes the logarithm of X using base e.

EXP(X)   Computes the number whose LØG base e is X.

TAB(X)   Moves the printing mechanism to the (X + 1)st position of the carriage unless the printing mechanism is already past that point, in which case there is no effect

LEN(A$)   Returns the number of characters in the string A$.

EXT$(A$,I,J)   String extract function. Isolates a substring in A$ from the Ith to the Jth character inclusive.

FILES

Hewlett-Packard Files

FILES   Names files to be used by the present program and makes them available for access. File names are separated by commas.

READ #N,R   Sets the file pointer to the beginning of the Rth record of the Nth file named in the files statement. In addition, when followed by a semicolon and variable list, this statement reads values from the file to the variables.

READ #N;   When followed by a variable list, this statement reads from the file at a point previously established.

MAT READ #   Reads values from a file with the same options allowed for READ #.

PRINT #N,R   Sets the file pointer in the Nth file named in the files statement to the beginning of the Rth rcord and erases the contents of that record. In addition, when followed by a semicolon and a variable list, this statement causes the contents of the variables to be printed into the file.

PRINT #N;   When followed by a variable list this statement causes the contents of the variables to be printed wherever the file pointer has been previously set.

IF END #N THEN n   When executed, this statement sets a flag. If at any later time an attempt is made to read past the end of data or past the physical end of the file or to print past the physical end of the file, control passes to line n.

TYP(N)   The TYP (N) function takes on values from 1 to 4, depending on the nature of the next information in the file TYP(N) becomes 1 for number, 2 for string, and 3 for end of file. If the argument is negative, the value 4 will be returned for end of record.

General Electric Files

FILES   Names files to be used by the current program and makes them available for access. File names are separated by semicolons.

ASCII Files

READ #N,   Reads data from the Nth file named in the program into the variables of the variable list following the comma.

WRITE #N,   Writes data from the variable list following the comma to the file. The variables in the list may be separated by semicolons or commas to achieve corresponding spacing in the file.

IF MØRE #N   Determines whether or not there is more data in the file.

IF END #N   Determines whether or not the end of the file has been reached.

APPEND #N   Allows additional data to be written to an existing file by setting the file pointer to the end of the Nth file and placing the file in the WRITE mode.

SCRATCH #N   Sets the pointer of the Nth file to the beginning of the file, erases the file, and places it in write mode.

RESTORE #N   Sets the pointer of the Nth file to the beginning of the file and places it in the READ mode.

Binary Sequential Files

Binary sequential files may be processed by all of the above statements by substituting a colon (:) for the pound sign (#). Binary files should be less expensive to work with; however, ASCII files are very convenient due to the fact that they may be listed at the terminal.

Random Access Files

READ :N,   Same as ASCII.

WRITE :N,   Same as ASCII.

IF MØRE :N   Tests true, except when the file pointer is at the physical end of file.

IF END :N   Tests false, except when the file pointer is at the physical end of file.

SCRATCH :N   Places the file pointer at the beginning of the file and fills the file with binary zeros.

RESTØRE :N

SETW N TØ X

Places the file pointer at the beginning of the file without altering the contents of the file.

Places the file pointer to the Xth word of file N. To access a random file by record, the formula $W*(R-1)+1$ places the pointer at the beginning of the Rth record if there are W words per record.

APPENDIX F

Index of Programs in Text

238 *Basic BASIC*

Program	Description	Page
SCØRE1	Listing of ASCII file (GE)	118
SEG$1	Demonstrates string subscripts (HP)	103
SEG$2	Prints one digit numeric using string output (HP)	104
SØLVE	Solves four equations and four unknowns	192
SRVEY1	More processing of data in SURVEY	88–89
SUM1	Adds integers 1 through 50	17
SUM2	Modifies SUM1	17
SUM3	Modifies SUM2	20
SUM3+	SUM3 using machine loop	29
SURVEY	Uses a 15 by 5 array to analyze a questionnaire	86–87
SYNDIV	Divides a polynomial by X − R	158
TCHB	Tabulates four items per family	76
TCHB+	TCHB done with an array	83–84
TØLL-1	Reads and prints data for TØLL-2	182
TØLL-2	Prints schedule of tolls paid	184–185
TØLL-3	TØLL-2 with matrix operation	186
TØTAL	Finds total cost of five different items	21
TØTAL+	TØTAL using machine loop	29
TRAGL	Demonstrates variable loop limit	34
TRI•BI	Multiplies a trinomial by a binomial	156
TRIG1	Prints trig table 0 to 80 degrees	134
TRPØS1	Takes the transpose of a column vector	195
TRPØS2	Takes the transpose of a 2 by 4 matrix	195–196
TV'S	Tabulates survey of TV sets per family	74
WRITEAVG	Loads file SCØRE1 from file SCØRE (GE)	118

Answers to
Even-Numbered Problems

Answers to Even-Numbered Problems

Each two-page spread should be read from top to bottom as one individual page.

CHAP. 1

Problem No. 2

The answer to this will vary from 286 for computers permitting only single letters of the alphabet, upward. Some systems permit dollar signs and ampersands as variables. Other systems permit several letters of the alphabet, such as ABX, as simple variables.

Problem No. 4

The quote is an instruction to the computer that the printed message is terminated. Here again, systems differ. Some systems permit printing double quotes (") by including them between single quotes ('), such as: 'HE SAID, "HELLO."'

Problem No. 6

```
10  READ A,B
20  PRINT A*B
35  DATA 1.E-06,.001
40  END
RUN
6

1.00000E+06

DONE
```

Problem No. 8

```
10  PRINT 2/3
20  END
RUN
8

.666667

DONE
```

Problem No. 16(d)

```
10  LET N=(23.481+7.048)*4
20  LET D=4.98+3-81-8*2
30  PRINT N/D
40  END
RUN
16D

-9.61374

DONE
```

CHAP. 2

Problem No. 2

The READ statement calls for two variables. A single zero would have caused the program to terminate, as the variable P would find no data.

Problem No. 4

```
5   REM   THE LINES USED TO MODIFY PROGRAM SUM2 ARE 75, 15 AND 35
10  LET N=5
15  LET G=5
20  LET S=0
30  LET S=S+N
35  LET T=T+1
40  IF N=1191 THEN 70
45  LET G=G+1
50  LET N=N+2
60  GOTO 30
70  PRINT "SUM OF ODD NUMBERS FROM 5 TO 1191 IS"S
75  PRINT "THE NUMBER OF NUMBERS SUMMED IS"T
80  END
RUN
NO.4

SUM OF ODD NUMBERS FROM 5 TO 1191 IS 355212.
THE NUMBER OF NUMBERS SUMMED IS 594

DONE
```

Problem No. 12

```
10   PRINT "INITIAL BALANCE = $14.23"
20   READ B
30   LET B=14.23
35   READ T
35   IF T=0 THEN 110
40   LET B=B+T
50   PRINT B
60   GOTO 30
100  DATA 9,-3.24,-1.98,-3.85,0
110  END
RUN
NO.12

INITIAL BALANCE = $14.23
23.23
19.99
18.01
14.16

DONE
```

Problem No. 14

```
10   LET G=0
20   LET D=1
30   REM  G KEEPS TRACK OF THE NUMBER OF GIFTS
31   REM  D IS THE DAY NUMBER
32   REM  T TOTALS THE NUMBER OF GIFTS ON A GIVEN DAY
40   LET T=0
50   LET T=T+1
70   IF T=D THEN 80
75   GOTO 50
80   LET G=G+1
90   IF D <= 12 THEN 40
100  PRINT "TOTAL NUMBER OF GIFTS IS"G
110  END
RUN
NO.14

TOTAL NUMBER OF GIFTS IS 364

DONE
```

240

Problem No. 10

```
10  READ A,B,C,D,E,F,G,H,I,J
20  PRINT A+B+C+D+E+F+G+H+I+J
30  DATA 1,2,3,4,5,6,7,8,9,10
40  END
RUN
10

55

DONE
```

Problem No. 12

```
10  READ A,B,C,D
20  PRINT A*C,A*D+B*C,B*D
30  DATA 1,2,3,4,2,3,3,2
40  GOTO 10
50  END
RUN
12

 3     10     8
 6     13     6

OUT OF DATA  IN LINE 10
```

Problem No. 14

```
10  READ N1,D1,N2,D2
20  LET N=N1*D2+N2*D1
30  LET D=D1*D2
40  PRINT N/D
50  DATA 1,2,5,6
60  END
RUN
14

(1/2)+(5/6) = 16  / 12

10.

DONE
```

Problem No. 16(a)

```
10  LET N=1/2+1/3
20  LET D=1/3-1/4
30  PRINT N/D
40  END
RUN
16A

10.

DONE
```

Problem No. 16(b)

```
10  LET A=(2/3)+(5/6)
20  LET B=(3/4)/(2/3)
30  PRINT A+B
40  END
RUN
16B

1.925

DONE
```

Problem No. 16(c)

```
10  LET A=(1/2+3/7)/(2/3-3/1)
20  LET B=((4*3-3*2)/5)/(11/4)
30  PRINT A+B
40  END
RUN
16C

.332613

DONE
```

Problem No. 6

```
10   LET N=1001
20   LET S=0
30   LET T=0
35   LET T=T+1
40   LET S=S+N
45   LET N=N+11
50   IF N = 2213 THEN 100
70   GOTO 35
100  PRINT "THE SUM OF THE NUMBERS IS";S
110  PRINT "THE NUMBER OF NUMBERS IS";T
200  END
RUN
NO.6

THE SUM OF THE NUMBERS IS 178266.
THE NUMBER OF NUMBERS IS 111

DONE
```

Problem No. 8

```
10  LET I=1
20  PRINT I,1/I
30  IF I=25 THEN 50
35  LET I=I+1
40  GOTO 20
50  END
RUN
NO.8

 1            1
 2            .5
 3            .333333
 4            .25
 5            .2
 6            .166667
 7            .142857
 8            .125
 9            .111111
10            9.09091E-02
11            8.33333E-02
12            7.69231E-02
13            7.14286E-02
14            6.66667E-02
15            .0625
16            5.88235E-02
17            5.55556E-02
18            5.26316E-02
19            .05
20            .047619
21            4.54545E-02
22            4.34783E-02
23            4.16667E-02
24            .04

DONE
```

Problem No. 10

```
5    REM THIS IS NO.10
20   DATA 2,-35,3,2,65,11,-25,1,9,49,35,1,59,0,0
25   READ N
30   LET T=0
35   READ N,P
40   IF N=0 THEN 100
50   LET T=T+1
60   GOTO 30
100  PRINT "THE NUMBER OF DIFFERENT ITEMS IN THE ORDER IS";T
110  END
RUN
NO.10

THE NUMBER OF DIFFERENT ITEMS IN THE ORDER IS 5

DONE
```

Problem No. 16

```
10   LET T=0
15   LET C=0
20   READ S
30   IF S=0 THEN 70
40   LET C=C+1
50   LET T=T+S
60   GOTO 20
70   PRINT "GEORGE TOOK";C;"TESTS"
80   PRINT "FOR AN AVERAGE OF";T/C
90   DATA 83,91,97,100,89,0
200  END
RUN
NO.16

GEORGE TOOK 5    TESTS
FOR AN AVERAGE OF 92

DONE
```

CHAP. 3

SEC. 3-1

Problem No. 2

```
10  LET C=0
20  LET T=0
30  FOR N=1001 TO 2213 STEP 11
40  LET C=C+1
50  LET T=T+N
60  NEXT N
70  PRINT "TOTAL IS";T
80  PRINT "THE NUMBER OF NUMBERS IS";C
90  END
RUN
NO.2

TOTAL IS 178266.
THE NUMBER OF NUMBERS IS 111

DONE
```

Problem No. 4

```
10  FOR X=1 TO 25
20  PRINT X,1/X
30  NEXT X
40  END
RUN
NO.4

 1            1
 2            .5
 3            .333333
 4            .25
 5            .2
 6            .166667
 7            .142857
 8            .125
 9            .111111
10            9.09091E-02
11            8.33333E-02
12            7.69231E-02
13            7.14286E-02
14            6.66667E-02
15            .0625
16            5.88235E-02
17            5.55556E-02
18            5.26316E-02
19            .05
20            .047619
21            4.54545E-02
22            4.34783E-02
23            4.16667E-02
24            .04

DONE
```

SEC. 3-1 Cont'd

Problem No. 6

```
10 LET S=0
20 FOR X=1 TO 1000
30 LET S=S+1/X
40 NEXT X
50 PRINT "SUM OF RECIPROCALS FROM 1 TO 1000 IS";S
60 END
RUN
NO.6
```

```
SUM OF RECIPROCALS FROM 1 TO 1000 IS 7.48547
DONE
```

Problem No. 8

```
5 LET P=100
10 FOR Q=1 TO 4
20 LET P=.01*P
30 LET P=P+1
40 NEXT Q
50 PRINT "AMOUNT AFTER ONE YEAR IS";P
60 END
RUN
NO.8
```

```
AMOUNT AFTER ONE YEAR IS 104.06
DONE
```

Problem No. 10

```
10 READ D
20 IF D=0 THEN 110
30 LET S=0
40 FOR X=1 TO D
50 LET S=S+X
60 NEXT X
70 PRINT "SUM UP TO";D;"DAYS IS";S
90 GOTO 10
100 DATA 12,30,0
110 END
RUN
NO.10
```

```
SUM UP TO 12    DAYS IS 78
SUM UP TO 30    DAYS IS 465
DONE
```

SEC. 3-2

Problem No. 2

```
10 FOR I=1 TO 12
20 PRINT I*C
30 NEXT C
40 NEXT I
50 PRINT
60 NEXT X
70 END
RUN
NO.2
```

1	2	3	4	5	6	7	8	9	10	11	12
2	4	6	8	10	12	14	16	18	20	22	24
3	6	9	12	15	18	21	24	27	30	33	36
4	8	12	16	20	24	28	32	36	40	44	48
5	10	15	20	25	30	35	40	45	50	55	60
6	12	18	24	30	36	42	48	54	60	66	72
7	14	21	28	35	42	49	56	63	70	77	84
8	16	24	32	40	48	56	64	72	80	88	96

```
RUN
NO.8
```

```
999 IS THE LARGEST AND IS IN POSITION 9
DONE
```

Problem No. 10

```
5 LET I=0
10 FOR R=1 TO 5
20 FOR C=1 TO 10
30 LET I=I+1
35 PRINT I;
40 NEXT C
50 PRINT
60 PRINT
70 END
RUN
NO.10
```

1	2	3	4	5	6	7	8	9	10
11	12	13	14	15	16	17	18	19	20
21	22	23	24	25	26	27	28	29	30
31	32	33	34	35	36	37	38	39	40
41	42	43	44	45	46	47	48	49	50

```
DONE
```

Problem No. 12

```
10 PRINT "SQUARE",
20 FOR X=0 TO 9
40 NEXT X
45 PRINT
50 PRINT
75 PRINT
80 FOR C=0 TO 9
90 PRINT (L+C)*2J
100 NEXT C
105 PRINT
106 PRINT
110 NEXT L
130 END
RUN
NO.12
```

SQUARE	0	1	2	3	4	5	6	7	8	9
0	0	1	4	9	16	25	36	49	64	81
10	100	121	144	169	196	225	256	289	324	361
20	400	441	484	529	576	625	676	729	784	841

```
DONE
```

SEC. 3-3

Problem No. 2

```
10 FOR I=1 TO 10
20 LET L(I)=I*2
30 NEXT I
40 FOR J=1 TO 10
50 PRINT J;L(J)
60 END
RUN
NO.2
```

1	1
2	4
3	9
4	16
5	25
6	36
7	49
8	64
9	81
10	100

```
DONE
```

```
220 FOR J=1 TO A
230 PRINT T(J);
240 NEXT J
255 DATA 6,11,15,17,26,63,15,19,27,83,91
260 END
NO.8
```

```
FIRST LIST 6    11    15    27    17    24    83
SECOND LIST 15   19    17    83    91
NUMBERS IN LIST F OR LIST S
6    11    15    17    26    83    19    27    63    91
DONE
```

Problem No. 10

```
10 FOR I=1 TO 10
20 LET L(I)=2*I-1
30 NEXT I
40 FOR J=1 TO 10
50 LET S=0
60 FOR K=1 TO J
70 LET S=S+L(K)
80 NEXT K
90 LET M(J)=S
100 PRINT M(J);
110 NEXT J
120 END
RUN
NO.10
```

1	4	9	16	25	36	49	64	81	100

```
DONE
```

Problem No. 12

```
10 FOR X=1 TO 6
20 READ F(X)
30 PRINT F(X);
40 NEXT X
45 PRINT
50 FOR Y=1 TO 6
60 READ S(Y)
70 PRINT S(Y);
80 NEXT Y
85 PRINT
90 FOR I=1 TO 6
100 LET A(I)=F(I)+S(I)
110 PRINT A(I);
120 NEXT I
130 DATA 6,1,3,7,2,9,8,2,3,9,7,4
140 END
RUN
NO.12
```

6	1	3	7	2	9
8	2	3	9	7	4
14	3	6	16	9	13

```
DONE
```

SEC. 3-4

Problem No. 2

```
5 PRINT "ORIGINAL ORDER";
10 FOR X=1 TO 5
20 READ L(X)
30 NEXT X
35 PRINT
40 FOR I=1 TO 4
50 FOR J=1 TO 5
60 IF L(I) <= L(J) THEN 110
70 LET S=L(I)
80 LET L(I)=L(J)
90 LET L(J)=S
100 NEXT J
110 NEXT I
120 NEXT J
130 PRINT "LEAST FIRST    ";
140 FOR I=1 TO 5
150 IF L(U)=L(U-1) THEN 180
160 FOR U=2 TO 5
170 PRINT L(U)
```

Problem No. 4

```
5 PRINT "YEAR  PRINCIPLE"
10 LET P=1000
20 FOR Y=1 TO 10
30 FOR Q=1 TO 4
40 LET I=P*.05/4
50 LET P=P+I
60 NEXT Q
70 PRINT Y;P
80 NEXT Y
90 END
RUN
NO-4
```

```
YEAR   PRINCIPLE
 1     1050.95
 2     1104.49
 3     1160.75
 4     1219.89
 5     1282.04
 6     1347.35
 7     1415.99
 8     1488.13
 9     1563.94
10     1643.62
```

DONE

Problem No. 6

```
10 PRINT "RATE\YEARS",1,2,3,4
15 PRINT
20 FOR R=4 TO 5.5 STEP .5
25 LET P=1000
30 PRINT R,
40 FOR Y=1 TO 4
50 FOR Q=1 TO 4
60 LET I=P*R/100/4
70 LET P=P+I
80 NEXT Q
90 PRINT P,
100 NEXT Y
120 PRINT
130 END
RUN
NO-6
```

RATE\YEARS	1	2	3	4
4	1040.6	1082.86	1126.82	1172.58
4.5	1045.77	1093.62	1143.67	1196.01
5	1050.95	1104.49	1160.75	1219.89
5.5	1056.14	1115.44	1178.07	1244.21

DONE

Problem No. 8

```
10 READ S
20 LET P=1
28 FOR P=2 TO 10
50 IF S>P THEN 80
60 LET S=M
70 LET P=F
80 NEXT P
90 PRINT P,"IS THE LARGEST AND IS IN POSITION";P
100 DATA 87,32,153,-999,876,321,-2,18,9999,3
110 END
```

Problem No. 4

```
5 PRINT "FIRST LIST",
20 FOR X=1 TO 5
30 READ F(X)
40 PRINT F(X)
50 NEXT X
55 PRINT
60 PRINT "SECOND LIST",
70 FOR Y=1 TO 4
80 READ S(Y)
90 PRINT S(Y);
100 NEXT Y
105 PRINT
110 PRINT "ALL PAIRS"
120 FOR A=1 TO 5
130 FOR B=1 TO 4
140 PRINT F(A);S(B),
150 NEXT B
160 NEXT A
165 DATA 6,4,11,51,17,51,12,11,16
170 END
RUN
NO-4
```

```
FIRST LIST   6    4    11    51    17
SECOND LIST  51   12   11    16
ALL PAIRS
  6    51      6    12      6    11      6    16
  4    51      4    12      4    11      4    16
 11    51     11    12     11    11     11    16
 51    51     51    12     51    11     51    16
 17    51     17    12     17    11     17    16
```

DONE

Problem No. 6

```
10 PRINT "TOTAL COST = $";
20 DATA 2,.35,3,2.65,11,.25,1,9,.49,35,1.59,0,0
25 LET T=0
27 LET I=0
28 LET N(I+1)=P(I)
30 READ N(I),P(I)
40 IF N(I)=0 THEN 45
40 LET T=T+N(I)*P(I)
45 GOTO 28
50 PRINT T
60 END
RUN
NO-6
```

TOTAL COST = $ 76.54

DONE

Problem No. 8

```
5 REM USE THREE LISTS F,S,T FOR FIRST SECOND AND THIRD
10 PRINT "FIRST LIST";
20 FOR X=1 TO 6
30 READ F(X)
40 LET T(X)=F(X)
50 PRINT F(X);
60 NEXT X
70 PRINT
80 PRINT "SECOND LIST";
90 FOR Y=1 TO 5
100 READ S(Y)
110 PRINT S(Y);
130 PRINT
140 LET A=6
145 PRINT "NUMBERS IN LIST F OR LIST S"
150 FOR X=1 TO 5
170 IF S(X)=T(I) THEN 210
180 LET A=A+1
190 LET T(A)=S(X)
210 NEXT X
```

DONE

```
180 NEXT U
190 DATA 45,76,-76,45,98
200 END
RUN
NO-2
```

```
ORIGINAL ORDER  45    76    -76   45   98
LEAST FIRST     -76   45    76    45   98
DONE
```

Problem No. 4

```
10 LET A=0
15 LET T=0
20 FOR X=1 TO 6
35 READ S
35 IF S=-1 THEN 130
40 LET T=T+S
60 NEXT X
70 LET G=T/6
80 PRINT "AVG =";G
110 LET G(A1)=G
120 GOTO 15
130 LET M(X)=X
140 LET M(X)=X
150 NEXT X
155 LET T=0 TO A-1
170 IF G(Y) >= G(Y+1) THEN 240
180 LET S1=G(Y)
190 LET G(Y)=G(Y+1)
200 LET G(Y+1)=S1
205 LET S=M(Y)
210 LET M(Y)=M(Y+1)
220 LET M(Y+1)=S2
230 LET S=1
240 NEXT Y
250 IF S=1 THEN 155
255 PRINT "GRADE AVERAGE","ORIGINAL LOCATION"
260 FOR S=1 TO A
270 PRINT G(S),M(S)
280 NEXT S
290 DATA 65,68,73,85,82,87
292 DATA 74,87,90,85,87,88
294 DATA 88,91,92,90,89
296 DATA 91,83,78,89,79,87
298 DATA 65,76,67,50,60,66
299 DATA -1
300 END
RUN
NO-4
```

					AVG =
65	68	73	85	82	87
74	87	90	85	87	88
88	91	92	90	89	89
91	83	78	89	79	87
65	76	67	50	60	66

```
GRADE AVERAGE   ORIGINAL LOCATION
91.1667          3
85.6667          2
84.5             1
76.6667          4
64               5
```

```
AVG =  76.6667
AVG =  85.6667
AVG =  91.1667
AVG =  84.5
AVG =  64
```

DONE

Problem No. 6

```
5 LET L=0
6 LET H=0
10 FOR X=1 TO 7
20 READ L(X),H(X)
30 LET L=L+L(X)
40 LET H=H+H(X)
50 LET R(X)=H(X)-L(X)
60 NEXT X
80 PRINT "AVG LOW =";L/7
80 PRINT "AVG HIGH =";H/7
90 LET R=R(1)
```

SEC. 3-4 Cont'd

Problem No. 6 Cont'd

```
100 LET D=1
110 FOR X=2 TO 7
120 IF R= R(X) THEN 150
130 LET R=R(X)
140 LET D=X
150 NEXT X
160 PRINT "HIGHEST RANGE ="R
170 PRINT "ON DAY NUMBER "D
180 DATA 51,71,48,67,50,77,55,78,55,76,55,75,49,79
RUN
N0.6
```

```
AVG LOW = 51.8571
AVG HIGH = 74.2143
HIGHEST RANGE = 30
ON DAY NUMBER  7

DONE
```

Problem No. 8

```
10 LET X=0
20 LET T=0
30 LET X=X+1
40 READ L(X)
50 IF L(X)=0 THEN 90
60 PRINT L(X)
70 LET T=T+L(X)
80 GOTO 30
90 LET A=T/(X-1)
95 PRINT
100 PRINT "AVERAGE ="A
110 FOR B=0 TO X-2
120 FOR C=1 TO X-1
130 IF L(B) <= L(B+1) THEN 180
140 LET S=L(B)
150 LET L(B)=L(B+1)
160 LET L(B+1)=S1
180 NEXT C
190 IF S=1 THEN 110
200 FOR C=1 TO X-1
210 IF A>L(C) THEN 240
240 PRINT C-1"SCORES WERE BELOW AVERAGE"
250 PRINT "TROUBLE"
260 FOR D=X-1 TO 1 STEP -1
270 IF A<L(D) THEN 300
280 PRINT X-C"TEST SCORES WERE ABOVE AVERAGE"
300 PRINT "TROUBLE"
310 PRINT "TROUBLE"
320 PRINT L(INT((X-1)/2+.5))"IS THE MEDIAN SCORE"
325 DATA 65,71,82,63,90,58,66,67,68
336 DATA 0
340 END
RUN
N0.8
```

```
65  71  82  63  90  58  66  67  68
AVERAGE = 70
 6  SCORES WERE BELOW AVERAGE
 3  TEST SCORES WERE ABOVE AVERAGE
67  IS THE MEDIAN SCORE

DONE
```

CHAP. 4

SEC. 4-1

Problem No. 2

```
RUN
N0.6
```

```
237     - 3  = 711
 79     = 9  = 711
  1     = 711  = 711

  1     = 991  = 991
        = -991  =-991
        = 991  = 991

-1     =-991  =-991
151     = 3  = 453
  3     = 6  = 453
  1     = 453  = 453

-327     = 2  =-654
-327     =-2  =-654
 218     = 3  =-654
-109     =-3  =-654
 109     = 6  =-654
-1     = 654  =-654
  1     = 654  =-654

  1     = 1009  = 1009
        =-1009  =-1009
-1     = 1009  =-1009
  1     = 9001  = 9001

DONE
```

Problem No. 8

```
10 FOR X=1001 TO 1500 STEP 2
20 FOR I=3 TO SQR(X) STEP 2
30 IF X/I=INT(X/I) THEN 60
40 NEXT I
50 PRINT X;
60 NEXT X
70 END
RUN
N0.8
```

1009	1013	1019	1021	1031	1033	1039	1049
1051	1061	1063	1069	1087	1091	1093	1097
1103	1109	1117	1123	1129	1151	1153	1163
1171	1181	1187	1193	1201	1213	1217	1223
1229	1231	1237	1249	1259	1277	1279	1283
1289	1291	1297	1301	1303	1307	1319	1321
1327	1361	1367	1373	1381	1399	1409	1423
1427	1429	1433	1439	1447	1451	1453	1459
1471	1481	1483	1487	1489	1493	1499	

```
DONE
```

SEC. 4-2

Problem No. 2

```
10 READ N,D
11 IF N=0 THEN 150
12 PRINT N"/"D"="
13 IF N<D THEN 17
15 LET X=D
16 GOTO 20
17 LET Y=N
18 LET Y=D
19 LET X=N
20 FOR P=X TO 2 STEP -1
30 IF X/P=INT(X/P) THEN 70
```

Problem No. 8

```
10 READ F,S
20 IF F=0 THEN 999
25 PRINT F;S;"GCF=";
30 FOR X=F TO 1 STEP -1
40 IF S/X=INT(S/X) THEN 60
50 GOTO 70
60 IF F/X=INT(F/X) THEN 110
70 NEXT X
80 PRINT 1
90 GOTO 10
110 PRINT X
120 GOTO 10
200 DATA 19,0,1083,27,35,27,36,16,34,12,20,0,0
999 END
RUN
N0.8
```

```
237     1083     GCF= 19
 27       35      GCF=  1
 27       36      GCF=  9
 16       34      GCF=  2
 12       20      GCF=  4

DONE
```

Problem No. 10

```
10 LET F[1]=1
20 LET F[2]=1
30 FOR I=3 TO 10
40 LET F[I]=F[I-1]+F[I-2]
50 NEXT I
60 FOR I=3 TO 9
70 LET J=I+1 TO 10
80 LET F=F[I]
90 GOSUB 1000
110 NEXT J
110 NEXT I
130 LET Z=1 TO C
140 PRINT L(Z);
150 NEXT Z
160 GOTO 1120
1000 FOR X=F TO 1 STEP -1
1020 IF S=X*INT(S/X) THEN 1030
1030 GOTO 1040
1030 IF F/X=INT(F/X) THEN 1060
1040 NEXT X
1050 GOTO 1110
1060 FOR Y=1 TO C
1070 IF X=L[Y] THEN 1110
1080 NEXT Y
1090 LET C=C+1
1100 LET L(C)=X
1110 RETURN
1120 END
RUN
N0.10
```

```
 1     2     3     5

DONE
```

SEC. 4-3

Problem No. 2

```
10 LET P=5
20 FOR W=1 TO 25
30 FOR W=1 TO 12
40 LET P=P+.045/12
50 LET P=P+5
60 NEXT W
70 NEXT M
80 LET P=N
90 PRINT P
100 END
```

```
10 PRINT
15 READ N
17 IF N=0 THEN 110
20 FOR D=2 TO SQR(N)
30 IF N/D=INT(N/D) THEN 70
40 NEXT D
50 PRINT I"*"N"="N
75 IF N>0 THEN 60
80 GOTO 10
85 DATA 1946,1949,1001,0
110 END
N=.2
```

```
973  *  2  =  1946
278  *  7  =  1946
139  *  14  =  1946
1  *  1946  =  1946

143  *  7  =  1001
91  *  11  =  1001
77  *  13  =  1001
1  *  1001  =  1001
```

Problem No. 4

```
5  PRINT "NUMBER","ABSOLUTE VALUE"
10 READ A
20 GOSUB 1000
30 GOSUB 10
1000 IF A >= 0 THEN 1020
1010 LET A=-A
1020 PRINT A
1030 RETURN
1040 DATA 11,-3,0,-17,13,-31,2,-11,-1
1050 END
RUN
N=.4
```

```
NUMBER     ABSOLUTE VALUE
11.3         11.3
-17          17
13           13
-31.2        31.2
-11.1        11.1

OUT OF DATA IN LINE 10
```

Problem No. 6

```
10 PRINT
15 READ N
17 IF N=0 THEN 110
20 FOR D=2 TO SQR(ABS(N))
30 IF N/D=INT(N/D) THEN 70
40 NEXT D
50 PRINT I"*"N"="N
51 IF N>0 THEN 60
52 PRINT -I"*"-N"="-N
70 IF N>0 THEN 75
71 IF N>0 THEN 75
73 IF N<0 THEN 10
75 GOTO 40
85 DATA 711,-991,-991,453,-654,1009,-1009,9001,0
110 END
```

```
40 NEXT P
50 PRINT N"/"D
60 GOTO 10
70 IF Y/D=INT(Y/P) THEN 90
80 GOTO 40
90 PRINT N/P"/"D/P
100 GOTO 10
110 DATA 5,6,82,48,3,4,36,48
120 DATA 0,0
RUN
N=.2
```

```
5   /  6   =  5   /  6
82  /  48  =  41  /  24
3   /  4   =  3   /  4
36  /  48  =  3   /  4
```

Problem No. 4

```
10 PRINT "INCHES =","YARDS FEET   INCHES"
20 READ I
30 IF I=0 THEN 999
40 PRINT I,
50 LET Y=INT(I/36)
60 LET I1=I-36*Y
70 LET F=INT(I1/12)
80 LET I2=I1-F*12
90 PRINT Y,F,I2
100 DATA 20,197,150,608,83,31,0
999 END
RUN
N=.4
```

```
INCHES =    YARDS  FEET  INCHES
20            0     1     8
197           5     4     5
150           4     2     6
608           16    2     8
83            2     0     11
31            0     2     7
```

Problem No. 6

```
10 READ H,Q,DO,N
15 PRINT "DOLLARS","HALF QUARTER DIMES NICKEL PENNIES"
20 READ D
21 IF D=0 THEN 9999
25 PRINT D,
27 LET D=D*100
30 LET H=INT(D/H)
40 LET D=D-H*H
50 LET Q1=INT(D1/Q)
60 LET D1=D1-Q1*Q
70 LET D2=INT(D1/DO)
80 LET D1=D1-D2*DO
90 LET N1=INT(D1/N)
100 LET D1=D1-N1*N
110 PRINT H;Q1;D2;N1;D1
120 GOTO 20
1010 DATA 50,25,10,5
1020 DATA 1.56,.35,1.76
1030 DATA -.01,0
9999 END
RUN
N=.6
```

```
DOLLARS   HALF QUARTER DIMES NICKEL PENNIES
1.56       3     0     0     1     1
.35        0     1     1     0     0
1.76       3     1     0     0     1
-.01       0     0     0     0     1
```

RUN
N=2

2780.36

DONE

Problem No. 4

```
10 LET P=0
20 FOR Y=1 TO 25
30 FOR M=1 TO 12
40 LET P=P+5
50 FOR D=1 TO 30
60 LET P=P+P*.045/360
70 NEXT D
80 NEXT M
90 NEXT Y
100 PRINT "$";INT(P*100+.5)*.01
120 END
RUN
N=.4
```

$ 2778.71

Problem No. 6

```
10 DEF FNK(X)=INT(100*X+.5)*.01
20 LET P1=P2=P3=99
30 FOR Y=1 TO 15
40 FOR M=1 TO 12
50 LET P1=P1+P1*4.75/100/12
60 NEXT M
70 FOR Q=1 TO 4
80 LET P2=P2+P2*5/100/4
90 NEXT Q
100 FOR D=1 TO 365
110 LET P3=P3+P3*4.5/100/365
120 NEXT D
130 NEXT Y
140 PRINT "  ***$99.00 FOR 15 YEARS***"
150 PRINT "4.75% COMPOUNDED MONTHLY...";
160 LET X=5
170 GOSUB 500
180 PRINT FNK(P1)
190 PRINT "5% COMPOUNDED QUARTERLY...";
200 LET X=X+1
210 GOSUB 500
220 PRINT FNK(P2)
230 PRINT "4.5% COMPOUNDED DAILY...";
240 LET X=X+2
250 GOSUB 500
260 PRINT FNK(P3)
500 FOR Z=1 TO X
510 PRINT " ";
520 NEXT Z
530 PRINT "$";
540 RETURN
999 END
RUN
N=.6
```

```
          ***$99.00 FOR 15 YEARS***
4.75% COMPOUNDED MONTHLY...      $ 201.59
5% COMPOUNDED QUARTERLY...       $ 208.41
4.5% COMPOUNDED DAILY...         $ 194.43
```

DONE

SEC. 4-3 Cont'd

Problem No. 8

```
10 DEF FNK(C)=2*C+2*86C-1
30 PRINT " X   Y "
40 PRINT X-4 TB 8
40 PRINT X=2FNK(X)
50 NEXT X
60 END
RUN
NO.8
```

X	Y
-6	23
-5	9
-4	-1
-3	-7
-2	-9
-1	-7
-0	-1
0	9
2	23

DONE

SEC. 4-4

Problem No. 2

```
5 DEF FNR(X)=INT(40*RND(X)-200)
10 DIM L(25)
20 FOR X=1 TO 25
30 LET L(X)=FNR(X)
40 PRINT L(X)
50 NEXT X
60 PRINT
70 LET I=26
75 REM CAN IMPROVE THE EFFICIENCY BY HAVING THE
76 REM COMPUTER LOOK AT ONE LESS NUMBER EACH TIME THROUGH
80 LET I=I-1
90 LET S=0
100 FOR X=1 TO I-1
110 IF L(X)=<L(X+1) THEN 160
120 LET L(X)=L(X+1)
130 LET L(X+1)=L(X)
140 LET L(X)=S
150 LET S=0
160 FOR Y=1 TO 25
180 PRINT L(Y)
190 PRINT L(Y)
200 NEXT Y
210 END
RUN
NO.2
```

```
108  -151  -79  -117  -190  116  -200  169  -52  -31   80  109
155    8   59   82  161   28  122  -124  -41  -130  191  -31
-40  -190  -151  -130  -124  -79  -60  116  155  182   41  -37
-200   59   80   82  108  108  109  116  122  155  161  169
```
191
DONE

Problem No. 4

```
10 DIM F(18),G(18)
20 LET A=1
30 LET G(1)=1
40 LET F(1)=F(2)=1
50 FOR X=3 TO 18
60 LET F(X)=F(X-1)+F(X-2)
70 NEXT X
80 FOR X=1 TO 17
```

```
360 PRINT F(K)
370 NEXT K
500 DATA 7,6,1,0,9,8,7,1,8,9
501 DATA 6,1,0,3,6,5,9,2,0,1
599 REM N8 WE COULD NOT USE JUST TWO LISTS••••••••
RUN
END
NO.8
```

	1	6	7	6	3	8	7	6	6
6	1	6	7	8	3	9	7	6	6
1	3	4	2	3	4	5	8	9	

DONE

Problem No. 10

```
10 DEF FNR(X)=INT(X*RND(1))
20 READ N
25 IF N=0 THEN 999
30 FOR Z=1 TO 5
40 LET B=FNR(N)
50 LET X=A+B
60 PRINT A" "B" "      "")
70 GOSUB 700
80 LET X=A+B
90 GOSUB 700
100 PRINT "  -  "
105 GOSUB 700
110 NEXT Z
115 PRINT
180 GOTO 20
700 LET L=X/N+X
710 LET W=INT(X/N)
720 LET W=X+W*N
730 PRINT W"MOD  "N)
900 DATA 5,6,0
999 END
RUN
NO.10
```

4	+3	=	2	MOD	5
4	+0	=	4	MOD	5
4	+2	=	1	MOD	5
4	-3	=	2	MOD	5
4	+0	=	4	MOD	5
3	+1	=	4	MOD	6
3	+2	=	5	MOD	6
3	-1	=	2	MOD	6
3	+2	=	5	MOD	6
3	-3	=	0	MOD	6

Problem No. 12

```
5 REM SUBTRACT  S FROM  F  MOD 7
10 READ F,S
15 IF F=0 THEN 999
20 LET D=F-S
30 IF D<0 THEN 100
40 IF D>7 THEN 60
50 LET D=D-7
60 PRINT F" - "S" = "D"MOD 7"
70 GOTO 10
110 LET D=D+7
110 GOTO 60
500 DATA 3,6,4,0,0,4,5,2,2,5,0,1,0
999 END
RUN
NO.12
```

3	-	6	=	4	MOD 7
5	-	0	=	4	MOD 7
5	-	4	=	3	MOD 7
2	-	2	=	0	MOD 7
2	-	5	=	4	MOD 7

DONE

```
255 LET A=20
270 FOR U1=1 TO 20
285 FOR U=1 TO 20
300 IF U(U)=T(U1) THEN 325
330 LET A=A+1
345 LET U(A)=T(U1)
360 NEXT U1
375 PRINT "ELEMENTS OF EITHER SET"
390 FOR X=1 TO A
400 PRINT U(X))
420 NEXT X
435 PRINT
450 PRINT "ELEMENTS WHICH APPEAR IN BOTH LISTS"
465 FOR X=1 TO B
480 PRINT I(X))
495 NEXT X
500 IF B>0 THEN 510
505 PRINT "NO ELEMENTS COMMON TO BOTH LISTS"
510 STOP
520 STOP
525 LET B=B+1
540 LET I(B)=U(U)
555 IF U=20 THEN 360
570 GOTO 315
590 END
RUN
NO.18
```

FIRST LIST								
88	-77	54	-85	-94	-97	-42	-76	18	90	76	-58

SECOND LIST								
28	33	45	80	-28	16	43	13	-5	-49	50	38

```
77  19  -82  44  -100  -94  23  96
```
ELEMENTS OF EITHER SET
| 88 | -77 | 54 | -85 | -94 | -97 | -42 | -76 | 18 | 90 | 76 | -58 |

| 80 | 96 | 16 | 43 | 51 | 13 | -48 | 33 | 19 | 45 | 80 |

```
-28  16  43  13  -49  50
```
| -100 | -96 | 23 | 96 |
ELEMENTS WHICH APPEAR IN BOTH LISTS
| 3 | 80 | -49 | 96 |

DONE

Problem No. 20

```
5 PRINT "TIME NOW","ADD TIME","TIME LATER"
10 DEF FNT(T)=INT(T*RND(1)+1)
20 FOR P=1 TO 10
30 LET N=FNT(12)
40 LET H=FNT(59)
50 LET M1=FNT(36)
60 LET M1=FNT(59)
70 LET H2=H+H
75 LET H2=H+H1
90 IF M2=60 THEN 110
90 LET M2=M2-60
100 LET H2=H2+1
110 IF H2 <= 12 THEN 150
130 LET H2=H2-12
140 GOTO 110
150 PRINT H":"M,H1":"M1,H2":"M2
170 NEXT P
170 END
RUN
NO.20
```

TIME NOW		ADD TIME		TIME LATER	
12	: 30	18	: 56	7	: 26
9	: 36	12	: 3	12	: 39
3	: 20	36	: 55	7	: 14
6	: 49	24	: 55	7	: 44
4	: 41	13	: 28	6	: 9
3	: 38	34	: 21	11	: 59
2	: 23	12	: 12	6	: 35
1	: 17	20	: 14	7	: 31
11	: 49	33	: 29	11	: 18

DONE

CHAP. 5

SEC. 5-1

Problem No. 2

```
10  FOR I=1 TO 5
20  LET C(I)=0
30  NEXT I
35  LET P=0
40  FOR R=1 TO 5
50  READ C
60  IF C=-1 THEN 100
61  LET A(R)=C
70  LET C(R)=C(R)+C
80  NEXT R
81  IF A(1)=0 THEN 90
82  IF A(3)=0 THEN 90
83  LET P=P+1
90  GOTO 40
100 PRINT "CHEMISTRY","PHYSICS","FRENCH","SPANISH","CALCULUS"
110 PRINT "PHYSICS IS=P
120 PRINT C(I),
130 NEXT I
145 PRINT "THE NUMBER OF PEOPLE TAKING CHEMISTRY AND ";
990 REM  "1" MEANS YES    "0" MEANS NO
     REM  DATA IS IN ORDER CHEMISTRY PHYSICS FRENCH SPANISH CALCULUS
1000 DATA 1,0,1,1,0,0,0,1,0,1,1,0,1,1,0,0,1
1010 DATA 0,1,1,0,0,0,0,1,0,1,1,0,1,1,0,0,1
1080 DATA 0,0,1,0,1,1,0,0,0
1100 DATA -1
9999 END
RUN
NO-2
```

CHEMISTRY	PHYSICS	FRENCH	SPANISH	CALCULUS
7	5	7	6	6

THE NUMBER OF PEOPLE TAKING CHEMISTRY AND PHYSICS IS 4

DONE

Problem No. 4

```
10  FOR I=1 TO 5
20  LET C(I)=0
30  NEXT I
35  LET P=0
40  FOR R=1 TO 5
50  READ C
60  IF C=-1 THEN 100
70  LET C(R)=C(R)+C
80  NEXT R
81  IF A(2)=0 THEN 90
82  IF A(5)=1 THEN 90
83  LET P=P+1
90  GOTO 40
110 PRINT "CHEMISTRY","PHYSICS","FRENCH","SPANISH","CALCULUS"
120 PRINT C(I),
130 NEXT I
140 PRINT "THE NUMBER OF PEOPLE TAKING PHYSICS BUT NOT CALCULUS"P
995 REM  "1" MEANS YES  "0" MEANS NO
     REM  DATA IS IN ORDER CHEMISTRY PHYSICS FRENCH SPANISH CALCULUS
1000 DATA 1,0,1,1,0,0,0,1,0,1,1,0,1,1,0,0,1
1010 DATA 0,1,1,0,0,0,0,1,0,1,1,0,1,1,0,0,1
1020 DATA 0,0,1,0,1,1,0,0,0
1030 DATA -1
9999 END
NO-4
```

CHEMISTRY	PHYSICS	FRENCH	SPANISH	CALCULUS
7	5	7	6	6

TAKING PHYSICS BUT NOT CALCULUS 1

DONE

Problem No. 14

```
10  DEF FNR(X)=INT(X*RND(0)+1)
20  FOR X=1 TO 10
30  LET I=FNR(999)
40  LET I1=FNR(300)    "OCF ="
45  PRINT I(I1);"OCF ",
50  FOR Y=1 TO 2 STEP -1
70  IF 1/Y=INT(I(I)/T) THEN 200
70  NEXT Y
80  PRINT I,
85  GOTO 400
200 IF I1/Y=INT(I1/T) THEN 300
205 GOTO 70
400 PRINT X
999 END
RUN
NO-14
```

864	1308	OCF	=	6
454	924	OCF	=	6
304	1195	OCF	=	1
585	783	OCF	=	37
445	1147	OCF	=	5
73	869	OCF	=	5
740	495	OCF	=	1
915	1387	OCF	=	1

DONE

Problem No. 16

```
10  DEF FNR(X)=INT(X*RND(0)+1)
20  FOR X=1 TO 10
30  LET I=FNR(100)
40  LET I1=FNR(100)    "LCM ="
45  PRINT I(I1);"LCM ",
50  FOR Y=1 TO 2 STEP -1
70  IF 1/Y=INT(I(I)/T) THEN 800
70  NEXT Y
80  PRINT I=1
85  GOTO 400
300 IF 1/Y=INT(I1/T) THEN 300
305 GOTO 70
400 PRINT X,
999 END
RUN
NO-16
```

99	39	LCM	=	1287
1	67	LCM	=	8
35	69	LCM	=	2415
7	51	LCM	=	1333
6	31	LCM	=	194
15	73	LCM	=	1095
52	9	LCM	=	468
72	65	LCM	=	3276
		LCM	=	4680

DONE

Problem No. 6

```
90  FOR X=X-1 TO 18
100 FOR Z=FIX) TO G(A)=1 STEP -1
110 IF F(T)/2=INT(F(X)/2) THEN 140
130 NEXT Z
140 GOTO 210
140 LET I=FNR(500)
150 IF F(T)/Z <> INT(F(Y)/Z) THEN 120
160 LET Z=G(W) THEN 810
170 NEXT Z
180 LET A=A+1
190 LET G(A)=Z
200 NEXT X
210 PRINT Y,
220 PRINT X,
230 FOR X=1 TO A
240 PRINT G(B),
250 NEXT X
260 PRINT B
     END
NO-6
```

-1	2	3	5	8	13	21	34

Problem No. 8

```
5   REM  WE MULTIPLY 7610987189 BY 8103659801
10  DIM B(20);T(20),P(20)
20  FOR Y=1 TO 10
30  FOR X=1
40  READ B(Y)
50  NEXT X
60  READ T(X)
70  FOR P(0)=0
74  FOR Y=1 TO 20
78  LET P(D)=0
80  FOR X=10 TO 1 STEP -1
90  LET P(P-3)=P(P-3)+B(P)*T(S)
100 LET P(P-3)=P(P-3)-8(P)*T(S)
110 NEXT 3
140 IF P(A)=10 THEN 300
150 LET P(A)=P(A)-1041
160 LET P(A)=P(A)-1041
300 FOR X=1 TO 80
     END
```

0	4	7	2	0	4	2	5	9	1	4	3
0	0	4	0	4	0	6	4	8	2	7	1

Problem No. 18

```
15  DIM B(20);T(20),I(20),U(40)
30  DEF FNR(X)=INT(20*RND(0)-100)
40  LET B=0
45  PRINT "FIRST LIST"
75  LET B(X)=FNR(X)
80  LET U(X)=B(X)
105 PRINT B(X),
135 NEXT X
150 PRINT
150 PRINT "SECOND LIST"
180 FOR Y=1 TO 80
195 LET T(Y)=FNR(Y)
810 PRINT T(Y),
285 NEXT Y
840 PRINT
```

Problem No. 6

```
10 FOR I=1 TO 5
20 LET C[I]=0
30 NEXT I
33 REM THIS LOOP SIMULATES 500 PEOPLE
40 FOR R=1 TO 500
42 REM THIS LOOP LOOKS AT FIVE COURSES FOR EACH PERSON
50 LET C=INT(7*RND(1))
52 LF C=3 THEN 58
54 GOTO 70
58 LET C=1
70 LET C[R]=C[R]+C
78 REM NEXT COURSE
80 NEXT R
88 REM NEXT PERSON
90 NEXT X
100 PRINT "CHEMISTRY","PHYSICS","FRENCH","SPANISH","CALCULUS"
110 FOR I=1 TO 5
120 PRINT C[I],
130 NEXT I
9999 END
RUN
NO.6
```

CHEMISTRY	PHYSICS	FRENCH	SPANISH	CALCULUS
204	232	234	205	219

DONE

SEC. 5-2

Problem No. 2

```
10 FOR R=1 TO 6
20 FOR C=1 TO 3
30 LET B[R,C]=1
40 NEXT C
50 NEXT R
60 REM ARRAY B IS FILLED WITH ONES
70 FOR R=1 TO 6
80 FOR C=1 TO 3
90 PRINT B[R,C];
100 NEXT C
110 PRINT
120 NEXT R
130 END
RUN
NO.2
```

DONE

Problem No. 4

```
10 FOR R=1 TO 7
20 FOR C=1 TO 7
30 LET D[R,C]=0
40 IF R <> C THEN 60
50 LET D[R,C]=1
60 NEXT C
70 NEXT R
80 FOR R=1 TO 7
90 FOR C=1 TO 7
100 PRINT D[R,C];
110 NEXT C
120 PRINT
130 NEXT R
140 END
```

Problem No. 6 (cont'd)

```
115 PRINT "2 TIMES ENTRIES OF FIRST ARRAY"
120 GOSUB 1000
130 STOP
1000 FOR A=1 TO 4
1010 FOR B=1 TO 7
1030 PRINT T[A,B];
1040 NEXT B
1050 PRINT
1060 NEXT A
1070 RETURN
9999 END
RUN
NO.5
```

FIRST ARRAY

210	258	158	132	-132	-479	-186
-207	232	-416	240	14	-427
-78	335	343	-452	-293	-198	-52
241	335	343	-293	-198	-52

2 TIMES ENTRIES OF FIRST ARRAY

420	516	316	264	-264	-958	-372
-414	464	492	-16	480	28	854
-158	-832	-268	136
482	670	686	-904	-586	-396	-104

DONE

Problem No. 10

```
10 FOR A=1 TO 10
20 FOR B=1 TO 10
30 LET M[A,B]=A*B
40 NEXT B
50 NEXT A
60 FOR I=1 TO 10
70 FOR J=1 TO 10
80 PRINT M[I,J];
90 NEXT J
95 PRINT
100 NEXT I
110 END
RUN
NO.10
```

1	2	3	4	5	6	7	8	9	10
2	4	6	8	10	12	14	16	18	20
3	6	9	12	15	18	21	24	27	30
4	8	12	16	20	24	28	32	36	40
5	10	15	20	25	30	35	40	45	50
6	12	18	24	30	36	42	48	54	60
7	14	21	28	35	42	49	56	63	70
8	16	24	32	40	48	56	64	72	80
9	18	27	36	45	54	63	72	81	90
10	20	30	40	50	60	70	80	90	100

DONE

Problem No. 12

```
20 FOR I=1 TO 5
30 FOR J=1 TO 5
60 LET P=(I-1)*(J-1)
70 IF P<5 THEN 90
75 GOTO 70
85 GO TO 70
90 LET P[I,J]=P
100 NEXT J
140 PRINT "MULTIPLICATION MOD 5"
150 FOR J=1 TO 5
160 FOR J=1 TO 5
170 PRINT P[I,J];
180 NEXT J
190 PRINT
200 PRINT
205 PRINT I
210 FOR N=1 TO 6
220 LET A=INT(5*RND(1))
230 LET B=INT(5*RND(1))
```

RUN
NO.2

QUEST NUMBER	MALE 21+	MALE UNDER	FEMALE 21+	FEMALE UNDER	TOTAL
1	2	2	1	-	7
2	2	-	2	1	5
3	2	1	1	-	5
4	2	-	2	1	5
5	2	-	1	2	5
6	2	-	1	1	4
7	2	-	1	1	4
8	3	-	2	1	6
9	2	-	-	2	4
10	2	1	2	-	4
11	2	1	2	-	6
12	2	2	3	-	6
13	3	2	3	2	6
14	2	2	2	2	4
15	3	2	4	2	6
	24	8	25	30	79

DONE

Problem No. 4

```
10 DIM S[15,10]
20 REM LINE 30 ENTERS THE ROW NUMBER IN THE FIRST COLUMN
28 FOR R=1 TO 15
30 LET S[R,1]=R
40 REM LINE 50 SETS THE LAST 9 COLUMNS AT ZERO
48 FOR C=2 TO 10
50 LET S[R,C]=0
60 NEXT C
70 NEXT R
80 FOR N=1 TO 50
90 LET P=INT(4*RND(1)+2)
98 REM Q GOES THROUGH THE 15 QUESTIONS
100 FOR Q=1 TO 15
110 LET A=INT(2*RND(1))
120 LET S[Q,P]=S[Q,P]+A
130 NEXT Q
140 NEXT N
145 FOR R=1 TO 15
150 LET S[R,6]=S[R,2]+S[R,3]
160 LET S[R,8]=S[R,4]+S[R,5]
170 LET S[R,8]=S[R,2]+S[R,4]
180 LET S[R,9]=S[R,3]+S[R,5]
185 LET S[R,10]=S[R,6]+S[R,7]
190 NEXT R
198 REM THE PRINTING BEGINS HERE
200 PRINT "QUEST MALE FEMALEFEMALE"
205 PRINT "NUMBER 21+ UNDER MALE  FEMALE UNDER MALE  FEMALE UNDER 21+")
211 PRINT " TOTAL"
220 FOR R=1 TO 15
230 FOR C=1 TO 10
250 PRINT S[R,C];
260 NEXT C
270 PRINT
280 NEXT R
9999 END
RUN
NO.4
```

QUEST NUMBER	MALE 21+	MALE UNDER	FEMALE 21+	FEMALE UNDER	FEMALE MALE	FEMALE UNDER	MALE 21+	FEMALE UNDER	TOTAL
1	5	10	5	5	15	10	10	10	25
2	5	11	8	8	16	16	13	19	23
3	3	7	6	8	15	14	11	15	34
4	5	11	8	6	20	14	13	18	29
5	9	11	4	6	20	10	13	11	31
6	7	6	6	6	13	12	13	12	26
7	6	8	4	10	14	14	10	16	29
8	7	8	8	4	15	12	15	12	20
9	7	6	7	7	13	14	14	13	22
10	7	6	4	3	13	7	11	9	20
11	7	4	7	8	11	15	14	12	22
12	7	10	4	7	17	11	11	17	27
13	6	8	7	6	14	13	13	14	27
14	5	8	3	10	13	13	9	16	27
15	4	7	9	11	11	16	11	16	27

DONE

Problem No. 6

```
10 DIM M(12,12)
20 FOR R=1 TO 12
30 FOR C=1 TO 12
40 LET M(R,C)=R*C
50 NEXT C
60 NEXT R
70 FOR R=10 TO 12
80 FOR C=1 TO 12
90 PRINT M(R,C);
100 NEXT C
110 PRINT
120 NEXT R
130 END
RUN
NO.6
```

10	20	30	40	50	60	70	80	90	100	110	120
11	22	33	44	55	66	77	88	99	110	121	132
12	24	36	48	60	72	84	96	108	120	132	144

DONE

CHAP. 6

SEC. 6-1

Problem No. 2

```
10 PRINT "MULTIPLY TWO FRACTIONS"
20 PRINT " TO STOP RUN INPUT -01 FOR N1"
30 PRINT "N1,D1";
40 INPUT N1,D1
42 IF N1=-01 THEN 999
50 PRINT "N2,D2";
60 INPUT N2,D2
70 LET N=N1*N2
75 LET D=D1*D2
80 LET D3=D
85 REM HERE IS THE EUCLIDEAN ALGORITHM
90 LET I=INT(N/D)
100 LET P=N-I*D
110 IF P=0 THEN 160
120 LET N=D
130 LET D=P
140 LET D=R
150 GOTO 100
160 PRINT "PRODUCT IS"N*3/D""/"D3/D
180 GOTO 30
999 GOTO 30
END
RUN
NO.2
```

```
MULTIPLY TWO FRACTIONS
 TO STOP RUN INPUT -01 FOR N1
N1,D1?1,2
N2,D2?3
PRODUCT IS 2    / 3

N1,D1?45,72
N2,D2?2,3
PRODUCT IS 105  / 64

N1,D1?-01,1
```

DONE

SEC. 6-2

Problem No. 2

```
5 DIM L(21)
10 READ N
15 LET T=0
20 FOR X=1 TO N
```

```
240 PRINT A"*"B"="P(A*1,B+1)"MOD 5"
250 NEXT M
260 END
RUN
NO.12
```

MULTIPLICATION MOD 5

0	*	0	=	0	MOD 5
0	*	1	=	0	MOD 5
0	*	2	=	0	MOD 5
0	*	3	=	0	MOD 5
0	*	4	=	0	MOD 5
3	*	4	=	2	MOD 5
2	*	1	=	2	MOD 5
2	*	2	=	4	MOD 5
4	*	4	=	1	MOD 5
4	*	2	=	3	MOD 5

DONE

SEC. 5-3

Problem No. 2

```
10 DIM S(16,10)
20 REM LINE 30 ENTERS THE ROW NUMBER IN THE FIRST COLUMN
30 LET S(R,1)=R
40 FOR C=2 TO 10
48 REM LINE 50 SETS THE LAST 9 COLUMNS AT ZERO
50 LET S(R,C)=0
60 NEXT C
70 NEXT R
78 REM 80 READS THE CATAGORY FOR THE NEXT PERSON IN THE SURVEY
80 READ P
95 IF P=-1 THEN 145
98 REM GOES THROUGH THE 15 QUESTIONS
100 FOR Q=1 TO 15
110 READ A
115 LET S(16,P)=S(16,P)+A
120 LET S(Q,P)=S(Q,P)+A
130 NEXT Q
138 REM LINE 140 SENDS THE COMPUTER BACK TO READ ANOTHER LINE OF DATA
140 GOTO 80
145 FOR R=1 TO 15
160 LET S(R,6)=S(R,2)+S(R,3)
165 LET S(R,7)=S(R,4)+S(R,5)
170 LET S(R,8)=S(R,2)+S(R,4)
180 LET S(R,9)=S(R,3)+S(R,5)
185 LET S(R,10)=S(R,6)+S(R,7)
190 LET S(16,C)=S(16,C)+S(R,C)
195 NEXT C
196 NEXT R
198 REM THE PRINTING BEGINS HERE
200 PRINT "QUEST MALE   MALE  'FEMALEFEMALE"
210 PRINT "NUMBER 21+ UNDER 21+ UNDER MALE  FEMALE UNDER 21+";
215 PRINT "  TOTAL"
220 FOR R=1 TO 16
230 FOR C=1 TO 10
240 PRINT S(R,C);
250 NEXT C
260 NEXT R
270 PRINT
280 REM
499 REM A LINE LIKE 500 MAY HELP TO LINEUP THE DATA LINES
500 DATA 1,1,1,1,1,...
501 DATA 1,1,1,0,0,1,1,1,1,0,1,0,0,0,1
502 DATA 4,1,0,0,0,0,1,1,1,0,0,1,1,0,1
503 DATA 4,1,1,1,0,1,0,1,0,1,0,0,0,1,0
504 DATA 2,1,1,1,1,0,1,0,0,0,1,0,0,0,1
505 DATA 3,0,0,1,1,1,0,0,0,1,0,0,1,1,0
506 DATA 3,0,0,1,1,1,0,1,1,1,1,1,0,0,1
507 DATA 2,1,1,1,1,1,1,0,0,1,0,0,0,0,1
508 DATA 3,0,0,1,1,1,0,1,1,0,1,0,0,0,1
509 DATA 2,1,1,0,1,0,1,0,0,0,1,0,0,1,0
510 DATA 2,1,1,0,1,0,0,1,0,1,0,0,0,0,1
999 DATA -1
END
```

```
RUN
NO.4
```

(matrix of 0's and 1's)

DONE

Problem No. 6

```
10 DEF FNR(C)=INT(C*RND(1))-50
20 PRINT "FIRST ARRAY"
30 FOR R=1 TO 3
40 FOR C=1 TO 7
50 LET E(R,C)=FNR(100)
60 PRINT E(R,C);
70 NEXT C
80 PRINT
90 NEXT R
95 PRINT "SECOND ARRAY"
100 FOR R=1 TO 3
110 FOR C=1 TO 7
120 LET F(R,C)=FNR(200)
130 PRINT F(R,C);
140 NEXT C
150 PRINT
160 NEXT R
170 FOR R=1 TO 3
180 FOR C=1 TO 7
190 LET G(R,C)=F(R,C)+E(R,C)
200 NEXT C
210 NEXT R
220 PRINT "SUMS ENTERED IN SECOND ARRAY"
230 FOR R=1 TO 3
240 FOR C=1 TO 7
250 PRINT G(R,C);
260 NEXT C
270 PRINT
280 NEXT R
290 END
RUN
```

```
FIRST ARRAY
 17   14  -33   18  -42   28   -1
-12  -13  -24   26   16    9  -39
-35  -45  -45  -31  -34   23   -7

SECOND ARRAY
 46   41  128   99  139   36   65
-35  107   54   56  148   79   37
 13   39   14   31  -42  -30   97

SUMS ENTERED IN SECOND ARRAY
-45   55   95  117   97   64   44
-47  -91   30   82   14   55   -2
 46   40  -31  -16  -76   -7   90
```

DONE

Problem No. 8

```
5 PRINT "FIRST ARRAY"
20 FOR X=1 TO 4
30 FOR Y=1 TO 7
40 LET I(X,Y)=INT(100*RND(1))-500)
50 NEXT Y
60 NEXT X
70 GOSUB 1000
80 FOR I=1 TO 4
90 FOR Y=1 TO 7
100 LET I(I,Y)=2*I(1,Y)
110 NEXT Y
```

```
30 READ L(X)
35 LET T=T+L(X)*2^(N-X)
40 IF L(X)=1 THEN 70
50 PRINT "0"
60 GOTO 80
70 PRINT "1";
80 NEXT X
90 PRINT " BASE TWO ="T"BASE TEN"
100 GOTO 10
110 DATA 5,1,0,1,1,1
120 DATA 5,1,1,0,0,1
130 DATA 15,1,0,0,0,1,1,0,0,1,1,0,0,1,0,0,1,0,0,1,0
999 END
NO.2
```

```
99999.  BASE TWO = 23      BASE TEN
10  BASE TWO = 2      BASE TEN
10001001100010  BASE TWO = 18018  BASE TEN
OUT OF DATA IN LINE 10
```

Problem No. 4

```
10 READ N
15 LET T=0
20 PRINT N;"BASE TEN =";
30 FOR E=20 TO 0 STEP -1
42 LET I=INT(N/3^E)
44 IF T=0 THEN 60
45 IF I=1 THEN 55
47 IF I=2 THEN 58
50 PRINT "0";
55 GOTO 60
57 PRINT "1";
58 PRINT "2";
60 LET R=N-I*3^E
65 NEXT E
85 PRINT "  BASE THREE"
90 GOTO 10
110 DATA 99999.,1,16
110 END
NO.4
```

```
99999.      BASE TEN =121210202000  BASE THREE
1   BASE TEN =1   BASE THREE
16  BASE TEN =121  BASE THREE
OUT OF DATA IN LINE 10
```

Problem No. 6

```
5 REM N1 IS NUMBER OF DIGITS
10 READ N1
15 LET N=0
20 FOR X=N1 TO 1 STEP -1
22 READ A
24 IF A=1 THEN 30
26 LET N=N+3^34
28 PRINT "0";
30 GOTO 40
32 PRINT "2";
40 LET N=N+A*3^(X-1)
50 NEXT X
60 PRINT " BASE THREE"
60 PRINT " EQUALS"
110 FOR T=0 TO 0 STEP -1
140 LET I=INT(N/2^E)
150 LET T=T+I
160 IF T=0 THEN 210
180 PRINT "0";
```

```
150 LET N(W(+I*10)=E)
160 LET R=N-I*10^E
170 LET N=R
180 NEXT E
190 PRINT N2;N1"G.C.F. =",
200 LET N2=INT(N2/N1)
210 LET R=N2-INT(N2/N1)
220 IF R=0 THEN 260
230 LET N2=N1
240 LET N1=R
250 GOTO 200
260 GOTO 30
350 END
NO.4
```

```
INPUT INTEGER?25
25  52  G.C.F. = 1

INPUT INTEGER?456
456  654  G.C.F. = 6

INPUT INTEGER?779
779  977  G.C.F. = 1

INPUT INTEGER?0

DONE
```

CHAP. 7

SEC. 7-2

Problem No. 2

```
95 REM * PRINTING A NUMERIC OF MORE
96 REM THAN ONE DIGIT USING STRING
97 REM SEE LINES 165, 182 AND 185
100 DIM D$(10)
110 D$="0123456789"
120 PRINT"POSITIVE INTEGER LESS THAN 1000000".
130 INPUT N
140 IF N=0 THEN 260
150 PRINT "#"INJ"#"
160 PRINT "$";
165 LET T=0
170 FOR E=5 TO 0 STEP -1
180 LET I=INT(N/10^E)
182 LET T=T+I
185 PRINT D$(I+1,I+1);
190 PRINT D$(I+1,I+1);
200 LET R=N-I*10^E
210 LET N=R
220 NEXT E
230 PRINT "$"
250 GOTO 120
260 END
NO.2
```

```
POSITIVE INTEGER LESS THAN 1000000?189231
#189231#
$189231$

POSITIVE INTEGER LESS THAN 1000000?0
```

Problem No. 4

```
2 REM ** NOTICE THAT THIS IS MUCH SHORTER
3 REM THEN A PROGRAM WITHOUT THE USE OF
4 REM STRINGS
8 DIM D$(12)
9 D$="0123456789TE"
10 READ N,B
```

```
110 PRINT "B$";
120 INPUT B$
130 CHANGE B$ TO B
140 FOR I = 1 TO B(0)
150 LET A(B(I)) = A(B(I)) + 1
160 NEXT I
170 LET B(0)=1
180 PRINT "CHAR NUM CODE"
190 FOR I = 0 TO 127
200 IF A(I) = 0 THEN 240
210 LET B(I) = I
220 CHANGE B TO A$
230 PRINT "'"; A$ ": "; A(I); " "; I
240 NEXT I
250 END
NO.2
```

```
B$? SUPPOSE I DON'T WISH TO PLAY THIS GAME
CHAR NUM CODE
' '   7    32
'.'   1    39
'A'   2    65
'D'   1    68
'E'   2    69
'G'   1    71
'H'   3    72
'I'   1    73
'L'   1    76
'N'   1    78
'O'   3    79
'P'   3    80
'S'   3    83
'T'   4    84
'U'   1    85
'W'   1    87
'Y'   1    89
```

Problem No. 4

```
100 DIM W$(7)
105
108 REM * READ DATA AND FIND LONGEST STRING
110 LET L=0
110 FOR I = 1 TO 7
120 READ W$(I)
130 IF LEN(W$(I)) <= L THEN 160
140 LET L = LEN(W$(I))
160 NEXT I
165
168 REM * PRINT DAYS OF THE WEEK VERTICALLY
170 FOR I = 1 TO L
180 FOR J = 1 TO 7
190 PRINT TAB(3*J); EXT$(W$(J),I,I)
200 NEXT J
210 PRINT
220 NEXT I
225
228 REM * DATA
230 DATA SUNDAY, MONDAY, TUESDAY, WEDNESDAY
240 DATA THURSDAY, FRIDAY, SATURDAY
250 END
NO.4
```

```
S M T W T F S
U O U E H R A
N N E D U I T
D D S N R D U
A A D A S A R
Y Y A Y D Y D
      Y     A     A
            Y     Y
```

Problem No. 6

```
100 DIM WS[7]
105
108 REM * READ DATA AND FIND LØNGEST STRING
110 LET L=0
120 FØR I = 1 TØ 7
130    READ WS[I]
140    IF LEN(WS[I]) <= L THEN 160
150    LET L = LEN(WS[I])
160 NEXT I
165
168 REM * PRINT DAYS ØF THE WEEK AT A SLANT
170 FØR L = 1 TØ 7
180    FØR J = 1 TØ 7
190       PRINT TAB(#*J+1); EXTS(WS(J),I,1))
200    NEXT J
210    PRINT
220 NEXT I
225
228 REM * DATA
230 DATA SUNDAY, MONDAY, TUESDAY, WEDNESDAY
240 DATA THURSDAY, FRIDAY, SATURDAY
250 END
RUN
NØ.6
```

```
        S  M  T  W  F  S
           U  O  U  E  R  A
              N  N  E  D  I  T
                 D  D  S  N  D  U
                    A  A  D  E  A  R
                       Y  Y  A  S  Y  D
                             Y  D  A
```

SEC. 7-5
Problem No. 2

```
92  REM * FILE PRINT ØNE TØ A RECØRD
92  REM * WITH RESTART FEATURE
100 DIM WS[72]
110 FILES TEST
120 FØR I=1 TØ 1000
121    IF END #1 THEN 130
123    READ #1,I,INS
130 GØTØ 150
130 READ NS,A,B
132 IF NS="STØP" THEN 230
138 IF END #1 THEN 155
140 PRINT #1,I,INS,A,B
145 PRINT NS
150 NEXT I
152 STØP
155 PRINT "FILE FULL"
160 DATA "WAGNER, WILHELM RICHARD",1813,1883
170 DATA "VERRAZANØ, GIØVANNI",1480,1527
180 DATA "BRØNTE, ANNE",1820,1849
190 DATA "CURIE, MARIE",1867,1934
210 DATA "VERNE, JULES",1828,1905
225 DATA "STØP",0,0
230 END
RUN
NØ.2
```

```
WAGNER, WILHELM RICHARD
VERRAZANØ, GIØVANNI
CURIE, MARIE
VERNE, JULES
```

```
20  LET T=0
30  PRINT N)"BASE TEN =";
40  FØR E=20 TØ 0 STEP -1
50  LET I=INT(N/B*E)
60  LET T=T+I
70  IF T=0 THEN 430
80  PRINT DS[I+1,I+1]);
430 .R=N-I*B*E
440 LET N=R
450 NEXT E
460 PRINT " BASE "B
470 PRINT "."
485 DATA 99862.,12.79324,.,9
490 DATA 64.2,999999.,.3
RUN
NØ.4
```

```
99862.      BASE TEN =499ST    BASE 12
79324.      BASE TEN =307027   BASE 9
64.2 BASE TEN =000000000SE  EASE  3
999999.     BASE TEN =121221020202000

ØUT ØF DATA IN LINE 10
```

Problem No. 6

```
100 DIM DS[10]
110 DS="0123456789"
120 GØTØ 140
130 PRINT "ØUT ØF RANGE"
140 PRINT "#";
150 PRINT
160 INPUT N
170 IF ABS(N)<.000001 THEN 130
180 IF ABS(N)>.999999. THEN 130
190 PRINT "#","N","#"
200 PRINT "S";
210 IF N>0 THEN 240
220 PRINT "-.";
230 LET N=ABS(N)
240 FØR E=5 TØ 0 STEP -1
250 FØR E=5 TØ 0 STEP -1
250 LET E = 10*E THEN 280
260 NEXT E
270 GØTØ 350
280 FØR E1=E TØ 0 STEP -1
290 LET I=INT(N/10*E1)
300 PRINT DS[I+1,I+1]);
310 LET R=N-I*10*E1
320 LET N=R
330 NEXT E1
340 PRINT "-.";
350 FØR E1=-1 TØ -6 STEP -1
360 LET I=INT(N/10*E1+.05)
370 PRINT DS[I+1,I+1]);
380 LET R=N-I*10*E1
390 LET N=R
400 NEXT E1
410 IF N<.000001 THEN 430
420 NEXT E1
430 STØP
440 END
RUN
NØ.6
```

```
#?.10023
#-1.10023
5-1.10023S
```

SEC. 7-3
Problem No. 2

```
98  REM * TABULATE CHARACTER FREQUENCY
100 DIM A[127],B[72]
```

```
190  GØTØ 210
200  PRINT ",",
210  LET R=N-I*2*E
220  LET N=R
240  PRINT " BASE TWO"
245  LET T=0
250  GØTØ 10
260  DATA 5,1,0,0,1,2
265  DATA 10,2,0,0,0,1,1,2,1,0,1
270  END
RUN
NØ.5
```

```
10012 BASE THREE
EQUALS
1010110 BASE TWO

2000112101 BASE THREE
EQUALS
10011010101001010 BASE TWO

ØUT ØF DATA IN LINE 10
```

SEC. 6-3
Problem No. 2

```
5   PRINT "TEST FØR DIVISIBILITY BY THREE"
6   PRINT
10  PRINT "INPUT INTEGER";
20  INPUT N
25  LET T=0
30  IF N=0 THEN 999
40  FØR E=5 TØ 0 STEP -1
50  LET I=INT(N/10*E)
60  LET T=T+I
70  LET R=N-I*10*E
80  LET N=R
90  NEXT E
100 PRINT "SUM ØF DIGITS IS"T
105 IF T/3=INT(T/3) THEN 130
110 PRINT "NØT DIVISIBLE BY THREE"
120 GØTØ 6
130 PRINT "3 IS A FACTØR"
140 GØTØ 6
999 END
NØ.2
```

```
TEST FØR DIVISIBILITY BY THREE

INPUT INTEGER?23*972
SUM ØF DIGITS IS 27
3 IS A FACTØR

INPUT INTEGER?37
SUM ØF DIGITS IS 10
NØT DIVISIBLE BY THREE

INPUT INTEGER?0

DØNE
```

Problem No. 4

```
30  PRINT
40  PRINT "INPUT INTEGER";
50  INPUT N
55  LET N2=N
60  LET T=0
70  LET I=0
80  IF N=0 THEN 350
90  LET E1=-1
100 LET I=INT(N/10*E)
110 LET I=INT(N/10*E)
120 LET T=T+I
130 IF T=0 THEN 160
140 LET E1=E1+1
```

SEC. 7-5 Cont'd

Problem No. 4

```
90  REM * ALPHABETIZE NAMES IN A FILE
92  REM * (ANY NUMBER OF NAMES)
100 DIM A$(72),B$(72)
110 FILES TEST
112 IF END #1 THEN 119
114 FOR N=1 TO 1000
116 READ #1,N;A$
118 NEXT N
119 LET N=N-1
130 READ #1,I;A$,A,A1
140 FOR J=I+1 TO N
150 READ #1,J;B$,B,B1
160 PRINT #1,I;B$,B,B1
170 PRINT #1,J;A$,A,A1
190 NEXT J
200 PRINT "FILE ALPHABETIZED"
210 NEXT I
230 END
RUN
NO.4

FILE ALPHABETIZED
RUN
NO.3
```

```
DBB       NAME
1820   ANTHONY, SUSAN B.
1847   BELL, ALEXANDER GRAHAM
1820   BRONTE, ANNE
1857   CURIE, MARIE
1747   JONES, JOHN PAUL
1828   VERNE, JULES
1480   VERRAZANO, GIOVANNI
1813   WAGNER, WILHELM RICHARD
1859   WASHINGTON, BOOKER T.
```

Problem No. 6

```
100 DIM A$(72),B$(72),A(250)
110 FILES TEST
120 REM * COUNT NAMES AND SAVE
130 REM   POSITION IN A ARRAY
140 IF  END #1 THEN 190
150 FOR I=1 TO 250
160 READ #1,I;A$
180 LET A(I)=I
190 NEXT I
200 REM * ARRANGE POSITIONS IN
210 REM   A ARRAY
220 READ #1,A(R);A$
230 FOR R=1 TO I-1
240 FOR J=R+1 TO I
250 READ #1,A(J);B$
260 IF A$<=B$ THEN 310
270 LET A(R)=A(J)
280 LET A(J)=X
290 LET A$=B$
300 LET X=B$
310 NEXT J
320 NEXT R
330 REM * NOW PRINT NAMES.
340 PRINT "NAMES IN ORDER"
350 FOR I=1 TO I
360 READ #1,A(N1);A$,A
370 READ #1,A(N1);A$,A
380 PRINT A;A$
```

```
170 LET S1$ = "ZZZZ"
180 RESTORE #1 TO C
190     = #1 TO NS
200 READ #1, NS
204 REM * GET THE NEXT NAME GREATER THAN THE LAST
205 REM   NAME PRINTED
210     IF NS <= SS THEN 240
220     IF NS > S1$ THEN 240
230     LET S1$ = NS
240 NEXT I
250 PRINT S1$
260 LET SS = S1$
270 NEXT P
280 END
RUN
NO.2

CHRISTIE AGATHA
GOOSE MOTHER
TRUMAN HARRY
TWIST OLIVER
WHITE SNOW
```

Problem No. 4

```
100 FILES NAMES1
110 PRINT " ** BEFORE **"; TAB(25); " ** AFTER **"
120 FOR I = 1 TO 10
130     SETW 1 TO 8*(I-1) + 1
140     READ #1, A$
150     PRINT A$; TAB(25);
160     FOR J = 1 TO LEN(A$)
170         IF EXT$(A$,J,J) = " " THEN 210
180     NEXT J
190     PRINT "SPACE MISSING"
200     GOTO 280
210     LET B$ = EXT$(A$,J+1,J+LEN(A$))
220     LET C$ = ", "
230     LET D$ = EXT$(A$,1,J-1)
240     LET A$ = B$ + C$ + D$
250     SETW 1 TO 8*(I-1) + 1
260     PRINT A$
270     NEXT I
280 END
RUN
NO.4
```

```
** BEFORE **          ** AFTER **
AGATHA CHRISTIE       CHRISTIE, AGATHA
HARRY TRUMAN          TRUMAN, HARRY
SNOW WHITE            WHITE, SNOW
MOTHER GOOSE          GOOSE, MOTHER
OLIVER TWIST          TWIST, OLIVER
SAMUEL SPADE          SPADE, SAMUEL
LEMONT CRANSTON       CRANSTON, LEMONT
DELORES SPIELER       SPIELER, DELORES
EDGAR MARKS           MARKS, EDGAR
DOROTHY WOODSON       WOODSON, DOROTHY
```

CHAP. 8

Problem No. 2

```
10  READ A,B,C
15  IF A=0 THEN 99
16  PRINT A;B;C
17  LET D=B↑2-4*A*C
20  IF D<0 THEN 72
25  LET X1=(-B+SQR(B↑2-4*A*C))/(2*A)
30  LET X2=(-B-SQR(B↑2-4*A*C))/(2*A)
40  PRINT "REAL ZEROS "X1;X2
45  GOTO 10
50  DATA 1,3,2
60  DATA 1,-1,-3,-2,4
70  DATA 0,0,0
```

Problem No. 4

```
10  LET G=ATN(SQR(96)/2)
20  LET G=G*180/3.14159
30  LET D=INT(G)
40  LET M=INT((G-D)*60+.5)
45  PRINT "TWO ANGLES ARE"M"DEGREES "M"MINUTES"
50  PRINT D"DEGREES "M"MINUTES"
60  LET G1=180-2*G
65  PRINT "THE THIRD ANGLE MEASURES"
70  PRINT INT(G1)"DEGREES   ",
90  PRINT INT((G1-INT(G1))*60+.5)"MINUTES"
90  END
NO.4

TWO ANGLES ARE
74  DEGREES      28  MINUTES
THE THIRD ANGLE MEASURES
23  DEGREES       4  MINUTES

DONE
```

Problem No. 6

```
10  LET G=ATN(12/5)
20  LET G=G*180/3.14159
40  LET M=INT((G-D)*60+.5)
50  PRINT D"DEGREES "M"MINUTES"
70  PRINT INT(G1)"DEGREES   ",
90  PRINT INT((G1-INT(G1))*60+.5)"MINUTES"
90  END
NO.6

67   DEGREES      23   MINUTES
22   DEGREES      37   MINUTES

DONE
```

Problem No. 8

```
10  LET H=1000*TAN((7+30/60)*3.14159/180)
20  PRINT "HEIGHT IS"H"FEET"
30  END
NO.8

HEIGHT IS 131.652     FEET

DONE
```

SEC. 9-3

Problem No. 2

```
10  LET K=3.14159/180
20  DEF FNT(X)=SIN(X*K)
30  DEF FNR(X)=INT(X*100+.5)/100
35  READ X
37  IF X=-1 THEN 999
38  IF X=0 THEN 62
40  READ A1,B1,A
50  REM  FIND THE THIRD ANGLE
58  REM  70 AND 80 COMPUTE THE OTHER TWO SIDES
60  LET C1=180-(A1+B1)
62  GOTO 70
64  LET A1=B1;A
66  LET A1=180-(C1+B1)
68  REM  70 AND 80 COMPUTE THE OTHER TWO SIDES
70  LET B=A*FNT(B1)/FNT(A1)
80  LET C=A*FNT(C1)/FNT(A1)
99  REM  NOW PRINT THE RESULTS
100 PRINT "A ="A,"B ="B,"C ="C1
110 PRINT "THE ANGLES ARE"A1,B1,C1
120 PRINT "THE SIDES ARE",FNR(A),FNR(B),FNR(C)
140 GOTO 35
150 GOTO 35
```

```
390 NEXT N
400 END
RUN
N0-6
```

```
NAMES IN ORDER
DBB     NAME
1820    ANTHONY, SUSAN B.
1847    BELL, ALEXANDER GRAHAM
1820    BRONTE, ANNE
1867    CURIE, MARIE
1747    JONES, JOHN PAUL
1828    VERNE, JULES
1480    VERRAZANO, GIOVANNI
1813    WAGNER, WILHELM RICHARD
1859    WASHINGTON, BOOKER T.
```

Problem No. 8

```
90 DIM A$(72)
100 FILES TEST
105 IF END #1 THEN 999
110 FOR I=1 TO 1000
115 READ #1,I
116 PRINT
120 PRINT "RECORD";I
200 IF TYP(-1)>1 THEN 300
205 READ A1
220 PRINT A1
230 GOTO 200
300 IF TYP(-1)>2 THEN 400
310 READ A$
320 PRINT A$;
330 GOTO 200
400 IF TYP(-1)=4 THEN 600
500 PRINT "END OF FILE"
600 NEXT I
999 END
N0-8
```

```
RECORD 1
FIRST 999812.   7612    -123.45
RECORD 2
SECOND RECORD
RECORD 3
END OF FILE

RECORD 4
1234  12456  -999999.      123
RECORD 5
END OF FILE
```

SEC. 7-6
Problem No. 2

```
NAMES

100 CHRISTIE AGATHA
110 TRUMAN HARRY
120 WHITE SNOW
130 GOOSE MOTHER
140 TWIST OLIVER
N0-2
```

```
100 FILES NAMES
104 REM * FIRST COUNT NAMES
110 LET C = 0
120 LET C = C + 1
130 READ #1, N$
140 IF MORE #1 THEN 120
150 LET S$ = "AAAAA"
160 FOR P = 1 TO C
```

Problem No. 4

```
10 READ A,B,C
20 IF A=.01 THEN 999
30 PRINT "X"+A"X12 +"B"X +"C
40 FOR X=-12 TO 12 STEP 3
60 PRINT X;A*X12+B*X+C
70 GOTO 10
80 DATA 2,-3,4
90 DATA .01,1,1
RUN
N0-4
```

	X	X12 **-3	X + 4
-12	328		
-9	193		
-6	94		
-3	31		
0	4		
3	13		
6	58		
9	139		
12	256		

```
DONE
```

```
72 PRINT "NON-REAL ZEROS ";-B/(2*A);SQR(-D)/(2*A),
75 PRINT -B/(2*A);-SQR(-D)/(2*A)
80 GOTO 10
99 END
RUN
N0-2
```

```
                1         2      REAL ZEROS -1   -2
                1         1
NON-REAL ZEROS -.5    .866025       -.5      -.866025
                3        -2    4
NON-REAL ZEROS 1.10554  .333333    .333333   -1.10554

DONE
```

Problem No. 4

```
2 DEF FNR(X)=INT(X*100+.5)/100
5 LET K=180/3.14159
7 PRINT "  ","  ","A","B"," C"
10 READ A,B1,C
15 IF A=0 THEN 1000
30 LET T=COS(B1/K)
35 LET B=SQR(A12+C12-2*A*C*T)
40 LET T1=(B12+C12-A12)/(2*B*C)
50 LET A1=K*ATN(SQR(1-T1*2)/T1)
60 LET C1=180-(A1+B1)
65 PRINT "THE SIDES ARE",A,B,C
70 PRINT "THE ANGLES ARE",FNR(A1),FNR(B1),FNR(C1)
80 GOTO 10
500 DATA 3,53,13,5
540 DATA 0,0,0
1000 END
N0-4
```

	A	B	C
THE SIDES ARE	3	3.99999	5
THE ANGLES ARE	36.87	53.13	90

```
DONE
```

```
497 REM  '!' MEANS AAS
498 REM  '0' MEANS ASA
499 REM  '-!' MEANS STBP
500 DATA 1,24,51,10
510 DATA 0,90,60,15
520 DATA -1
999 END
RUN
N0-2
```

	A	B	C
THE ANGLES ARE	24	51	105
THE SIDES ARE	10	19.11	23.75
THE ANGLES ARE	30	60	90
THE SIDES ARE	15	25.98	30

```
DONE
```

Problem No. 6

```
5 PRINT "  "," A"," B"," C"
10 DEF FNR(X)=INT(X*100+.5)/100
15 LET K=180/3.14159
20 READ B1,C,B
25 IF B1=0 THEN 9999
30 IF ABS(SIN(B1/K)-B/C)<.00001 THEN 1000
40 IF B<C*SIN(B1/K) THEN 1100
80 IF B>C THEN 1200
90 PRINT "THERE ARE TWO TRIANGLES"
95 PRINT "ONE"
100 GOTO 1210
110 PRINT "TWO"
130 LET C1=180-C1
140 LET S1=M-M1
150 GOTO 1230
1000 PRINT "RIGHT TRIANGLE"
1010 LET A=SQR(C12+B12)
1020 PRINT "SIDES ARE",FNR(A),B,C
1030 PRINT "ANGLES ARE",90-B1,B1,90
1040 GOTO 20
1100 PRINT "NO TRIANGLE"
1110 GOTO 20
1200 PRINT "SINGLE TRIANGLE"
1205 LET S1=0
1210 LET S=C*SIN(B1/K)/B
1220 LET C1=ATN(S/SQR(1-S12))*K
```

CHAP. 9
SEC. 9-2
Problem No. 2

```
10 LET G=ATN(SQR(36-8*2)/8)
15 PRINT G;"RADIANS"
17 PRINT "   ","OR"
28 PRINT "",G*180/3.14159
28 LET D=INT(G)
30 PRINT D"DEGREES"
35 LET M=60*(G-INT(G))
40 LET M1=INT(M)
45 PRINT M1"MINUTES"
55 LET S=M-M1
55 PRINT S*60"SECONDS"
60 END
RUN
N0-2
```

```
1.3467      RADIANS
            OR
77          DEGREES
9           MINUTES
37.7161     SECONDS

DONE
```

SEC. 9-3 Cont'd

```
1230 LET A1=180-(B1+C1)
1240 LET A=SIN(A1/K)*B/SIN(B1/K)
1250 PRINT "SIDES ARE",A,B,C
1260 PRINT "ANGLES ARE",FNR(A1),FNR(B1),FNR(C1)
1270 GOTO 120
1300 DATA 30,8,9
1310 DATA 30,9,8
1320 DATA 30,2,1
1400 DATA 0,0,0
999 END
RUN
NO.6
```

	A	B	C
SINGLE TRIANGLE			
SIDES ARE	14.9905	9	8
ANGLES ARE	123.61	30	26.39
THERE ARE TWO TRIANGLES			
ONE			
SIDES ARE	14.4086	8	9
ANGLES ARE	115.77	30	34.23
TWO			
SIDES ARE	1.17985	8	9
ANGLES ARE	4.23	30	145.77
RIGHT TRIANGLE			
SIDES ARE	2.24	1	2
ANGLES ARE	60	30	90

DONE

Problem No. 8

```
5 LET K=180/3.14159
10 READ A,B2,B3,B4,C
15 IF A=0 THEN 1000
17 LET B1=B2+B3/60+B4/3600
20 LET T=COS(B1/K)
30 LET B=SQR(A*2+C*2-2*A*C*T)
40 LET T1=(A*2+B*2-C*2)/(2*A*B)
50 LET A1=K*ATN(SQR(1-T1*2)/T1)
60 LET C1=180-(A1+B1)
65 PRINT "THE SIDES ARE",A,B,C
70 PRINT "THE ANGLES ARE"
80 LET A2=INT(A1)
90 LET A3=INT((A1-A2)*60)
100 LET A4=INT(((A1-A2)*60-A3)*60+.5)
110 LET B2=INT(B1)
120 LET C2=INT(C1)
130 LET C3=INT((C1-C2)*60)
135 PRINT "ANGLE  DEG  MIN  SEC"
150 PRINT "A1 = ";A2;B3;B4
160 PRINT "B1 = ";B2;B3;B4
165 PRINT "C1 = ";C2;C3;C4
170 GOTO 10
500 DATA 3,53,7,48,5
530 DATA 0,0,0,0,0
1000 END
RUN
NO.8
```

THE SIDES ARE	A	B	C
	3	3.99999	5

THE ANGLES ARE			
ANGLE	DEG	MIN	SEC
A1 =	36	52	12
B1 =	53	7	48
C1 =	90	0	0

DONE

Problem No. 2(e),(f)

```
10 LET K=3.14159/180
20 PRINT " X"," Y"," X*"," Y*","ANGLE"
30 DEF FNX(R)=R*COS(G*K)
35 DEF FNY(R)=R*SIN(G*K)
40 DEF FNR(X)=INT(X*100+.5)/100
50 FOR G=0 TO 360 STEP 15
60 LET E=SIN(G*K)
65 PRINT FNR(FNX(E)),FNR(FNY(E)),
70 IF ABS(COS(G*K))<.0001 THEN 90
80 PRINT FNR(FNX(F)),FNR(FNY(F)),G
85 GOTO 100
90 PRINT " "," X OR Y UNDEFINED",G
100 NEXT G
170 NEXT G
180 END
RUN
NO.2EF
```

X	Y	X	Y	ANGLE
0	0	1	0	0
.18	.48	-.27	.48	15
.5	.43	.5	.48	30
.5	.71		1.73	45
.5	0	3.73	3.73	60
-1	0	-1	-3.73	75
0	0		X OR Y UNDEFINED	90
.18	-.13	-.5	-3.73	105
.5	-.43	-.5	-1.73	120
.5	-.71	-.87	-.58	135
.5	0	-.68	-.27	150
-1	0	-.18	.18	165
0	0	1	0	180
```
RCOS(G)*1
```

Problem No. 2(g),(h)

```
10 LET K=3.14159/180
20 PRINT " X"," Y"," X*"," Y*","ANGLE"
25 PRINT " X*"," Y*",   R=1*RCOS(G)"   R=SIN(G)+COS(G)"
30 DEF FNX(R)=R*COS(G*K)
```

X	Y	X	Y	ANGLE
.68	.68	.18	-.27	0
.87	.5	.5	.58	15
.5	.5	.5		30
.5		.5	1.73	45
.18	-1		3.73	60
0	0		-3.73	75
.18	0		X OR Y UNDEFINED	90
.5	.18	.5	-3.73	105
.87	.5	.5	-1.73	120
.5		.87	-.58	135
.18	-.68	.68	-.27	150
0	-.68		-.18	165
	0		0	180

DONE

Problem No. 4

```
10 READ A,B,C,D
11 IF A=.01 THEN 999
12 PRINT "("*A*","*B*")("*C*","*D*")("*"A-C","*"B-D")"
20 PRINT "("*A*","*B*")("*C*","*D*")("*"C-A","*"D-B")"
30 PRINT "("*A*","*B*")("*C*","*D*")("*"*")"
40 PRINT "("*A*","*B*")("*C*","*D*")("*"*")"
45 PRINT "(A*C-B*D)/(C*2+D*2)","*(B*C-A*D)/(C*2+D*2)")"
50 PRINT "(("*C*","*D*")("*A*","*B*")("
55 PRINT "(A*C-B*D)/(A*2+B*2)","*(A*D-B*C)/(A*2+B*2)")"
65 GOTO 10
100 DATA 1,0,0,1;1;2;3;4;5;-8;2;4
110 DATA .01;0;0;0
999 END
RUN
NO.4
```

(	1	,	0	)/(	0	,	0	)	> (	1	,	0	)	
(	1	,	0	)/(	0	,	0	)	> (	-1	,	0	)	
(	3	,	4	)/(	2	,	1	)	> (	2	,	1	)	,-2)
(	3	,	4	)/(	2	,	1	)	> (	2	,	-1	)	,2)
(	5	,	-8	)/(	2	,	4	)	> (	-1	,	.44	)	,-.08)
(	5	,	-8	)/(	2	,	4	)	> (	-1	,	2.2	)	,-.4)
(	2	,	4	)/(	5	,	1	)	> (	-3	,	-1.1	)	,-1.8)
(	2	,	4	)/(	5	,	1	)	> (	-3	,	-.247191	)	,.404494)

DONE

Problem No. 6

```
5 FOR K=1 TO 5
10 READ C,D
20 PRINT "("*1*,0)/("*C*","*D*")("*"C/(C*2+D*2)")","("
25 PRINT "-D/(C*2+D*2)")"
30 NEXT K
40 DATA 1,2;1;0;0;1;2;3;-3;-4
50 END
RUN
NO.6
```

(	1	,	0	)/(	1	,	2	)	> (	.2	,	.0	)	
(	1	,	0	)/(	0	,	1	)	> (	0	,	-1	)	
(	1	,	0	)/(	2	,	3	)	> (	.153846	,	-230769	)	
(	1	,	0	)/(	-3	,	-4	)	> (	-.12	,	.16	)	

DONE

SEC. 10-2 Problem No. 2

```
10 LET R=1
20 LET G=45
30 LET G1=0
40 LET R1=R+R*T8
50 LET R1=R1+R*T8
60 LET R1=R1+R*G
70 LET G1=G1+G
80 PRINT "(1,45)*"*N*"*"R1",*"G1")"
90 NEXT N
100 END
RUN
NO.2
```

(1,45)*	1	*(	1	,	45	)
(1,45)*	2	*(	1	,	90	)
(1,45)*	3	*(	1	,	135	)
(1,45)*	4	*(	1	,	180	)
(1,45)*	5	*(	1	,	225	)
(1,45)*	6	*(	1	,	270	)
(1,45)*	7	*(	1	,	315	)
(1,45)*	8	*(	1	,	360	)

DONE

THE SIDES ARE   10   12.5786   20
THE ANGLES ARE
ANGLE DEG MIN SEC
B1 =   31   23   44
B1 =   24   18   18
C1 = 124   18   11
DONE

SEC. 9-4

Problem No. 2(a),(b)

```
5 LET K=3-14159/180
10 DEF FNR(X)=INT(X*100+-5)/100
15 PRINT " X°," Y°," X°," Y°,"ANGLE"
20 PRINT "  COS(2*G)","  COS(4*G)"
30 FOR G=0 TO 360 STEP 15
40 LET A=COS(2*G*K)
50 LET B=COS(4*G*K)
60 PRINT FNR(A*COS(G*K)),FNR(A*SIN(G*K)),
70 PRINT FNR(B*COS(G*K)),FNR(B*SIN(G*K)),G
90 NEXT G
100 END
RUN
N8-2AB
```

COS(2*G)		COS(4*G)		ANGLE
X	Y	X	Y	
-.84	0	.98	0	0
-.43	-.25	.75	.13	15
		-.25	.43	30
		-.71		45

COS(2*G)		COS(4*G)		ANGLE
X	Y	X	Y	
-.84	0	.98	0	
-.25	-.22	.13	.75	
.43	-.43	-.84	-.43	
-.25	-.25	-.25	-.43	
-.43	0	-.22	0	
-.84	.43	-.43	-.84	
-.25	.22	-.25	-.25	
-.43	.43	.13	-.75	
-.71		-.71		

Problem No. 2(c),(d)

```
5 LET K=3-14159/180
10 DEF FNR(X)=INT(X*100+-5)/100
15 PRINT " X°," Y°," X°," Y°,"ANGLE"
20 PRINT "  COS(4*G)","  SIN(8*G)"
30 FOR G=0 TO 360 STEP 15
40 LET C=COS(4*G*K)
50 LET D=SIN(8*G*K)
70 PRINT FNR(C*COS(G*K)),FNR(C*SIN(G*K)),
75 PRINT FNR(D*COS(G*K)),FNR(D*SIN(G*K)),G
90 NEXT G
100 END
RUN
N8-2CD
```

COS(4*G)		SIN(8*G)		ANGLE
X	Y	X	Y	
-.48	0	0	.13	0
-.75	.25	.75	-.43	15
-.71	-.25	-.71	-.71	30
				45

Problem No. 4

```
10 LET K=3-14159/180
20 PRINT "CONVERT FROM (A,B) TO (R,G)"
30 PRINT
40 PRINT "A,B")
50 INPUT A,B
60 A=-.01,.03 FORM = (")
70 IF A <> 0 THEN 130
90 IF B>0 THEN 130
100 PRINT "0,0")"
110 GOTO 30
...
240 END
N8-4
```

```
CONVERT FROM (A,B) TO (R,G)

A,B?-1,1
(R,G) FORM = ( 1.41421    , 90)

A,B?-.01,0
```

Problem No. 6

```
10 PRINT "FIND INTEGRAL POWERS OF (A,B)"
20 PRINT
30 PRINT "WHAT POWER?"
40 INPUT N
50 PRINT "A,B")
60 INPUT A,B
70 LET C=C+1
100 LET C=A*C-B*F
110 LET D=A*F+B*C
120 LET E=C
130 LET F=D
140 PRINT X"("C"),"D")"
150 NEXT X
RUN
N8-6
```

```
FIND INTEGRAL POWERS OF (A,B)

WHAT POWER?4
A,B?-1,-1
1   (-1    ,-1    )
2   ( 0    , 2    )
3   ( 2    ,-2    )
4   (-4    , 0    )

DONE
```

CHAP. 10

SEC. 10-1

Problem No. 2

```
10 PRINT "ROOTS OF AX↑2+BX+C"
20 PRINT
30 PRINT "A,B,C")
40 INPUT A,B,C
50 IF A=0 THEN 160
60 LET D=B↑2-4*A*C
70 IF D=0 THEN 120
80 PRINT "REAL ROOTS"
90 PRINT "NON-REAL ROOTS"
110 GOTO 20
130 PRINT "("-B/(2*A)","  SQR(ABS(D))/(2*A)")"
140 PRINT "("-B/(2*A)",""-SQR(ABS(D))/(2*A)")"
160 END
RUN
N8-2
```

```
ROOTS OF AX↑2+BX+C

A,B,C?6,13,6
REAL ROOTS
-.666667    -1.5

A,B,C?2,2,6
NON-REAL ROOTS
(-.25    , 1.71391    )
(-.25    ,-1.71391    )

A,B,C?0,0,0

DONE
```

SEC. 10-3

Problem No. 2

```
20 DEF FNR(X)=INT(X*1000+-5)/1000
30 PRINT "TAKE ROOTS OF COMPLEX NUMBERS IN (A,B) FORM"
40 READ A=B=N
60 LET R=SQR(A↑2+B↑2)
80 PRINT "THE"N"TH ROOTS OF ("A","B") ARE:"
102 IF A <> 0 THEN 120
```

		ANGLE
		15
		30
		45
		60
		75
		90
		105
		120
		135
		150
		165
		180
		195
		210
		225
		240
		255
		270
		285
		300
		315
		330
		345
		360

SEC. 10-3 Cont'd

```
104 LET G=3.14159/2
106 IF B>0 THEN 240
120 GOTO 140
128 LET G=ATN(B/A)
140 IF A>0 THEN 200
160 LET G=G-3.14159
180 GOTO 240
200 IF B>0 THEN 240
240 FOR G=G-3.14159
260 LET R1=R*(1/N)
280 LET G1=G/N
300 LET A1=R1*COS(G1)
320 LET B1=R1*SIN(G1)
340 PRINT "("FNR(A1)","FNR(B1)")"
360 LET G=G+3.14159
380 NEXT X
400 PRINT
420 GOTO 60
440 DATA 0,1,4
440 DATA 1,1,2
460 DATA 1,0,3
480 END
NO.6
```

```
TAKE ROOTS OF COMPLEX NUMBERS IN (A,B) FORM
THE 4 , 4  TH ROOTS OF ( 0 , 1 ) ARE:
( .924 ,  .383 )
(-.383 ,  .924 )
(-.924 , -.383 )
( .383 , -.924 )

THE 2 , 2  TH ROOTS OF ( 1 , 1 ) ARE:
(-1.099 ,  .455 )
(-1.099 , -.455 )

THE 3 , 3  TH ROOTS OF ( 1 , 0 ) ARE:
(-.5 ,  .866 )
(-.5 , -.866 )
(-1 , 0 )

OUT OF DATA IN LINE 60
```

CHAP. 11

SEC. 11-1

Problem No. 2

```
5 REM SUBTRACT TWO POLYNOMIALS
10 FOR X=1 TO 10
20 LET B(X)=T(X)=S(X)=0
30 NEXT X
40 FOR X=N TO 2 STEP -1
50 READ N
60 READ G(X)
70 PRINT G(X)"X"X"X-1"+"";
80 NEXT X
90 READ B(1)
100 PRINT B(1)
110 READ N1
120 FOR X=N1 TO 2 STEP -1
130 READ T(X)
140 PRINT T(X)"X"X"X-1"+"";
150 NEXT X
160 READ T(1)
170 PRINT T(1)
180 LET S(X)=G(X)-T(X)
190 FOR X=10 TO 2 STEP -1
200 LET S(X)=G(X)-T(X)
210 NEXT X
220 FOR X=10 TO 2 STEP -1
230 LET S=S-S(X)
240 IF S=0 THEN 260
250 PRINT S(X)"X"X"X-1"+"";
260 NEXT X
270 PRINT S(1)
280 DATA 4,3,2,6,-8
280 DATA 5,6,-7,8,0,1
299 END
```

```
120 NEXT I
125 FOR Z=A+B-1 TO 1 STEP -1
135 NEXT Z
140 PRINT P(Z)
145 PRINT
150 NEXT T
155 END
RUN
NO.6
```

```
0    10    8     9
3    14   -8     9
0    30   164  -61   102   27

-8
-14
-112

4     8     0     4
7    56     0    28
28

4    13     6     1
24   110   182   154   67    9

DONE
```

Problem No. 8

```
10  PRINT "POWERS OF (X+1)"
20  DIM P(12),F(12)
30  FOR W=1 TO 12
40  LET P(W)=0
50  NEXT W
60  LET F(1)=F(2)=1
70  LET S(1)=S(2)=1
80  LET A=B=2
90  PRINT F(1),F(2)
100 FOR I=1 TO 10
110 FOR J=1 TO A
120 LET B=B+1
130 LET P(I+J-1)=P(I+J-1)+F(I)*S(J)
140 NEXT J
150 NEXT I
160 FOR X=1 TO B-1
190 PRINT P(Z)
200 PRINT P(Z)
210 NEXT Z
220 FOR W=1 TO 12
250 LET A=A+1
270 NEXT T
280 END
NO.8
```

```
POWERS OF (X+1)
1
1   1
1   2   1
1   3   3    1
1   4   6    4    1
1   5  10   10    5    1
1   6  15   20   15    6    1
1   7  21   35   35   21    7    1
1   8  28   56   70   56   28    8    1
1   9  36   84  126  126   84   36    9    1
1  10  45  120  210  252  210  120   45   10    1
1  11  55  165  330  462  462  330  165   55   11   1

DONE
```

```
260 IF X=1 THEN 10
270 PRINT "NONE FOUND"
290 DATA 4,1,-2,3,-4
300 DATA 5,2,-1,-11,-2
310 DATA 4,1,3,-78,-80
315 DATA -91
320 IF ABS(P) >= 2 THEN 180
330 LET K(Q-1)=X
340 LET K(Q,2)=X
350 LET Q=Q+1
360 GOTO 180
380 FOR I=N TO 1 STEP -1
390 LET P=P+P(I)*X*(I-1)
400 NEXT I
410 RETURN
420 END
NO.4
```

```
1    -2    3    -4
INTEGRAL ZERO(S)   NONE FOUND

1    -2   -11   11   -2
INTEGRAL ZERO(S)   2

1    3   -78   -80
INTEGRAL ZERO(S)   8    -1    -10

DONE
```

SEC. 11-3

Problem No. 2

```
10  PRINT "SEARCH FOR REAL ZEROS OF A POLYNOMIAL"
20  PRINT "START, END, INCREMENT";
30  LET S3=0
40  INPUT F,L,S
50  DEF FNT(X)=12*X^3-64*X^2+17*X+195
60  LET A=0
70  FOR X=F TO L STEP S
80  LET S1=FNT(X)
90  LET S2=FNT(X+S)
100 IF S1*S2>0 THEN 130
110 LET A=A+1
120 LET S(A)=X
125 IF S3=1 THEN 190
130 NEXT X
140 IF A>0 THEN 190
150 PRINT "NO INTERVALS FOUND **** TRY AGAIN "
160 PRINT "WITH EITHER GREATER LIMITS OR SMALLER INCREMENT"
180 GOTO 20
190 PRINT "INTERVAL(S) BEGIN AT:"
200 FOR I=1 TO A
210 PRINT S(I)
220 NEXT I
230 PRINT
240 PRINT "NOW ";
250 GOTO 20
270 END
RUN
NO.2
```

```
SEARCH FOR REAL ZEROS OF A POLYNOMIAL
START, END, INCREMENT?-195,195,1
INTERVAL(S) BEGIN AT:

NOW START, END, INCREMENT?2,3,.1
2.8
INTERVAL(S) BEGIN AT:

NOW START, END, INCREMENT?1,1,0

DONE
```

```
RUN
NO.2
      X↑3   + 2    X↑2   + 6    X↑2   +-8    X↑1   +-1
-6    X↑4   +-7    X↑3   + 8    X↑3   + 0    X↑1   +-1
      X↑4   + 10   X↑3   +-6    X↑2   + 6    X↑2   +-9
DONE
```

Problem No. 4

```
80  DIM P[20]
100 FOR W=1 TO 10
120 LET F[W]=S[W]=P[W]=P[W+10]=0
140 NEXT W
160 READ W
180 IF F[W]=-1 THEN 680
180 FOR X=A TO 1 STEP -1
200 READ F[X]
220 PRINT F[X]
240 NEXT X
260 PRINT X
280 READ B
300 FOR Y=B TO 1 STEP -1
320 READ S[Y]
340 PRINT S[Y]
360 NEXT Y
380 PRINT Y
400 FOR J=1 TO B
420 LET P[I+J-1]=P[I+J-1]+F[I]*S[J]
440 NEXT J
460 NEXT I
500 FOR Z=A+B-1 TO 1 STEP -1
580 PRINT P[Z]
560 NEXT Z
540 PRINT
580 GOTO 100
590 DATA 5,3,2,2,0,2,1
595 DATA 3,2,5,2
600 DATA 2,3,2
605 DATA 2,2,3
610 DATA -1
420 END
RUN
NO.4
```

```
   2    5    0    0    1
3  6    2    16   8    12   9    2

   2    2
6  13   6
```

DONE

Problem No. 6

```
5   DIM P[20]
10  DEF FNR(X)=INT(X*RND(1)-X/2)
15  DEF FNK(X)=INT(X*RND(X)+1)
20  FOR W=1 TO 10
25  LET F[W]=S[W]=P[I]=P[W+10]=0
30  NEXT W
35  LET A=FNK(10)
45  FOR X=A TO 1 STEP -1
50  LET F[X]=FNR(20)
55  PRINT F[X]
60  NEXT X
70  LET B=FNK(5)
75  FOR Y=B TO 1 STEP -1
80  LET S[Y]=FNR(16)
85  PRINT S[Y]
90  NEXT Y
95  PRINT
99  PRINT
100 FOR I=1 TO A
105 FOR J=1 TO B
110 LET P[I+J-1]=P[I+J-1]+F[I]*S[J]
115 NEXT J
```

SEC. 11-2

Problem No. 2

```
10  DEF FNR(X)=INT(X*RND(1)+1-X/2)
15  FOR T=1 TO 3
20  PRINT
30  PRINT "ZEROS ARE:    ";
40  FOR S=1 TO 4
60  LET P[X]=0
70  NEXT X
80  LET F[2]=S[2]=1
90  LET A=B=2+FNR(20)
100 PRINT -F[1]
110 LET S[1]=2*FNR(20)
120 PRINT -S[1]
130 PRINT -S[1]
140 FOR I=1 TO A
160 FOR J=1 TO B
170 LET F=S[I]
180 LET I=I+1
190 IF S=0 THEN 270
210 LET F[X]=P[X]
230 LET P[X]=0
240 NEXT X
250 LET A=3
260 GOTO 120
270 PRINT
275 PRINT "THE COEFFICIENTS ARE:    ";
280 FOR X=A TO 1 STEP -1
290 PRINT P[X]
300 NEXT X
305 PRINT
310 NEXT T
320 END
RUN
NO.2
```

```
ZEROS ARE:         1    4    7    -12    39    -28
THE COEFFICIENTS ARE:    1

ZEROS ARE:        -4    8    -9    5      -68   -288
THE COEFFICIENTS ARE:    1

ZEROS ARE:         6    -7    -6    7     -36   -252
THE COEFFICIENTS ARE:    1
```

DONE

Problem No. 4

```
10  PRINT
20  READ N
25  IF N=-.01 THEN 420
30  FOR S=N TO 1 STEP -1
40  READ P[S]
50  PRINT P[S]
70  NEXT S
80  LET Q=1
90  PRINT "INTEGRAL ZERO(S):    ";
100 LET X=0
110 FOR X=-P[1] TO P[1] STEP SGN(P[1])
120 READ P[S]
130 IF P[1]/X <> INT(P[1]/X) THEN 180
140 GOSUB 370
150 IF P <> 0 THEN 320
160 NEXT X
180 IF Q=1 THEN 260
190 PRINT "ABS(P)=2"
200 PRINT X
210 PRINT "ABS(P)=2"
215 LET Q=1
225 FOR X=1 TO Q-1
230 PRINT K[X,2]*K[X,1]
240 NEXT X
250 GOTO 10
```

Problem No. 4

```
10  DEF FNT(X)=12*X↑3-64*X↑2+17*X+195
30  FOR R=-5 TO 5
40  LET S1=FNT(X)
50  LET S2=FNT(X+1)
60  IF S1*S2=0 THEN 90
82  LET X=R
82  IF X <> F THEN 90
84  IF S1 <> 0 THEN 90
86  PRINT X"IS A ZERO"
90  NEXT X
92  IF S2 <> 0 THEN 100
94  PRINT *+S"IS A ZERO"
100 PRINT "INTERVAL(S) BEGIN AT:"
110 FOR I=1 TO A
120 PRINT S[I]
130 NEXT I
140 FOR I=1 TO A
150 PRINT
160 FOR I=1 TO A
170 LET F=S[I]
180 LET I=I+1
190 LET S=S+1
210 LET D=(I*FNT(F))/(FNT(F)-FNT(S))
230 IF FNT(X) <> 0 THEN 250
230 PRINT X;"IS A ZERO"
240 GOTO 340
250 IF ABS(FNT(X))>-.0001 THEN 280
260 PRINT X;"YIELDS FNT(X)="FNT(X)
270 GOTO 340
280 IF FNT(F)*FNT(X)>0 THEN 310
290 LET I=I0
300 GOTO 190
310 LET I1=I1-D
320 LET F=X
330 GOTO 190
340 NEXT I
350 END
RUN
NO.4
```

```
INTERVAL(S) BEGIN AT:
-2       -2       3
-1.44714       YIELDS FNT(X) = 6.10352E-05
2.87573        YIELDS FNT(X) =-6.10352E-05
3.90475        YIELDS FNT(X) =-3.05176E-05
```

DONE

SEC. 11-4

Problem No. 2

```
10  DEF FNA(X)=P[9]*X↑8+P[8]*X↑7+P[7]*X↑6+P[6]*X↑5+P[5]*X↑4
20  DEF FNB(X)=P[4]*X↑3+P[3]*X↑2+P[2]*X+P[1]
30  DEF FNF(X)=FNA(X)+FNB(X)
40  PRINT
41  FOR X=1 TO 9
51  LET P[X]=0
60  NEXT X
70  READ N
75  IF N=-.0101 THEN 500
80  FOR S=N TO 1 STEP -1
90  READ P[S]
110 PRINT P[S]
120 NEXT S
130 PRINT "INTEGRAL ZERO:    ";
140 FOR X=-P[1] TO P[1] STEP SGN(P[1])
160 IF X=0 THEN 200
170 IF P[1]/X <> INT(P[1]/X) THEN 200
180 PRINT X
190 GOTO 210
200 NEXT X
210 PRINT
220 PRINT "SYNTHETIC DIVISION BY    X -"X;"YIELDS:"
230 PRINT P[N]
240 FOR X=N-1 TO 1 STEP -1
```

SEC. 11-4 Cont'd

```
250 LET P(X)=P(X)+P(X+1)*R
260 IF X=1 THEN 280
270 PRINT P(X),
280 NEXT X
300 FOR X=1 TO N-1
310 LET P(X)=P(X+1)
320 NEXT X
325 LET P(N)=0
330 IF N=-1 THEN 360
340 LET N=N-1
350 GOTO 30
360 LET F=2*P(3)
370 LET F=2*P(2)/F
380 LET A=-P(2)/F
390 LET B=SQR(ABS(D))/F
400 IF D=0 THEN 440
410 PRINT "REAL ZEROS:"
420 PRINT A+B;"AND";A-B
430 GOTO 40
440 PRINT "NON-REAL ZEROS:"
450 PRINT "(";A;")+(";B;")I";"AND";"(";A;")-(";B;")I"
460 PRINT
470 DATA 4,1,-2,-1,-2
480 DATA 5,2,-5,-31,-21,45
490 DATA .0101
500 END
RUN
NO.2
```

```
              2    -1   -2      INTEGRAL ZERO:   1
SYNTHETIC DIVISION BY   X - 1      YIELDS:
1     3     2               REAL ZEROS:      -1   AND   -2

              2    -5   -31  -21   45   INTEGRAL ZERO:  -5
SYNTHETIC DIVISION BY   X + 5      YIELDS:
2    -5    -9               INTEGRAL ZERO:   1
SYNTHETIC DIVISION BY   X - 1      YIELDS:
2    -3    -9               REAL ZEROS:      3   AND   -1.5
```

DONE

CHAP. 12

SEC. 12-1

Problem No. 2

```
10 DIM A(3,12)
20 MAT READ A
30 FOR X=1 TO 12
40 LET A(3,X)=A(2,X)+A(1,X)
50 NEXT X
60 MAT PRINT A;
65 DATA 1,2,3,4,5,6,7,23,51,47,56,234
66 DATA 2,-3,43,90,45,32,-89,65,43,-96,0,1
67 DATA 0,0,0,0,0,0,0,0,0,0,0,0
70 RUN
END
NO.2
```

1	2	3	4	5	6	7	23	51	47	56	0	56
2	-3	43	90	45	32	-89	65	43	-96	0	1	23
3	-1	46	94	50	38	-82	88	94	-49	56	-49	56

DONE

Problem No. 4

```
10 DIM A(4,3)
20 MAT READ A
30 MAT PRINT A;
40 FOR R=1 TO 4
50 FOR C=1 TO 3
60 LET A(R,C)=3*A(R,C)
70 NEXT C
80 NEXT R
```

```
70 MAT PRINT A;
80 END
RUN
NC.10
```

```
0   0   0   0   0   0   0
0   0   0   0   0   0   0
```

DONE

SEC. 12-2

Problem No. 2

```
20 DIM A(4,3),B(1,4),C(1,3)
40 MAT READ A
60 DATA 6,3,2,5,3,2,4,3,2,3,2,1
140 MAT READ B
160 DATA 0,0,0,0
240 FOR C=1 TO 3
260 FOR R=1 TO 1
280 LET C(R,C)=0
300 FOR X=1 TO 4
320 LET C(R,C)=C(R,C)+B(R,X)*A(X,C)
340 NEXT X
360 NEXT C
380 NEXT R
500 PRINT "ROAD","TUNNEL","BRIDGE"
520 MAT PRINT C
999 END
NO.2
```

ROAD	TUNNEL	BRIDGE
0	0	0

DONE

Problem No. 4

```
20 DIM A(4,3),B(4,4),C(4,3)
40 MAT READ A
60 DATA 6,3,2,5,3,2,4,3,2,3,2,1
140 MAT READ B
160 DATA 0,0,0,1,0,0,1,0,0,1,0,0,0,1,0,0
240 FOR R=1 TO 4
260 FOR C=1 TO 3
280 LET C(R,C)=0
300 FOR X=1 TO 4
320 LET C(R,C)=C(R,C)+B(R,X)*A(X,C)
340 NEXT X
360 NEXT C
380 NEXT R
500 PRINT "ROAD","TUNNEL","BRIDGE"
520 MAT PRINT C
999 END
NO.4
```

ROAD	TUNNEL	BRIDGE
3	2	1
4	3	2
5	3	2
6	3	2

DONE

Problem No. 6

```
10 PRINT "BECAUSE THE DIMENSIONS ARE"
20 PRINT "NON-CONFORMING"
30 END
RUN
NO.6
```

```
BECAUSE THE DIMENSIONS ARE
NON-CONFORMING
```

DONE

```
61   55
123  97
```

DONE

Problem No. 8

```
10 DIM A(2,2),B(2,2),C(2,2),D(2,2)
20 MAT READ A,B
30 DATA -2,1,1,5,-5,1,2,3,4
40 MAT C=A+B
50 PRINT "A+B"
60 MAT PRINT C;
70 MAT D=B-A
80 PRINT "B-A"
90 MAT PRINT D;
100 END
RUN
NC.8
```

A+B
```
-1   0
 0   1
```

B-A
```
1   0
0   1
```

Problem No. 10

```
10 DIM A(1,12),B(12,1),C(12,12)
20 MAT READ A
30 RESTORE
40 MAT READ B
50 MAT C=B*A
60 MAT PRINT C;
100 DATA 1,2,3,4,5,6,7,8,9,10,11,12
200 END
RUN
NO.10
```

1	2	3	4	5	6	7	8	9	10	11	12
1	2	3	4	5	6	7	8	9	10	11	12
2	4	6	8	10	12	14	16	18	20	22	24
3	6	9	12	15	18	21	24	27	30	33	36
4	8	12	16	20	24	28	32	36	40	44	48
5	10	15	20	25	30	35	40	45	50	55	60
6	12	18	24	30	36	42	48	54	60	66	72
7	14	21	28	35	42	49	56	63	70	77	84
8	16	24	32	40	48	56	64	72	80	88	96
9	18	27	36	45	54	63	72	81	90	99	108
10	20	30	40	50	60	70	80	90	100	110	120
11	22	33	44	55	66	77	88	99	110	121	132
12	24	36	48	60	72	84	96	108	120	132	144

DONE

```
85 PRINT
90 MAT PRINT A;
95 DATA 3,56,78,3,20,45,3,9,673,564,90,234
100 END
RUN
NO.4

 2    56    78
 3    20    45

 3    90    673
564   90    234

 6   168   234

 9    60   135

 9    27  2019
1692  270   702

DONE
```

Problem No. 6

```
10 DIM X(2,5)
20 MAT READ X
30 MAT PRINT X;
40 FOR C=1 TO 5
50 FOR C=1 TO 5
60 IF (R*C)/2=INT((R*C)/2) THEN 90
70 LET X(R,C)=-3*X(R,C)
80 GOTO 110
90 LET X(R,C)=-18*X(R,C)
110 NEXT C
120 NEXT R
130 MAT PRINT X;
140 DATA 3,67,32,45,90,2,9,57,-3,1
150 END
RUN
NO.6

 3    67    32    45    90
 2     9    57    -3     1

-3  -201   -32  -135   -90
-6    -9  -171     3    -3

DONE
```

Problem No. 8

```
10 DIM X(2,6)
20 FOR R=1 TO 2
30 FOR C=1 TO 6
40 LET X(R,C)=1
50 NEXT C
70 MAT PRINT X;
80 END
RUN
NO.8

1   1   1   1   1   1
1   1   1   1   1   1

DONE
```

Problem No. 10

```
10 DIM X(2,R)
20 FOR X=1 TO 2
30 FOR Y=1 TO 2
40 LET A(X,Y)=0
50 NEXT Y
60 NEXT X
```

Problem No. 2

```
10 DIM A(4,4),B(4,1),C(4,1)
20 MAT READ A
40 MAT READ B
50 DATA -1,2,-3,-4
60 MAT PRINT C
70 MAT END
RUN
NO.2

 7

-23

64

-12

DONE
```

Problem No. 4

```
10 DIM A(2,2),B(2,2),C(2,2),D(2,2)
20 MAT READ A,B
30 DATA 3,12,1,4,-12,2,8,-3,-7
40 MAT C=A+B
50 MAT D=B+A
60 PRINT "A+B"
70 MAT PRINT C
80 PRINT "B+A"
90 MAT PRINT D;
100 PRINT "I CONCLUDE THAT MATRIX"
110 PRINT "MULTIPLICATION IS NOT"
120 PRINT "COMMUTATIVE"
130 END
RUN
NO.4

A+B
 0    0

B+A
-8   -32

 2    8

I CONCLUDE THAT MATRIX
MULTIPLICATION IS NOT
COMMUTATIVE

DONE
```

Problem No. 6

```
10 DIM A(2,2),B(2,2),C(2,2),D(2,2)
18 DIM E(2,2),F(2,2),G(2,2)
20 MAT READ A,B,C
30 DATA 1,2,3,4,-1,-2,5,3,2,-1,1,25,3
40 MAT D=A*B
50 MAT E=A*C
60 MAT F=E
70 PRINT "A*B+A*C"
80 MAT PRINT F;
90 MAT G=A+C
100 MAT F=A*(B+C)
110 PRINT "A*(B+C)"
120 MAT PRINT F;
130 END
RUN
NO.6

A*B+A*C
 61    55

123    97

A*(B+C)
```

Problem No. 2

```
10 DIM B(2,2),C(2,2),D(2,2)
20 MAT READ B
30 MAT C=INV(B)
40 PRINT "INV(B)"
50 MAT PRINT C
60 MAT D=B*C
70 PRINT "B*INV(B)"
75 MAT PRINT D
80 MAT D=C*B
90 PRINT "INV(B)*B"
100 MAT PRINT D
200 DATA -8,-3,0,-1
300 END
RUN
NO.2

INV(B)
-.125    .375

   0      -1

B*INV(B)
   1       0

   0       1

INV(B)*B
   1       0

   0       1

DONE
```

Problem No. 4

```
10 DIM C(3,3),K(3,1),S(3,1),I(3,3)
20 MAT READ C,K
30 MAT X=INV(C)
40 MAT S=I*K
50 MAT PRINT S
100 DATA 2,-9,-5,7,-6,5,9,-6,5
105 DATA 2,-35,-39
RUN
NO.4
-2.

.999998

-3

DONE
```

Problem No. 6

```
10 DIM C(4,4),K(4,1),I(4,4),S(4,1)
20 MAT READ C,K
30 MAT S=INV(C)
40 MAT S=I*K
50 MAT PRINT S
100 DATA 6,3,6,5,-7,5,-7,-1
102 DATA -3,1,3,6,-2,-4,4,-7
110 DATA -12,77,31,-76
120 END
RUN
NO.6
-3.

-6

 6

DONE
```

SEC. 12-4 Cont'd

Problem No. 8

```
10 DIM C[3,3],K[3,1],S[3,1],I[3,3]
20 MAT READ C,K
30 MAT I=INV(C)
40 MAT S=I*K
100 MAT PRINT S
100 DATA 2,4,-3,-9,-3,0,-9,8,5
105 DATA -11,-9,58,5,66,6
110 END
RUN
NO.8
```

```
-6.7
.600001
-.299998
```

DONE.

Problem No. 10

```
10 DIM C[10,10],K[10,1],I[10,10],S[10,10]
12 REM WE ALLOW UP TO TEN UNKNOWNS
20 READ N
25 IF N=0 THEN 999
30 MAT READ C[N,N],K[N,1]
50 PRINT "COEFFICIENT MATRIX"
60 MAT PRINT C
60 PRINT "CONSTANT TERMS"
70 MAT PRINT K
80 MAT I=ZER[N,N]
90 MAT S=ZER[N,1]
100 MAT I=INV(C)
110 MAT S=I*K
120 PRINT "SOLUTIONS"
130 MAT PRINT S
140 GOTO 20
200 DATA 2,3,1,5,-3,7,21
210 DATA 3,2,0,-1,3,0,1,1,-2,-5
220 DATA 20,0,6
230 DATA 0
999 END
RUN
NO.10
```

```
COEFFICIENT MATRIX
3    1
5   -3

CONSTANT TERMS
7
21

SOLUTIONS
5.
-2.

COEFFICIENT MATRIX
3    0   -1
1   -2   -5

CONSTANT TERMS
20
0
6

SOLUTIONS
5.
-3
```

DONE

```
36   118    40
-5    -1     7
12    40    -8
```

TRN(A)*TRN(B)
```
3    31    12
26    7   -11
58    75    17
```

DONE

CHAP. 13

SEC. 13-2

Problem No. 2

```
10 LET N=1
20 FOR X=14 TO 1 STEP -1
30 LET N=N*X
40 LET N=N/2
50 PRINT N
70 END
RUN
NO.2
```

4.35891E+10

DONE

Problem No. 4

```
10 LET P=1
20 FOR X=25 TO 13 STEP -1
30 LET P=P*X
40 NEXT X
50 FOR X=12 TO 1 STEP -1
60 LET P=P*X
70 NEXT X
80 PRINT P
90 END
RUN
NO.4
```

1.55112E+25

DONE

Problem No. 6

```
10 LET C=1
20 FOR X=52 TO 52-5+1 STEP -1
30 LET C=C*X
40 NEXT X
50 FOR X=5 TO 1 STEP -1
60 LET C=C/X
70 NEXT X
80 PRINT C"HANDS"
90 END
RUN
NO.6
```

2.59896E+06   HANDS

DONE

Problem No. 8

```
5 LET N=1
10 FOR X=365 TO 365-5+1 STEP -1
20 LET N=N*X
30 NEXT X
40 PRINT N
50 END
```

```
40 NEXT X
50 FOR X=4 TO 1 STEP -1
60 LET C=C/X
70 NEXT X
80 PRINT C"STRAIGHT COMMITTEES"
90 LET C=(13*12)/(2*1)
100 LET C1=(16*15)/(2*1)
110 LET C2=C*C1
120 PRINT "TWO GIRLS AND TWO BOYS"C2
130 LET C=13*17*16*15/(1*2*3)
140 PRINT "ONE BOY AND THREE GIRLS"C
150 LET C1=17*16*15*14/(4*3*2*1)
160 PRINT "ALL GIRLS"C1
170 LET C=13*12*11*10/(4*3*2*1)
180 PRINT "ALL BOYS"C
200 END
RUN
NO.18
```

```
27405   STRAIGHT COMMITTEES
TWO GIRLS AND TWO BOYS 10608
ONE BOY AND THREE GIRLS 8840
ALL GIRLS 2380
ALL BOYS 715
```

DONE

Problem No. 20

```
10 LET H=H1=1
20 FOR X=52 TO 52-5+1 STEP -1
30 LET H=H*X
40 NEXT X
50 FOR X=5 TO 1 STEP -1
60 LET H1=H1*X
70 NEXT X
100 FOR X=52-5 TO (52-5)-5+1 STEP -1
110 LET H1=H1*X
120 NEXT X
130 FOR X=5 TO 1 STEP -1
140 LET H1=H1/X
150 NEXT X
160 PRINT H*H1"PAIRS OF FIVE CARD HANDS"
200 END
RUN
NO.20
```

3.98665E+12   PAIRS OF FIVE CARD HANDS

DONE

SEC. 13-3

Problem No. 2

```
10 LET N=2
20 FOR X=9 TO 1 STEP -1
30 LET N=N*X
40 NEXT X
50 FOR X=10 TO 1 STEP -1
60 LET D=1
70 PRINT N/D
100 END
RUN
NO.2
```

.2

DONE

Problem No. 4

```
10 LET N=1
20 FOR X=52 TO 52-5+1 STEP -1
30 LET N=N*X
40 NEXT X
50 FOR X=5 TO 1 STEP -1
60 LET N=N/X
70 NEXT X
```

Problem No. 2

```
10 DIM A(3,3),B(3,3),C(3,3)
20 MAT READ A
30 MAT B=TRN(A)
40 MAT C=A*B
50 PRINT "TRN(A)"
60 MAT PRINT B;
70 PRINT "A*TRN(A)"
80 MAT PRINT C;
90 MAT C=A-B
100 PRINT "A-TRN(A)"
130 MAT C=B-A
140 PRINT "TRN(A)-A"
150 MAT PRINT C;
300 DATA 5,3,1,6,-2,9,3,9,1
999 END
RUN
NO.2
```

TRN(A)
```
5    6    3
3   -2    9
1    9    1
```

A*TRN(A)
```
10    9    4
9    -4   18
4    18    2
```

A-TRN(A)
```
0   -3   -2
3    0    0
2    0    0
```

TRN(A)-A
```
0    3    2
-3    0    0
-2    0    0
```
DONE

Problem No. 4

```
10 DIM A(3,3),B(3,3),C(3,3),D(3,3),E(3,3)
20 MAT READ A,B
30 MAT C=A+B
40 MAT D=TRN(C)
50 PRINT "TRN(A+B)"
60 MAT PRINT D;
70 MAT C=TRN(A)
80 MAT D=TRN(B)
100 PRINT "TRN(B)+TRN(A)"
110 MAT PRINT E;
120 MAT E=C+D
130 PRINT "TRN(A)+TRN(B)"
140 MAT PRINT E;
300 DATA 2,-1,3,5,0,8,-3,4,2
310 DATA 6,3,6,8,9,5,4,11,-2,0
999 END
RUN
NO.4
```

TRN(A+B)
```
36   118   40
-5    -1    7
12    40   -8
```
TRN(B)+TRN(A)

DONE

RUN
NO.8

6.30855E+12

DONE

Problem No. 10

```
10 PRINT 26*3*10*3"DIFFERENT PLATES"
20 END
RUN
NO.10
```

1.75760E+07   DIFFERENT PLATES

DONE

Problem No. 12

```
5 LET T=0
10 FOR F=5 TO 0 STEP -1
15 LET P=1
20 FOR X=5 TO 5-F+1 STEP -1
30 LET P=P*X
40 NEXT X
50 LET T=T+P
70 PRINT F""FLAGS""P"SIGNALS"
70 NEXT F
75 PRINT "TOTAL NUMBER OF SIGNALS IS"T
80 END
RUN
NO.12
```

```
5    FLAGS 120    SIGNALS
4    FLAGS 120    SIGNALS
3    FLAGS 60     SIGNALS
2    FLAGS 20     SIGNALS
1    FLAGS 1      SIGNALS
0    FLAGS 1      SIGNALS
TOTAL NUMBER OF SIGNALS IS 326
```

DONE

Problem No. 14

```
10 LET G=1
20 FOR X=50 TO 50-25+1
30 LET G=G*X
40 NEXT X
60 FOR X=25 TO 1 STEP -1
70 LET G=G/X
80 NEXT X
90 PRINT G"GUEST LISTS"
100 END
RUN
NO.14
```

6.44695E-26   GUEST LISTS

DONE

Problem No. 16

```
10 LET N=1
20 FOR X=14 TO 1 STEP -1
30 LET N=N*X
40 NEXT X
45 LET N=N*2
60 PRINT N
60 END
RUN
NO.16
```

1.74357E+11

DONE

Problem No. 18

```
10 LET C=1
20 FOR X=30 TO 30-4+1 STEP -1
30 LET C=C*X
```

```
80 PRINT 1/N
90 END
RUN
NO.4
```

3.84769E-07

DONE

Problem No. 6

```
10 PRINT (1/2)*10
20 END
RUN
NO.6
```

9.76562E-04

DONE

Problem No. 8

```
10 LET P=(48/52)*(47/51)*(46/50)*(4/49)
20 PRINT P
30 END
RUN
NO.8
```

6.38877E-02

DONE

Problem No. 10

```
10 PRINT (5/6)*3*(1/6)
20 PRINT (5/6)*99*(1/6)
50 END
RUN
NO.10
```

9.64506E-02
3.23011E-02

DONE

Problem No. 12

```
10 PRINT 1-(364/365)*28
20 END
RUN
NO.12
```

7.39399E-02

DONE

SEC. 13-4

Problem No. 4

```
10 MAT S=ZER(1,4)
20 PRINT "LIGHT DEFECTIVE"
30 PRINT "LIGHT OPENER BOTH NEITHER"
40 FOR X=1 TO 1000
50 LET L=INT(20*RND(1))
55 LET C=INT(25*RND(1))
70 IF L>0 THEN 120
80 LET S(1,1)=S(1,1)+1
90 IF C>0 THEN 140
100 LET S(1,2)=S(1,2)+1
105 IF L>0 THEN 140
115 LET S(1,3)=S(1,3)+1
115 GOTO 140
120 IF C>0 THEN 90
130 LET S(1,4)=S(1,4)+1
140 NEXT X
150 MAT PRINT S;
160 END
RUN
NO.4
```

```
        DEFECTIVE
LIGHT OPENER BOTH NEITHER
42    35    3    926
DONE
```

SEC. 13-4 Cont'd

Problem No. 6

```
10 LET C=0
20 FOR X=1 TO 500
30 LET R=INT(6*RND(1)+1)
40 IF R=1 THEN 100
50 IF R=5 THEN 100
60 GOTO 200
100 LET C=C+1
200 NEXT X
210 PRINT C"FIVE OR ONE UP"
220 END
RUN
NO.6
```

162 FIVE OR ONE UP

DONE

Problem No. 8

```
10 LET N=1
20 DIM S(500)
30 MAT S=ZER
40 FOR X=1 TO 500
50 LET R=INT(6*RND(1)+1)
60 IF R=1 THEN 120
100 GOTO 60
120 LET S(N)=S(N)+1
130 LET N=N+1
140 IF N=N1=SEN>1
150 PRINT "ROLLS TIL ONE","NUMBER OF TIME
160 FOR X=1 TO N1
170 PRINT X,S(X,X)1
180 NEXT X
190 END
RUN
NO.8
```

ROLLS TIL ONE	NUMBER OF TIMES
1	84
2	60
3	57
4	60
5	39
6	42
7	23
8	17
9	16
10	14
11	15
12	11
13	8
14	5
15	5
16	5
17	2
18	5
19	2
20	3
21	0
22	4
23	1
24	1
25	2
26	0
27	0
28	1
29	0
30	0
31	1
32	0
33	0
34	0
35	1

DONE

Problem No. 10

```
10 DIM S(1,13)
15 MAT S=ZER
20 FOR X=1 TO 500
35 FOR R=0 TO 10
40 LET R1=INT(6*RND(1)+1)
50 IF R1>1 THEN 100
60 LET C=C+1
100 LET S(1,C+1)=S(1,C+1)+1
140 NEXT X
150 PRINT "NONE  ONE  TWO  THREE";
160 PRINT " FOUR  FIVE  SIX";
170 PRINT " SEVEN  EIGHT  NINE  TEN";
180 PRINT S;
RUN
NO.10
```

NONE	ONE	TWO	THREE	FOUR	FIVE	SIX	SEVEN	EIGHT	NINE	TEN
78	160	153	69	32	8	0	0	0	0	0

DONE

SEC. 13-5

Problem No. 2

```
5 PRINT "ONES  PROBABILITY","TOTAL"
7 LET T=0
10 FOR R=10 TO 0 STEP -1
15 LET C=1
20 FOR X=10 TO 10-R+1 STEP -1
30 LET C=C*X/(10-X+1)
40 NEXT X
50 LET P=C*(1/6)*R*(5/6)^(10-R)
55 LET T=T+P
60 PRINT R;P,T
70 END
RUN
NO.2
```

ONES	PROBABILITY	TOTAL
10	1.65382E-08	1.65382E-08
9	8.26908E-07	8.43447E-07
8	1.86054E-05	1.94489E-05
7	2.48072E-04	2.67591E-04
6	2.17063E-03	2.43816E-03
5	1.30238E-02	.015548
4	5.42449E-02	6.97979E-02
3	.155045	.224773
2	.29071	.515483
1	.323011	.838495
0	.161506	1.

Problem No. 4

```
10 REM C0MB 100 THINGS 1 AT A TIME=100
20 LET P=100*.001*1*.999^99
30 PRINT P
40 END
RUN
NO.4
```

9.05693E-02

DONE

Problem No. 6

```
10 LET P=1*.001*10*.999^100
20 PRINT 1-P
30 END
RUN
NO.6
```

9.5212?E-02

DONE

Problem No. 8

```
5 PRINT "ONES  PROBABILITY"
10 LET N=6
20 FOR R=0 TO 6
30 LET C=1
40 FOR X=N TO N-R+1 STEP -1
60 LET C=C*X
70 NEXT X
90 FOR X=R TO 1 STEP -1
100 LET C=C/X
110 NEXT X
120 PRINT R;C*(5/6)^(N-R)*(1/6)^R
130 NEXT R
150 END
RUN
NO.8
```

ONES	PROBABILITY
0	.334898
1	.401878
2	.200937
3	5.35837E-02
4	8.03755E-03
5	6.43004E-04
6	2.14335E-05

DONE

Problem No. 10

```
5 LET T=0
10 FOR R=6 TO 0
15 LET C=1
20 FOR X=10 TO 10-R+1 STEP -1
30 LET C=C*X/(10-X+1)
50 LET P=C*(1/2)*R*(1/2)^(10-R)
60 LET T=T+P
65 NEXT R
68 PRINT T
70 END
RUN
NO.10
```

.376953

DONE

Problem No. 12

```
5 PRINT "FLIPS  PROBABILITY"
10 FOR R=1 TO 10
20 LET P=R*(1/2)
40 PRINT R;P
50 NEXT R
60 END
RUN
NO.12
```

FLIPS	PROBABILITY
2	.5
3	.25
4	.125
5	.0625
6	.03125
7	.015625
8	7.8125E-03
9	3.90625E-03
10	1.95312E-03
	9.76562E-04

DONE

Index

Index

De Moivre's theorem, 152
Depressed polynomial, definition of, 169
Descartes' Rule of Signs, 173, 175
Dimension conversions, 50–51
Dimensioning
  arrays, 85–86
  lists, 66
DIM statement, 66, 103
  two-dimensional, 85, 86, 89
Division
  of polynomials, 156–158, 159
  synthetic, 158
Dummy argument, definition of, 62
Dummy data; *see* Artificial data

E-format, 8–9
END statement, 2, 12
Enumeration
  combinations, 200
  factorial, 198
  partitioning, 202
  permutations, 198–199, 200, 202
  Principle of, 197–198
Equality, matrix, 187, 190
Equals sign, 10
  in IF–THEN statement, 15
  as relational operator, 15
Error diagnosis, 218–224
Euclidean algorithm, 112–113
  greatest common factor, 91
Event, definition of, 205
Executive program, 4
Experiment in probability, definition of, 197, 207
Exponentiation, symbols used for, 4

Factorial, 198
Factoring integers, 48–49
Factor theorem, 160
Failure in probability, definition of, 197
Fibonacci numbers, 39, 46
FILES statement, 110, 117
Flowcharting, 13–14, 20
FØR–NEXT statement, 26, 28, 31, 32
Fractions, reducing, 50–51
Functions
  circular, 132, 133
  computer, *see* Computer functions

GØSUB statement, 41, 45
GØTØ statement, 3, 12, 18

Greatest common factor, 51, 54, 91

Identity matrix, 187
IDN, 187
IF END statement, 111
IF–THEN statement, 15, 18–19
IMAGE statement, 227
Initializing, 9–10
INPUT statement, 166
Integers
  computing greatest, 47
  factoring, 48–49
Integral zeroes of polynomials, 159–163
INT(X) function, 47, 48, 51
INV( ) statement, 191–192

Law of Cosines, 139–142
Law of Sines, 138–139, 141, 142
LEN( ) function, 103
LET statement, 5–6, 11, 56
  as assignment statement, 10
Lists; *see* Computer list
Location principle, 163
Logical end, definition of, 69
Log-on; *see* Sign-on
Loops, 24–25, 31–34
  FØR–NEXT, 26, 28
  machine-made, 26, 28–30
  nested, 32

Machine-made loops, 26, 28–30
MAT instructions, 176
MAT READ, 178–179
MAT PRINT, 177, 178, 179
Matrix, 179; *see also* Arrays
  coefficient, 192
  creating zero matrix (ZER), 187
  filling locations with 1 (CØN), 187
  forming identity matrix (IDN), 187
  identity, 187
  inverse of, 190–191
  transpose of, 195
Matrix addition, 186
Matrix algebra, 185–188
Matrix equality, 187, 190
Matrix inverse, 190, 191
  difference from transpose, 195
Matrix multiplication, 185–186
  scalar, 187
Matrix subtraction, 186
Maximum, 124